English
verb handbook

Fredrik Liljeblad

**Berlitz Publishing /
APA Publications GmbH & Co. Verlag KG,
Singapore Branch, Singapore**

English Verb Handbook

CONTACTING THE EDITORS
Every effort has been made to provide accurate information in this publication, but changes are inevitable. The publisher cannot be responsible for any resulting loss, inconvenience, or injury. We would appreciate it if readers would call our attention to any errors or outdated information by contacting Berlitz Publishing, 95 Progress Street, Union, NJ 07083, USA. Fax: 1-908-206-1103. email: comments@berlitzbooks.com

Reprinted September 2002
Printed in Canada
ISBN 2-8315-7296-7

Series Editor:

Christopher Wightwick is a former UK representative on the Council of Europ Modern Languages Project and principal inspector of Modern Languages f England.

CONTENTS

A
ENGLISH VERBS AND HOW TO USE THEM

The Way We Use Verbs

Most people **would agree** that the verb **is** the most important part of an English sentence. If we **want to give** or **get** information about an event or situation, a feeling, thought, or opinion, the verb **tells** us much of what we **need to know:** if something **happened** in the past or **is going to happen** in the future, who the situation **involves,** who **did** something, or what someone **said.** All the words in boldface in this paragraph **are** verbs, and you **can see** we **need** many of them **to express** our ideas.

Read the paragraph below and try to understand its meaning without any of the verbs to help you.

> **This morning, Margaret's doorbell _____. She _____ _____ her coffee and _____ to the door. When she _____ it, she _____ a delivery man _____ there. He _____ _____ five dozen roses in different colors. Margaret _____ roses, but she _____ _____ why someone _____ _____ her so many of them. The delivery man _____ her the flowers and then _____ her a note. She _____ it and _____ her boyfriend's writing. After she _____ _____ it, she finally _____ it _____ her birthday.**

Now read the same paragraph with the verbs in place.

This morning, Margaret's doorbell **_rang._** She **_put down_** her coffee and **_walked_** to the door. When she **_opened_** it, she **_saw_** a delivery man **_standing_** there. He **_was carrying_** five dozen roses in different colors. Margaret **_loves_** roses, but she **_couldn't understand_** why someone **_had sent_** her so many of them. The delivery man **_gave_** her the flowers and then **_handed_** her a note. She **_opened_** it and **_recognized_** her boyfriend's writing. After she **_had read_** it, she finally **_remembered_** it **_was_** her birthday.

Every complete English sentence must have a subject (a person, animal, thing, or situation that the verb relates to) and a verb (the word that shows what action, thought, feeling, change—or lack of change—is happening to the subject). The easy way to recognize a verb is to put *to* in front of it and ask yourself "Does this make sense?"

In English word order, unlike some other Western languages, the verb always comes after (although not always immediately after) the subject in a statement. Even in questions, the only verbs that come before the subject are auxiliaries and modals (see sections 5 and 6, pages 15 and 20, respectively).

A sentence, particularly a complex one, can have two or more verbs, but there is always a *main* verb—the one that most clearly talks about the subject. Look at this sentence.

> Carl *heard* Maria's voice in the hall several minutes before she actually *came* into the room and calmly *walked* over to his chair, while his heart *continued beating* wildly.

There are five verbs (*hear, come, walk, continue,* and *beat*), two people, and two things in the sentence: Carl, Maria, Maria's voice, and Carl's heart. Which is the main verb, and who or what is the subject? Ask yourself what is happening and who it is happening to. Something happened to *Carl*. What happened to him? *Carl* **heard** something (Maria's voice).

Verbs have several important characteristics you should know about.

- They show the time of an action or event through *tense*—part of the verb changes if it describes something in the past or future, or something that is happening as we speak (walk**ed**—**will** walk—**is/are** walk**ing**).

I *talked* to Bobby's teacher <u>yesterday</u>. My husband **will** *talk* to the principal <u>tomorrow</u>.

- They can confirm or deny that an action, situation, or event has happened by being in the *affirmative* (walk) or *negative* (not walk) form.

I *speak* French and German. I **do not** *speak* Spanish or Italian.

- They show if the speaker is talking about himself or herself (I speak) or one or more other people (he/she/it walks; we/they walk).

Donald *says* "how do you do," but Bill and Frank just *say* "hi."

Most English verbs have a consistent way to form tenses, such as adding *-ed* to make the past tense. Verbs that do this are called *regular verbs* (see Complete Conjugations for the pattern of Regular Verbs, Active Form, page 63).

Some verbs form these tenses in various other ways. These are called *irregular verbs,* even though most of them fall into groups that follow one of about six patterns (see Complete Conjugations for Irregular Verbs starting on page 118).

2. Verb Basics: Infinitives, Imperatives, and Participles; Negative Forms

Verb tenses show the time frame of an action or situation. It's sometimes necessary to use a verb for its basic meaning, without any time associations. Dictionaries and indexes list verbs in their most basic form (*read* instead of *reading*). This is usually called the *simple form* of the verb. This simple form, when it is used with *to* (to speak, to learn), is called the *infinitive.* Many sentences in English use the infinitive form, particularly if a verb comes after the main verb of the sentence, or after certain modals (see section 6, page 20)

I started *to leave,* but the train had begun *to move.*

Sarah forgot *to lock* the door.

To find a better life is the hope of every immigrant.

We want *to see* the World Trade Center.

Martha's baby is beginning *to walk.*

The simple form—the infinitive without *to*—is also used for the imperative—the form of the verb for giving "commands" or instructions, or to express the speaker's wishes in a basic way. Unless the speaker is discussing another conversation, the imperative is always used directly between the speaker and the listener.

to play (infinitive)   Play! (imperative)

"So the boss said, '*Get* those reports, now!'"

"I told Sally '*Don't touch* it!'"

Turn the fax machine off! Now *pull* the paper tray out.

Don't wear those muddy shoes indoors, Bobby!

Here comes the bus—*take* your coffee with you!

It's very important to remember that the imperative is especially dependent on your tone of voice. It can easily sound like an order. Adding "please" can frequently "soften" imperatives, but it doesn't work in every situation. If you are explaining a procedure, such as how to get to the train station, or when giving instructions on how to repair something, you shouldn't use *please.* If you add *would you* or *could you* along with *please,* it can soften an imperative even more. The negative form is *don't* (or *please don't*) plus the imperative.

Please is used with imperatives when

- asking an adult for a service

Please *call* a taxi for me.

- asking for a favor

Could you please turn down the stereo?

- trying to soften a "command"

(Could you) *turn* the stereo down, please?

Please is not used with imperatives when

- giving strong commands, such as in the military

Stand up straight, Private!

Boys, *be* quiet!

***Stop* meowing and *eat* your food, Morris!**

Pam, *give* me some more toast, would you please.

***Take* the Number 5 bus to Malden Street.**

***Add* the sugar gradually.**

Please *don't look* so sad.

Certain tenses (see section 8, page 28) are formed with one of two verb forms called *participles.* English has two: the *present participle* and the *past participle*. The present participle ends in *-ing;* the past participle ends in *-ed* for regular verbs, but the form varies with irregular verbs. Dictionaries and language books usually give the simple form, the past tense, and the past participle of irregular verbs (speak-spoke-spoken; take-took-taken).

SIMPLE FORM	PRESENT PARTICIPLE	PAST PARTICIPLE
ask	asking	asked
talk	talking	talked
be	being	been
drive	driving	driven
eat	eating	eaten

Participles can have other uses: both the present and past participles can be used as adjectives (a *roaring* fire; my *aching* knee, the car's *broken* windshield), and the past participle is used to form the passive voice (see section 9, page 43).

Ted *broke* the car windows in an accident. The car's windows *were broken* in an accident.

What's Happening: Action Verbs

The human ear is attracted by the sound of movement, just as the human eye is. Most verbs show things such as movement or change—actions, in other words. This is the characteristic that gives the verb its importance. Verbs show things happening, verbs describe things vividly, verbs are dynamic—they make you notice them. Choosing the right verb creates drama. Read these sentences. They show how much activity verbs can give a sentence.

The glass *shattered* into thousands of pieces that *scattered* everywhere.

The cat *shot* out of the chair when the dog *started barking.*

We *stared* at the fireworks as they *exploded* across the sky, slowly *cascading* down to earth.

The wind *howled* loudly as it *whipped* the trees back and forth.

Jane *dozed* as the small boat *glided* down the river as it *flowed* toward the sea.

Some of these verbs are admittedly not everyday words, but even less dramatic verbs (*break, fall, jump, burst, drop, blow, shake, sleep, move, run*) have much more power than most nouns or adjectives.

Action verbs, particularly in their progressive forms, can tell the listener many things about a situation. They can show

• a progression or a process of change

grow, age, decrease, increase, broaden, accelerate, slow, become, change, speed

---

The days *were growing* longer.

It *had become* chilly outside.

The years *sped* by, and Patricia *began to slow* down.

• daily or momentary activities

eat, drink, run, throw, ask, work, drive, read, write, watch, listen, talk

WHAT'S HAPPENING: ACTION VERBS

Billy *hit* the ball, *driving* it far away.
The students *had written* many notes while they *were listening* to the lecture.

> • a transition from one situation to another
>
> *travel, journey, move, seek, search, explore, investigate, uncover, discover*

Larry *traveled* endlessly from one place to another, *searching* for peace, *seeking* some greater truth.

> • physical symptoms of illnesses or physical responses
>
> *cough, ache, moan, groan, itch, scratch, sneeze, burn (with fever), sweat*

Elizabeth *watched* helplessly as her son *tossed* and *turned*, his skin *burning, coughing* until his chest *ached*.

Not all verbs show so much activity. A number of verbs show states of being where very little changes (see section 4, *Something to Think About: State-of-Being Verbs*, page 10).

When Anna *recalled* her childhood, she *remembered* best the way the apple orchards *smelled* in spring, the *feel* of the wind on her skin.

4 Something to Think About: State-of-Being Verbs

Although most verbs show action, change, or dynamic happenings, some verbs show existing states of being, usually grouped together in a general category known as *state-of-being* verbs. One way to distinguish between a state-of-being verb and an action verb, is by asking yourself if the verb shows the possibility of change *within the moment*. If you *hate* cats (*hate* is a state-of-being verb), your opinion may change in time, but at the moment you use the verb, the feeling of hate is a state of being, not action.

State-of-being verbs usually describe thought processes, moods and emotions, or one of the verbs relating to the five physical senses. The most common of all state-of-being verbs is *to be,* often used as an auxiliary (see Part B, page 66). Here are some other state-of-being verbs and the general categories they are sometimes divided into.

*Sense Verbs: also called *perception* verbs

appear
feel
look/look like   (= appear) when (*to*) *look* is
seem   followed by *at,* it is an action verb
smell
sound
taste

Thought-process and Emotion Verbs: also called *cognitive* verbs

believe
doubt
fear
forget

hate
know
like
love
prefer
remember
think *of*   (= opinion)
understand
want
wish

Relationship Verbs:

belong (to)
contain
have
lack
matter
mean
owe
own

*Other State-of-Being Verbs:

ache
be
cost
equal
hurt
itch
measure
weigh

Note: *Most of the verbs in these categories, as well as a few of the others, have action forms as well as state-of-being forms.

Sometimes the action and state-of-being forms of the verb are identical, sometimes they are quite different. For example, *to feel* can be either a state-of-being or an action verb. But *to sound* is a state-of-being form while *to listen to* is an action verb. One way to distinguish between such state-of-being and action forms of verbs, is to decide if the subject controls the action or not.

ENGLISH VERBS AND HOW TO USE THEM

Marcia *weighs* her new baby.
(active—Marcia is controlling the action: she's *doing* something)

Marcia's new baby *weighs* seven pounds.
(state-of-being—the baby can't control its weight or decide when it will be weighed)

Contrast the sense of the action and state-of-being forms of the verbs in these sentences:

Action	State-of-Being
I *feel* the rain on my face.	The rain *feels* good (to me).
Betty *is looking* at a magazine.	These magazine articles *look* interesting.
Do you *smell* the cookies baking?	Mmm, that stew *smells* delicious.
They've just *sounded* the fire alarm.	The news *sounds* really serious.
Have you *tasted* the rum punch?	These tomatoes *taste* bitter.

Sense verbs in their *state-of-being forms* can be followed only by an adjective, never an adverb (exception: adverbs of degree—*extremely, really, very*—that strengthen the adjective).

Tom *feels* good about his book's success.	(not *well;* feel well = healthy)
Our neighbor's party last night *sounded* really loud.	(not *loudly*)
I thought Lindsay's new dress *looked* cheap.	(not *cheaply*)
This curry *tastes* really hot.	(not *hotly*)

There is a practical reason to be able to recognize state-of-being verbs and to distinguish them from action verbs. As a general rule, state-of-being verbs are seldom used in any of the progressive tense forms (see section 8, *All About Tenses,* page 28). It's incorrect to use a progressive form with many state-of-being verbs (*I am loving Mozart* is wrong); the state-of-being verb's meaning becomes radically different from its action verb counterpart if it's used in one of the progressive tense forms (*is/was/will be/has been -ing*). Here are a few examples that contrast the meanings of some state-of-being verbs in their simple and progressive tense uses—you can see how the use of the progressive changes the meaning.

Simple	Progressive
John *is* charming. (= his natural character)	**John *is being* charming.** (= he is actively trying to use charm)
The boss *thinks* it's a bad idea. (= his opinion)	**The boss *is thinking* about it.** (= using the thought process)
I *see* the sign, but I can't read it. (= the sign is in front of him/her)	**I *'ve been seeing* Helena for a while.** (= meeting or dating)
The professor *knows* very much. (= has much knowledge)	**The professor *is* very *knowing*.** (= shrewd and clever)
The Carlssons *have* a large house. (= they own it)	**The Carlssons *are having* money problems.** (= experiencing now)
Anne *wants* to be manager. (= wishes to be)	**Reports find Anne *is wanting* in her current position.** (= lacks skill)

The verb *to be,* especially, needs to show the subject's conscious choice if it is used in a progressive form followed by an adjective. If the subject has no choice, it's wrong to use a progressive.

ENGLISH VERBS AND HOW TO USE THEM

Simple	Progressive
Greta *was* tiresome. (= a tiresome person)	**Greta *was being* tiresome at dinner.** (= she behaved badly that particular time)
The children *are* impossible! (= they are always difficult)	**The children *are* being impossible!** (= they are usually nice, but are difficult today)
Do you realize you *are* very sarcastic? (= your manner is naturally sarcastic)	**Are you *being* sarcastic?** (= did you intend to make a sarcastic remark)

Sentences with (*to*) *be* are not usual in everyday speech.

Lastly, some other differences to remember between many (not all) state-of-being and action verbs include the following:

- Many state-of-being verbs either lack an imperative form entirely, or the imperative only survives in out-of-date or idiomatic expressions (*Have* pity! *Know* this:... *Look* sharp!).

- The subject of these verbs in their state-of-being sense is often the "abstract" *it,* as in *It feels like rain,* or *It looks bad for the home team.*

Verb Helpers: Auxiliaries

There is an entire category of verbs in English known as *auxiliaries,* or *helping verbs.* The most frequently used auxiliaries are *be, do, have,* and *will.* Auxiliaries are not used for their own meanings. Instead, an auxiliary always appears together with another verb (called a *full verb*) that supplies true meaning to the sentence. Auxiliaries are also called helping verbs because they are needed in English to help form certain tenses and structures. Although *be, do,* and *have* are auxiliaries, they (but not *will*) can also be used independently as full verbs. Complete conjugations of *be, do,* and *have* as verbs are in Part B, sections 2, 3, and 4, respectively. Section 8, *All About Tenses,* (see page 28), explains the meaning and use of each tense. Here are the language functions of each of the four major auxiliaries.

Be is used as an auxiliary to form:

- All simple progressive tenses—present, past, and (together with the auxiliary *will*) future progressive

> My cat *is biting* my left ankle.
> She *was biting* my right ankle during breakfast.
> Our guests *will be arriving* shortly.

- The negative form of all simple progressive tenses

> Mr. Barr *isn't working* for this company anymore.

- The simple future tense with *going to,* including the negative form

> *I'm* not *going to write* that report today.

- All tense aspects of the passive voice, including the negative

15

ENGLISH VERBS AND HOW TO USE THEM

Was this book _printed_ in the United States?

- Questions in all progressive tenses

Are George and Joan still _sleeping?_

_Do_ is used as an auxiliary to form:

- Questions in the simple present and simple past tenses

How much _does_ Charles _know?_
Don't you _know_ how to play chess?
Did your train _arrive_ on time?
Did the protest march _succeed?_

- Questions with most modals (see Section 6, _More Help: Modals,_ page 20)

_Do_ you _want to eat_ dinner downtown?
Did Bernie _have to_ pay a lot of taxes last year?

- The emphatic and negative forms of the imperative

Do come and visit us again soon!
Please _don't smoke_ here.

Have is used as an auxiliary to form:

- All perfect tenses—present, past, and (together with the auxiliary _will_) future

Marianne _has felt_ ill for over a week.
All the guests _had arrived_ by the time Philippe got home.
They _will_ already _have left_ by the time we get out of this traffic!

- The negative form of all perfect tenses

We *haven't spoken to* Billy since he left for Guam.
The banks *hadn't expected* such an enthusiastic response.
Don't sit down! The paint *won't have dried* yet.

- All perfect progressive tenses (together with the auxiliaries *be* and *will*)

Have you *been waiting* long?
Next Friday, we *will have been living* in our new house for two years.
Willie *had been studying* Chinese for two years before the teacher introduced the written language.

- The negative form of all perfect progressive tenses

Mrs. Wilson *hasn't been living* in this house since 1992.
The deluxe model *hadn't been selling* well for some time when it was discontinued.
By this Christmas, Harry *won't have been speaking* to our neighbor for five years.

- The past conditional

If John *had taken* the train, he never *would have had* that accident.
Would you *have bought* that table if you had known it was a copy?

ENGLISH VERBS AND HOW TO USE THEM

Will is used as an auxiliary to form:

- The simple future and simple future progressive tenses

How expensive *will* Loretta's wedding *be?*
The meeting *will be ending* in another 10 minutes.

- The negative form of the simple future and simple future progressive tenses

I *won't listen* to any more of the news—it's too depressing.
We *won't be needing* a house of this size after the kids go to college.

- The future perfect tense

Sam *will have contributed* almost $180,000 to the retirement fund by the time he's 65.

- The negative form of the future perfect tense

Don't worry, they *won't have started* showing the movie yet.

- The future perfect progressive tense

Five more minutes and we *will have been* waiting for over an hour.

- The negative form of the future perfect progressive tense

This is the third year in a row we *won't have been showing* a profit.

- To form questions in the simple future, simple future progressive, and future perfect tenses

---

Who *will take* the dogs for their morning walk?

Will Janet *be sleeping* in her old room tonight?

Will the shipment *have gone* out yet?

Will you *have finished eating* by the time Chris gets there?

More Help: Modals

Modals are not easy to define. Few experts agree completely on which are "true" modals, but several other verbs are used as "semi-modals." Modals are, in fact, a form of auxiliary, but are different from "pure" auxiliaries (like *be, do,* and *have*) because they express the attitude of the speaker to the situation described by the *full verb.*

The general consensus is that these are "true" modals:

Modal	Meaning
can	ability; possibility/potential; permission (considered colloquial by some)
could	past forms of *can*; past ability; permission or requests (polite: more diffident than *will/would*, less than *might*); unlikely possibility (*couldn't*); possibility only in certain situations (*+ if*);
had better have got to	strong advice; suggested obligation, necessity; emphatic form of *have to*
have to	necessity
may	uncertain future possibility; making or granting requests in immediate future; speculate objectively on situations
might	past forms of *may*; uncertain possibility; permission (very polite/diffident)
must	strong/unavoidable necessity; strong likelihood
ought to shall	advisability; implied obligation suggestions; offering choices

should	obligation; probability; logical expectation
will*	definite future prediction; strong intention; offering/inviting
would	past form of *will*; speculating on (unlikely) events; making polite requests (more assertive than *could*)

Also widely used as if they were modals are:
be able to
like to
need to
want to

The complete conjugations of these modals, including the negative forms and whether they require the use of *to* before the verb, appear at the end of Section B, after the conjugations for irregular verbs (see page 221).

Note: * In this sense, *will* is a true modal because it is expressing the strong wish or determination (the will) of the speaker. When *will* is used to form the future tenses ("I will talk to my boss"), however, it is a "pure" auxiliary (like *be*, *do*, and *have*) because its function is entirely practical—it adds none of its own meaning other than a prediction of the future.

Shall is very rarely used in the United States (with two minor exceptions), and even in Britain it is used less frequently than it once was. The use of *shall* in a statement (*"I shall/shan't be able to....;" "We shall be late if...."*) is exclusively British.

In the United States, *shall* is used to make polite suggestions in question form that always include both the speaker and the listener. A secondary use is to ask about the listener's wishes. Many Americans tend to use *should I?* or *would you like me to,...* instead of *shall* in the second situation.

Shall we have dinner now, or would you prefer to wait?

Shall we have some wine while we're waiting?

What *shall* I call you, Marina or Mrs. Greer?/What *should* I call you, Marina or Mrs. Greer?

Shall I stay until you get the front door unlocked?/*Would* you like me to stay until you get the front door unlocked?

To understand modals we need to look at them in two ways.

First, modals need to be understood in terms of their general definition in the language, and by the function of the specific modal in the sentence:

- The purpose of a modal is to show the speaker's opinion on the subject of the sentence.

You *may* go.

- The choice of modal indicates what the speaker feels about the subject.

Sue wants to go, but she *may not* be able to.

- The modal helps the main verb complete the meaning of the sentence, but modals alone can't take the place of the full verb.

You *ought to* <u>have parked</u> within the white lines.

Second, modals also need to be understood in terms of practical usage:

- With a few exceptions, modals don't usually have the complete array of tenses that full (also called *finite*) verbs do; some have a kind of past tense, and a few have a future tense, but no true modal has any progressive tense.

I *may* go now. ➡ I *may* go tomorrow. ➡ I *might have* gone yesterday.

- Modals need a second (full or finite) verb to complete their meaning.

Harry *can* still <u>remember</u> things from 40 years ago.

- When it follows a modal, or a modal and auxiliary, the full verb usually, but not always, keeps its simple form (*read, play, drive*).

As a boy, I *could* <u>stay up</u> for 24 hours and not feel tired.

- Modals are often used together with auxiliaries (like *be, do,* and *have*); even then, both are usually followed by a full verb (modals used with *be* are sometimes an exception; they can make sense with only an adjective or noun phrase following them).

Mary and John are getting married? It *can't be* possible!

- When a modal is used together with a full verb, only the modal indicates the time frame—the *tense* (see Section 8, *All About Tenses*, page 28).

Teresita *had to sell* her house after she was fired.

- If a modal + auxiliary combination is used with a verb, only the auxiliary changes tense.

I know we *should* <u>*have taken*</u> heavier coats.

- The negative forms of modals are quite variable; each one needs to be studied carefully.

I *must* go today. ➡ I *don't have to* go tomorrow. You needn't go tomorrow. (= *need not;* Am: *don't need to*) ➡ Tommy *must* take his medicine. ➡ Tommy *must not* eat chocolate.

- Many modals have more than one meaning: the modal *should* can mean a degree of obligation, probability, or expectation, depending on how it is used in the sentence.

You should take off your hat indoors. ➡ Jon's plane should be landing in Amsterdam about now. ➡ The rain should end by morning.

We *can* sometimes have frost in April.

Bobby *can* spend the night here if you promise you'll go to bed on time.

I suppose the package *could* still get here by the 10th, but it seems unlikely.

That profit and loss sheet *had better* look good, or we'll all need new jobs.

I *had better* stop and see if Mom needs any groceries.

According to my broker, Antrim Industries stock *may* go up.

Tom *may* meet Deborah for drinks at 5:00. I *might* join them later for dinner—although there's a lot of work here that I *should* do.

Contractions

Mainly in conversation, but also in informal written English, many pronoun/auxiliary (or pronoun/modal/auxiliary) combinations are shortened—*contracted*—particularly negative forms. American English especially favors contractions. These are the standard contractions used in spoken English (but you may see others in fiction- or dialogue-writing that the writer is using for effect):

Contractions with *be:*

I am	= I'm
you are	= you're
he is	= he's
she is	= she's
it is	= it's*
we are	= we're
they are	= they're

Note: * Remember that the meaning of *it's,* the contraction of *it is,* differs from *its,* the possessive form of *it.*

It's my birthday.   (– it is)
I wish that dog would stop its barking.   (= his or her)

Negative contractions with *be:*

is not	= isn't
are not	= aren't
was not	= wasn't
were not	= weren't

Contractions with *will:*

I will	= I'll
you will	= you'll
he will	= he'll
she will	= she'll
it will	= it'll*
we will	= we'll
they will	= they'll

Note: * Contracting *it will* to *it'll* is not entirely accepted yet, particularly in written form.

ENGLISH VERBS AND HOW TO USE THEM

In British usage, both *I will* and *I shall* are contracted to *I'll* and *we will/shall* to *we'll,* so you'll have to be guided by context.

Negative contractions with *will:*

| will not | = won't |

Contractions with *have:*

I have	= I've
you have	= you've
he has	= he's
she has	= she's
it has	= it's
we have	= we've
they have	= they've

Negative contractions with *have:*

do not have	= don't have*
does not have	= doesn't have
have not	= haven't*
has not	= hasn't
had not	= hadn't

Note: *Be careful to distinguish these uses of *have:* don't/doesn't have = to not have a car, some matches, etc; have/has/had not = negative form of auxiliary *have,* used to form perfect tenses.

Contractions with *would/had:*

I would/I had	= I'd
you would/you had	= you'd
he would/he had	= he'd
she would/she had	= she'd
we would/we had	= we'd
they would/they had	= they'd

Negative contractions with *would*:

| would not | = wouldn't |
| would not have | = wouldn't have |

Note: * The same pattern is used for *could* and *should.*

Negative contractions with *do*/does/did:*

do not	= don't
does not	= doesn't
did not	= didn't

Note: * There are no contractions with *do* in the affirmative.

Other contractions:

That is	= That's
There is	= There's
There would (be)	= There'd (be)
What is?	= What's
Who is?/Who has?	= Who's
Who have?	= Who've
who had	= who'd*
Let us	= Let's

Other negative contractions:

That is not	= That isn't/That's not
There is not	= There isn't/There's not
There are not	= There aren't
What is not	= What isn't/What's not
Who is not?	= Who isn't?/Who's not?
Who has not?	= Who's not?/Who hasn't?
who have not	= who haven't*
Let us not	= Let's not

Note: * This contraction is used only with relative clauses, not in questions.

All About Tenses

Like most Western languages, English is very concerned about the time frame that something happens in. Each English verb goes through numerous systematized changes in spelling or pronunciation. These changes are markers that let the listener or reader know when an action or situation occurs. Such verb forms are called *tenses,* and each tense is used in a particular way. Tenses mainly focus on the time of an action or situation (or its length), but each tense also brings with it nuances that go beyond timelines. We will discuss all of them as we examine each tense. In terms of language, time concepts fall into three fairly neat categories with fairly little overlap:

- *The present tenses,* at or near the moment of speaking— which doesn't always literally mean "now"

Sampras *is playing* at Wimbledon on Saturday.
The sale at Saks *is ending* today.

- *The past tenses,* which comprise actions or events that are completely finished at the time of speaking

I *went to* the Picasso exhibit yesterday.

- *The future tenses,* which basically cover things that have not yet happened by the time of speaking

We *'ll visit* Marie tomorrow.
Tom *is going to leave* on a trip later this afternoon.

In addition to the concept of time, the actual tenses can be divided into categories based on other concepts that are actually considerably more logical groupings than purely time-based ones. (You will find that in the Complete Conjugations of verbs in Section B, we have taken this common-sense approach.) The categories are the following:

Simple tenses: the simple present, simple past, and simple future (two forms). *All* simple tenses show complete, often brief or habitual actions. Simple and progressive tenses sometimes intersect, depending on the length or brevity of two actions and who the subject(s) is/are.

Progressive tenses: the present progressive, past progressive, future progressive. Progressive tenses are all about continuous actions. They can be ongoing at the moment of speaking, go from one past point in time to another, or describe a continuous action that will either begin and end in the future, or (in the case of the present perfect progressive) begin in the present and continue to a future point. Verbs that show states of being (see Section 4, *Something to Think About: State-of-Being Verbs,* page 10) seldom have a progressive form, or else such a verb's meaning changes considerably if used in a progressive sense. All progressive tenses express continuity, but also carry overtones of unfinished or incomplete action, and repetitive (but not regular or habitual) actions as well. This is a major difference from the simple tenses.

Perfect tenses: the present perfect, past perfect, and future perfect. Perfect tenses always point to completed actions that carry over into another time frame or affect it in some way. There are also corresponding progressive tenses for each of the perfect tenses.

Finally, there are some grammar forms that deal with time frames to some degree, but are not tenses, strictly speaking. They are:

Participles: The present and the past participles are not tenses in themselves, but they are used to form several important tenses and other constructions.

Conditionals: the future conditional, the "unreal" conditional, and the past conditional. Conditional forms all contain *if* (or a similar word), and are less about time frames than how likely or unlikely it is for an event to take place. Each one has a fairly rigid structure, so the conditional forms all need to be understood and memorized. All conditional sentences are made up of two parts connected by a comma. One sentence contains the word *if* that sets up a situation with varying degrees of possibility or impossibility (*the if-clause*), and the second explains some possible or likely (or impossible) result (*the result clause*).

The Subjunctive: The subjunctive is almost nonexistent in modern English. Its main use is to form the unreal conditional. A secondary use is in clauses followed by *that.*

Used to + simple form verb: This construction is an exception in that while it looks like a past tense form, its real function is to talk *in the present* about a general preference or habitual act that was true in the past, but is no longer true. Because *used to* already points to a past situation, there is no past tense. In theory, the question form is *Did you/he use to . . . ?* The negative form is *didn't use to* (Carol *didn't use to* tire so quickly; I *used to like* beef, but nowadays I prefer fish). Note that the negative and interrogative forms of *used to* are spelled *use to*, without the *d.*

Let's look at the individual tenses and see how each is used.

Simple Present Tense

The simple present tense consists entirely of the verb's simple form (the infinitive without *to*), but changes for the 3rd person singular (*he/she/it*) by adding *-s* (or *-es,* depending on the spelling of the verb) in the simple present. The irregular verbs *be, do,* and *have* are the only exceptions (see individual verb conjugations in Section B).

This tense describes:

- Regular or habitual actions that can be daily, hourly, or merely frequent

This model *performs* well under all conditions.
The last train from the city *arrives* at 8:00.
Mr. Henson always *leaves* home at 7:00.
I *don't eat* bread at breakfast.
Tom and I *play* squash several times a month.

- Factual, mathematical, or scientific information

Hurricanes *strike* between August and November.
Spinach *contains* oxalic acid.
Four *times* five *makes* twenty.

• Eternal "truths;" timeless or general statements

> **All humans *experience* grief.**
> **Oil and water *don't mix*.**
> **The rain *ends* and the sun *comes out*.**

• States of being such as emotions and intellectual processes

> **Henry *doesn't drink* coffee.**
> **Margo *detests* sentimentality.**
> **I *didn't notice* Pearl's broken finger.**

Simple Past Tense

The simple past tense consists entirely of the verb's past form, which is the simple form of the verb with the past tense marker *-ed* for regular verbs, and often for many irregular verbs as well; for other forms of irregular past tense verbs, see Part B: Complete Conjugations for Irregular Verbs, pages 118–220. There are no changes for the 3rd person singular in any past tense.

This tense describes:

• Completed actions or situations—often brief—that began and ended in the past

> **Sara and I *went* to a wedding last Sunday.** (marriage continues, but wedding is over)
> **Mindy *bought* a Cadillac last September.** (she still drives it, but the act of buying is over)
> **What *did* you *get* on your birthday?**
> **I *enjoyed* the play we *saw* yesterday.**

• A recurring action or situation in the past, or a habitual action if it has not continued into the present

> **Harry *played* soccer in high school.** (he can still play soccer, but his high school days are over)

My father always *took* me for drives in the country when I was a boy.

Leslie *smoked* two packs of cigarettes a day for years until her doctor *insisted* that she quit.

Simple Future Tense

There are two forms of the simple future tense. One is formed with the auxiliary *will* and the simple form of the verb (the infinitive without *to*). The other is formed with three elements: the present tense of *be, going to,* and the simple form of the verb. *Be* is the only element that changes according to person (*is/am/are going to play,* etc.). The *will*-form is almost always contracted to pronoun + *'ll* (*I'll, you'll, they'll*); the *be going to*-form is contracted as for *be* (*I'm, you're, we're, it's*). The two forms are not quite interchangeable, although in many cases the meaning stays the same. Here are the differences.

The *will*-form describes:

- Predictions based on hopes or feelings, previous experience, or probability (but *not* objective logic)

They *'ll* never *get* seats to the football game at this late date.

I *'ll do* everything to make you happy—you *'ll* never *have to worry* about anything again!

During the holiday season, it *'ll take* an extra hour to get here.

- Spontaneous, unplanned future decisions, or last-minute changes of plan

Let's go to Mario's—we *'ll eat* dinner there instead.

Charles! I've decided that I *will come* to the party after all!   (emphatic—no contraction)

- The strong determination or emphatic will of the speaker

Just wait! I *will get promoted* to regional manager—if not this year, then next (year).
The Board of Directors *will be* sorry—I'*ll make* them pay for this!   (make pay = cause __ to suffer)

- The speaker's agreement to (or reconfirmation of) a specific future event, such as a party or business meeting

The Senator *will attend* the ceremony, but he *won't be able to stay* for the dinner.
I'*ll see* you on the 25th at 8:00.   (*will/won't be able to* = future form of modal *can*)

- Making and responding to requests

"*Will* Billy *come* and *feed* the cat while I'm away?" "He'*ll be* there, don't worry!"
"I'*m going to buy* a house this summer." "I'*ll buy* a house eventually, too."   (definite decision and objective plan vs. internalized hopes/feelings)

The *be going to*-form describes:

- Predictions based on objective logic, established or researched facts, or personal assessment and observation

The doctor's tests show that Dad *isn't going to live* much longer, but I'm sure we'*ll find* some treatment that works.   (objective medical facts vs. subjective hope)

- Fixed plans involving others—personal, business, and professional appointments, etc.

> **Darla***'s going to take* **the car in**   (= mechanical maintenance)
> **for a tune-up at 10:00.**
> **The Bradleys** *are going to fly* **to**
> **Bermuda next month, and we're**
> **going to join them on the 17th.**

- Plans or intentions for the immediate or distant future—often the speaker's plans regarding himself or herself

> **I'***m going to use* **the shuttle to get to the airport next time.**
> **We'***re going to paint* **the house at last!**

Present Progressive

The present progressive is formed with the present tense of the auxiliary *be* and the *present participle* of the verb (*-ing*).

This tense describes:

- Something that is happening at the moment of speaking

> **I'***m washing* **dishes at the moment.**
> **He'***s* **just** *leaving* **for the airport now.**

- A situation in the very near future—often a single, specific occasion

> **I'***m taking* **my final exam on Friday.**
> **What** *are you doing* **this weekend—***not staying* **in the city, I**
> **hope?**

- A temporary situation—perhaps ongoing, but not repetitive, or habitual

We*'re staying* with my mother until the renovations are completed.
Bill *is walking* with a cast.

- A frequent situation that may not actually be in progress at the moment of speaking

Linda tells me that Alex *is playing tennis* again.
Are you *joking?* I don't think that's funny.
Sally *is* always *teasing* the dog.
Stop the car now! I*'m getting out!*

Note: The pronoun and *be* are almost always contracted in normal speech *unless* the speaker wants to be emphatic ("I *am* speaking from home—where did you think I was?").

Past Progressive

The past progressive is formed with the past tense of the auxiliary *be* (*was/were*) and the *present participle* of the verb (*-ing*). An exception is the form *was/were going to* + simple form (*I was going to call you last week*). It is used to show an unfulfilled or interrupted intention in the past. The past progressive differs from the simple past because it talks about an *ongoing* action from one point in the past to another. It can be used only with actions or situations of some duration. It can also be used with *while* and a second verb in either the past progressive or simple past to show two intersecting or parallel actions (Anne *was making* breakfast *while* I *was taking* a shower; The doorbell *rang while* I *was speaking* to my mother in London).

This tense describes:

- Past events that continued from one point in the past to a less distant point that is also in the past

Marty *was snoring* throughout the entire concert.
A dog in our neighborhood *was barking* from 10:00 p.m. until dawn.

- A specific moment during an ongoing activity

The turkey *was browning* beautifully; then the electricity went out.

- Events leading up to the main action of a story

Paula *was* just *sitting* and *waiting* on the doorstep when I got home—she had locked herself out.

- A one-time incident of repetitive (*not* habitual) action in the past

When I left the house, a boy *was* *bouncing* a ball on the sidewalk.   (= *repeated* bouncing)

Just then, the boy *bounced* the ball off of my car.   (= a single bounce)

- A feeling of incompletion or interruption

The secretary *was* just *finishing* the keyboarding when our computer crashed.

Future Progressive

The future progressive is formed with *will* or *be going to* + the simple form of the auxiliary *be* and the *present participle* of the main verb (*-ing*)—The staff *will be working* during the weekend. All the characteristics of the progressive tenses apply. You may ask: Why not just use the simple future? The answer is that in English only a progressive tense can show an action's duration or continuity. Additionally, the simple future is inexact—it gives a general future time frame for an action or intention, with little beginning or ending. The future progressive tense narrows the time frame to focus on a specific, continuing action.

This tense describes:
- An action that will be happening at a specific point, or between two specific points in the future

The boss *will* still *be shouting* about cost cutting when you come back from the meeting.

Mr. Devrys *won't be taking* any phone calls between now and 4:00; *he'll be conducting* a seminar for the sales staff.

Margaret *will be exercising* in her aerobics class tomorrow morning.

- A future action that has been planned or scheduled, and that will be in progress at the future point we are discussing

***Are* Steve and Laurie *going to be coming* to the party on the 14th?**

David's father *is going to be undergoing* surgery at 7:00 tomorrow morning. He should be waking up around 3:00 p.m.*

- An action we predict will be ongoing during a future time frame

In another month Tommy *will be relaxing* at home, enjoying his retirement.

- Questions about the listener's plans for a future point in time

***Who'll be taking* your place in the golf tournament next Sunday?**

Note: * In the case of predictions, *will* is sometimes replaced by *should,* which in this case means "it is likely that . . . will be happening." This is used when the speaker isn't entirely sure of the situation (John's plane should be getting in about now—but it might be late).

Present Perfect Progressive

The present perfect progressive is formed with the present tense of the auxiliary *have* + the past participle of *be* (*been*) and the present participle of the verb (*-ing*)—She *has been soaking* in the bathtub for over two hours. The present perfect progressive tense follows the principles of the perfect tenses (see below), but also adds the feeling of continuity of the progressive tenses. It is frequently used with words that stress duration, such as *since* and *for.*

Note: There are also future perfect progressive and past perfect progressive tenses, both of which combine the characteristics of the perfect and progressive tenses involved.

This tense describes:

• An action or state that started in the past and is continuing into the present moment

I'*ve been trying* to get interested in this novel since my vacation, but I just can't concentrate on it.

We *have been waiting* for Kenneth's letter for weeks.

Why *has* John *been smoking* so much more than usual lately?

Anthony *has been writing* in his diary for years.

How long *has* Irene *been driving?*

Present Perfect

The present perfect is formed with the present tense of the auxiliary *have* and the past participle (*eaten, driven, won*) and is used mainly to show a connection between an action or state begun in the past, and something in the present. Either the action or state has continued into the present, or it has some connection with it. The present perfect tense is frequently used with the time indicators *since* or *for.*

This tense describes:

• A situation or action that started in the past and has continued into—or had an effect on—the present

Katherine *has had* this ring since her 18th birthday.

The Herrera family *has lived* in this house for 200 years.

Jeff and Miriam *have been* in love since high school.

- An action that has itself ended but that took place within a time frame that has not ended yet (often used with the time indicator *already*)

Have you *already heard* the news this morning about the merger?

- Whether or not within our lifetime we have had a particular experience (always used with *ever* or *never*)

Has Stan *ever visited* Boston?

Tina *has never eaten* a raw oyster.

- A physical condition that began in the past, but is still in progress.

We *'ve* had jet lag ever since we arrived.

Bella's mother *has suffered* from allergies for the last 15 years, and they *have gotten* worse recently.

Past Perfect

The past perfect is formed with the past tense of the auxiliary *have* (*had*) and the past participle (*spoken, cried, gotten*). It is frequently set off by the time words *before, when,* or *by the time.* The past perfect shows a *completed* action that starts from one past point in time and precedes another action that also is *in the past.* The second action is usually in the simple past.

This tense describes:

- The relationship between two past actions or events, one of which took place before the other

> Anna *had* already *left* the office by the time the fax came through.
>
> When they got to the airport, Bob discovered that he *'d left* the tickets in his other suit.
>
> By the time the rescue team arrived, Eric *had developed* frostbite in both feet.

Future Perfect

The future perfect is formed with *will* and the present tense of the auxiliary *have* + the past participle (*said, drunk, given*). It is frequently set off by the expression *by the time.* The future perfect shows that an action will have ended by a specific future point in time. *Going to* is seldom used to form the future perfect.

This tense describes:

- The length of an activity that may have started before "now" but will be ongoing up to a specific point in the future

> Do you realize that Frank and I *will have been married* for 50 years next month?
>
> By the time Cindy arrives, I *will* already *have finished cleaning* the house.
>
> The Rosenthals *will have spent* close to 70 thousand dollars on Herbie's education by the time he finishes graduate school.
>
> I got soaking wet in the rain this morning, but I'm sure I *will have dried out* by dinner time.

Future Conditional

The future conditional is formed by *if* + the simple form of the verb—*go, take, say*—(the *if-clause*), and *will* + the simple form of the verb (*the result clause*). The two clauses can be reversed, but the elements *cannot* be mixed within a single clause.

This form describes:

- A possible situation in the immediate or distant future with a 50% likelihood of attainment

If Carlo *wins* tickets to the concert I*'ll scream!*

I*'ll go if* I *can find* the time.

Dana *will take* sailing lessons *if* she *can get* the money together.

The company *will make* a good profit this year *if* sales *are* steady.

What *will* you *wear if* the   (keep = continue)
temperature *keeps* dropping?

Unreal Conditional

The unreal conditional's *if-clause* is formed by *if* + the simple past tense of the verb (*spoke, went, laughed*). If the verb is *be*, the subjunctive form is used. (*were*—for *all* persons). The *result clause* is formed with *would* (or *could, might,* etc.) + the simple form of the verb.

This form describes:

- Contrary-to-fact situations or unlikely/impossible wishes

If we *won* the lottery, what *would* you *want to do* first?

If Scott *were* in charge of the company, we *would* all *be looking* for new jobs.

If Debbie *spoke* Japanese, she *could* probably *get* a job in Tokyo.

If it *were* spring, the garden *wouldn't look* so bare.

I *could* give the boss a lot of good advice, *if* he *listened.*

My wife says that Charlie *might have* better luck in school *if* he *studied* more often.

Past Conditional

The past conditional is formed by *if* + the past tense of the auxiliary *have* (*had*) and the past participle (*spoken, cried, gotten*—the *if*-clause). The result clause is formed with *would* (or *could, might,* etc.) + the present tense of the auxiliary *have* + the past participle.

This form describes:

- Speculation on past events—what would have happened if I hadn't done this, etc.

If Dad *had* only *finished* high school, he *could have been* very successful.

Janice *might have found* the right man *if she had been* a bit more serious about looking.

Would things *be* a lot better *if* the country *had thought* more carefully about energy conservation?

If Betty *hadn't left* when she did, she never *would have met* Pedro.

You *wouldn't be* so critical *if* you *had had* to work as hard as I did.

The Passive Voice

Verbs show the effect of the subject on the object. The attention is largely focused on what the subject "does" (or doesn't do) to the object. Sometimes, it is more important to shift the focus to the effect the subject's "doing" has on the object. To accomplish that, we use a form called the *passive voice.* This form says to the listener or reader, "Never mind about the subject, look at what *is done* to me!"

The passive voice is formed by adding the appropriate tense of the auxiliary verb *to be** to the past participle, *-ed* for regular verbs (see Section 2, *Verb Basics: Infinitives, Imperatives, and Participles; Negative Forms,* page 5). So, the simple present of the verb *to learn* in the passive voice would become *is/are learned;* the simple past tense, *was/were learned.* As you can see, it is the auxiliary—*be*—that is conjugated, not the full verb, *learn.* That verb always keeps its past participle form.

Note: * Sometimes in idiomatic English *get* is substituted for *be* (Paul's book *got published;* Joe *got robbed* last night) in passive constructions (see final entry in this section).

It's important to remember that while any active verb can be transformed into the passive, in many cases it would only be a theoretical exercise. Practically speaking, many situations would never be described with the passive voice.

The turkey *was carved* by Bob.	(stuffy and artificial)
Bob *carved* the turkey.	(natural focus is who did the carving, not what was done to the turkey)
Timmy's teeth *were brushed.*	(completely artificial—who brushed them?)
Timmy *brushed* his teeth.	(natural)

In Section B, you will find complete conjugations of the passive voice for the regular verb *to be asked* (*ask*), and the irregular verb, *to be given* (*give*), on pages 78–80 and 81–83, respectively.

ENGLISH VERBS AND HOW TO USE THEM

Active	Passive
do	*be* do*ne*
drive	*be* driv*en*
eat	*be* eat*en*
make	*be* ma*de*
send	*be* sent
take	*be* tak*en*
use	*be* use*d*
watch	*be* watch*ed*

Understanding when and when not to use the passive voice is slightly more complex. Many people, particularly in creative writing, try to avoid using it. Excessive or inappropriate use can weaken and obscure the speaker's meaning, or can sound formal, legalistic, stuffy, or artificial. Still, the passive voice has many legitimate, even essential uses (the average paragraph in a newspaper article contains at least half a dozen examples), and it is often the only form to accurately and naturally express certain situations. The passive voice is not only appropriate but also optimal for certain situations.

The passive voice best describes:

- When the *effect* of the action is more important than the person or situation (the *agent*) that caused it

All my best dishes *were broken* during the move!

The thief *was caught* as he tried to cross the border.

The play *was cancelled* and our money *was refunded*.

A lot of people *were put* out of (put out of work = lose one's job
work when the factory shut down. due to company closure)

- When we are giving factual information about something

The "Mona Lisa" *has been exhibited* all over the world.

After Evalyne's death, her Estate *was sold* at auction.

Limestone *is composed* chiefly of calcium carbonate.

- When we know the result of the action, but not who or what caused it

No trace of the missing manuscript *was* ever *found.*
The cause of the fire *is* still *unknown.*
Drawers *were ripped open* and   (ripped open = pulled out violently)
clothing *scattered* everywhere.*

- When the focus is on what happened and the agent is understood by context or because it was established earlier

We *were served* a wonderful salad, but the entrée *was brought out* too soon.
I*'ve been given* two speeding tickets on that road.
Did you notice that Barbara's hair *is being styled* in a different way?

- When the speaker (or writer) wants to maintain an impersonal, objective tone—as in news reports, written notices, signs and announcements, or formal (verbal) statements

A ground invasion *hasn't been ruled out,* and missile attacks *are being launched* as we speak.   (news)

Several instances of looting in the Capital *have been reported.*   (news)

Access to the public beyond this point *is* strictly *forbidden.*   (sign)

Shoplifters *will be prosecuted.*   (sign)

The wedding *was held* at St. James Episcopal church.   (announcement)

Note: * If two different verbs in the passive are used about the same subject, it's seldom necessary to repeat the auxiliary unless the time frame of the two verbs differs. (The articles *were seized* in Customs and *have* never *been* claimed.)

The passive voice is often used with modals and "semi-modals." In such cases, the modal shows the tense and neither *be* nor the verb changes form.

The machine *can be operated* from either position.

The prisoner *had to be restrained* before the sentence *could be read.*

Is it so terrible *to want to be shown* some affection?

Didn't the seller tell you that the transfer *would have to be registered* with us?

Sometimes it *is* important for clarity to include the agent, even when the focus of the situation demands the use of the passive voice.

The house *was damaged* more by water than by the fire itself.

Fortunately, the impact of the crash *was lessened* by the airbags.

Paula *is being immobilized* by her broken leg.

Candles *were* actually *melted* by the recent heatwave.

In informal situations, *be* is frequently replaced as the passive voice auxiliary by *get,* in its sense of "becoming" or "receiving."

Joe *got fired* yesterday.

Some Verbs Need an Object: Transitive and Intransitive Verbs

In the first section, *The Way We Use Verbs,* we looked at how to recognize the subject and the main verb of a rather long sentence.

Carl *heard* Maria's voice in the hall several minutes before she actually *came* into the room and calmly *walked* over to his chair, while his heart *continued beating* wildly.

It was clear that *Carl* was the subject and *heard* was the main verb. In that case, what part did *Maria's voice* play in the sentence? It was the *object*—actually, the direct object. There are also indirect objects, but we will examine those elsewhere. When the action that the main verb talks about is directed at someone or something, then that person or thing is the direct object. Here are some more sentences with direct objects.

Joe ate six *sausages.*	(Joe did something to the sausages: he ate them.)
The cat scratched *the dog's nose.*	(The cat did something to the dog's nose: she scratched it.)
I was talking to *Leslie* at the office this morning.	(I "did" something to Leslie: I talked to her.)
Marc hadn't seen *his sneakers* since he came home.	(Marc didn't "do" something to his sneakers: he didn't see—couldn't find—them.)

It's important to be able to recognize the direct object of a sentence, because certain verbs must have an object to complete their meaning—without one, they don't make sense. These are called *transitive verbs.*

Other verbs have a complete meaning without needing anything else, although they can be—and often are—followed by an adverb that shows degree (*It rained heavily*). These are called *intransitive verbs.*

Many other verbs can be either transitive or intransitive. Some of these can have wildly different meanings depending on which way they are used. Usually, one of the two forms will be much more common than the other (*give,* transitive, meaning "to transfer something"; *give,* intransitive, meaning "to yield to pressure").

Sometimes the differences between transitive and intransitive verbs, especially in spelling or conjugation, can be very subtle. This can cause confusion—even among some native speakers. Often, we can see the difference more easily in the past tense than in the infinitive or the present.

The sun *shone* brightly.	(*to shine*—intransitive)
The boy *shined* my shoes.	(*to shine* something—transitive)
Alexander the Great *lived* in the 3rd century BC.	(*to live*—intransitive)
Alexander the Great *lived* his life to the fullest.	(*to live* one's life—transitive)
Keith *lay* on the grass.	(*to lie* = physical position—intransitive)
Keith first *laid* the blanket on the grass.	(*to lay* = to place something—transitive)
Keith *lies* all the time!	(*to lie* = speak untruthfully—intransitive)

Here are some of the most common transitive and intransitive verbs.

Transitive:

build	give	place
buy	have	put
carry	hear	say
clean	know	take
consider	make	tell
discover	lay	want
enjoy	let	wear
find	like	
force	love	

Intransitive:

appear	live
arrive	look
bark	rain
care	rise
come	sit
dance	sleep
die	snow
dream	stand
fall	step
go	talk
laugh	think
lie	wait
listen	

11 When One Verb Follows Another

Reaching a more advanced level in English requires that you deal with more complex sentence structures. Often, you will be creating sentences that have more than one verb per sentence.

A frequent question is when to use an infinitive after another verb, and when to use a *gerund*. Gerunds are verbs used as nouns. They resemble the present participle, but a gerund can be the subject of a sentence.

> *Taking* the subway during rush hour is exhausting.
>
> I hate *fixing* dinner when I have a cold.
>
> *Trying* to eat with chopsticks can be frustrating.

Why not say *To take the subway during rush hour is exhausting* or *I hate to fix dinner when I have a cold?* The answer is that English verbs fall into three groups: those that can only be followed by a gerund, those that can only be followed by an infinitive, and those that can be followed by either one.

> I *regret selling* my car.
>
> I *promise to sell* you my car.
>
> I *waited* six years *to buy* a new one.
>
> I *hated waiting* six years.

When these verbs are immediately followed by another verb, it is always a gerund:

admit, appreciate, avoid, complete, consider, delay, deny, discuss, dislike, enjoy, escape, finish, imagine, mind (= dislike), practice, recall, recommend, suggest, understand

When these verbs are immediately followed by another verb, it can be either a gerund or an infinitive:

afford, attempt, begin, choose, come, continue, go, hate, hesitate, intend, like, love, neglect, play, prefer, pretend, regret, remember, start, stop, try

WHEN ONE VERB FOLLOWS ANOTHER

When these verbs are immediately followed by another verb, it is always an infinitive:

ask, beg, care, choose, convince, decide, deserve, expect, fail, forget, happen, know how, need, plan, prepare, pretend, seem, tend, wait, want, wish

Sometimes, the meaning changes depending on whether you choose a gerund or an infinitive.

I stopped *to watch*.	(= stop walking in order to watch)
I stopped *watching*.	(= stop looking at something)
Try *to cook* stew.	(= attempt to cook successfully)
Try *cooking* stew.	(= decide to cook stew instead of something else)
Remember *to lock* the door.	(= *don't forget* to do it later)
Do you remember *locking* the door?	(= *do you remember* that you did it earlier)

Only gerunds can follow prepositions (think about *doing*, plan on *going*, succeed in *selling*).

We had some regrets *at being* unable to see the Louvre.
We *regret to say* we didn't see the Louvre.
Jane planned *on giving* a party for the authors.
Jane planned *to give* a party for the authors.
Mac felt sorry *about damaging* that chair.
Mac felt sorry *to have damaged* that chair.

12 Phrasal Verbs

A certain group of English verbs are called phrasal verbs because they are not a single word, but are made up of two, sometimes three, words. The first of these words is always the verb. It is followed (never preceded) by the second part, called the *particle*. With three-word phrasal verbs, the second and third words are particles. As a rule, particles are prepositions, but they can also sometimes be adverbs. In the case of three-word phrasal verbs, the final particle is almost always a preposition.

Phrasal verbs are sometimes considered "difficult" for a couple of reasons. In most cases, the meanings of phrasal verbs are highly idiomatic. Certainly, their meanings often have little in common with the original verb. For example:

(to) break	crack, crush, destroy, separate into pieces
break apart	separate into pieces
break down	a machine stops working
break into	enter a building with force
break out	escape; get a skin rash
break through	overcome a physical or intellectual barrier
break up	divide; laugh uncontrollably
break up with	end a relationship with someone

As you can see, almost none of the phrasal verbs above are close to the original meaning of *break*. The meaning of these verbs depends completely on which particle is used. The wrong choice of particle can totally change the speaker's intended meaning. *Step up* (come forward) is worlds apart in meaning from *step down* (get off of a train or, in another meaning, resign from a high position). Another thing to remember is that the verb part of phrasal verbs needs to be conjugated, just as any other verb. Phrasal verbs fall into three general groups:

Group 1: separable phrasal verbs

In this group, the verb can be separated from the particle with an object (see Section 10, page 47, for more on objects). You can put the object in two places, either between the particle and the verb or after the particle. In other words, a separable phrasal verb doesn't actually have to be separated except if the object is a pronoun (*he, them, me, it,* etc). In that case, the pronoun *must* come between the verb and the particle. Every *separable* phrasal verb can take an object.

I *picked out* <u>a new sweater</u>.	(correct)
I *picked* <u>a new sweater</u> *out.*	(correct)
I *picked* <u>it</u> *out.*	(correct)
I *picked out* <u>it</u>.	(incorrect)

Group 2: inseparable phrasal verbs that take an object

The particle and the verb must stay together, but they can still take an object. All three-word phrasal verbs belong to this group.

We know that we can *count on* <u>you</u>.

Please *look after* <u>the dogs</u>.

Bobby has so much energy, we can't *keep up with* <u>him</u>.

Don't *run out of* <u>milk</u>.

Group 3: inseparable phrasal verbs that don't take an object

These phrasal verbs have meanings that are complete without anything added. They *don't* have to take an object. The verb and particle are never separated, and what follows the phrasal verb is something other than an object. Such phrasal verbs can even be put at the end of a sentence.

Peter Pan never *grew up.*

My computer has just *broken down!*

This morning, I *woke up* at 5:00.

Separable phrasal verbs include:

add up	find the total amount of several figures
back up	move a car in reverse
bring out	reveal, show to advantage
bring up	raise children/introduce a new subject in conversation
bring/take back	return something
call off	cancel plans
check out	investigate
calm down	sooth *another* person who is upset
fill in/out	write information on a form
find out	discover information
give back	return something to a person
look up	check facts in a dictionary, etc.
pick out	choose from among several
pick up	lift from the floor/stop a car and get a person/thing
put away	return something to its proper place
put in	add or insert
put off	postpone
put on	add an article of clothing to the body
show off	display object or skill with pride
take off	remove an article of clothing from the body
take/pull out	remove
think over	carefully review an opinion/decision
try on	put on clothing to check for style, size, etc.
turn down	lower volume on TV, etc./reject an offer or request
turn into	make another person/situation change
work out	solve a problem/reach a compromise

Inseparable (two-word) phrasal verbs include:

call out	shout
call on	visit someone
care for	be fond of/take care of someone
check into	register at a hotel/research a subject
count on	rely on someone
go on	continue (often followed by a gerund)
go over	reexamine/review
go through	use something up/go over in sequence
hang up	put the phone receiver back/put clothes on a hanger
look after	take care of someone or something
look into	investigate a situation or a person
run across	accidentally find something
run into	accidentally meet someone
turn into	a person/situation becomes different

Inseparable (three-word) phrasal verbs include:

break up with	end a relationship (usually people, also businesses)
check out of	pay the bill on leaving a hotel, hospital, etc.
get along with	have friendly/smooth relations with
get rid of	throw something out/persuade a person to leave
get on with	start doing something (after hesitating, postponing)
get out of	leave a small vehicle (car, elevator, etc.)
go along with	agree with someone/something
keep up with	maintain the current speed or level

look forward to	anticipate an enjoyable future event
put up with	endure an unpleasant situation/behavior
run out of	the supply of something ends
stand up to	resist someone or some force

Inseparable phrasal verbs that take <u>no</u> object include:

act up	a person behaves badly
add up	something lacks logic (negative sense)
break down	a mechanism stops working
calm down	person returns to calm by himself/herself
come/go in(to)	enter a place (building, etc.)
come/go back	return to a place
eat in	eat at home
eat out	go to restaurants (vs. "eat in")
get by	manage in a difficult situation
get on	be successful/move upward, forward (career, life, etc.)
get up	leave one's bed and stand up
give in	stop resisting
give up	lose hope
go out	leave a place
grow up	become an adult
keep on	continue
look up	raise eyes
sit down	change from a standing to sitting position
stand up	rise to a standing position
take off	a plane/rocket leaves
throw up	to vomit
wake up	open one's eyes after sleeping
work out	do exercise (at gym)

Keep in mind two more important things about phrasal verbs: (1) one phrasal verb can have several different meanings and (2) whether the phrasal verb is separable or inseparable, whether it does or does not take an object, all depends on the particular meaning—determined by the context of the sentence.

I tried to *calm* <u>**Barbara**</u> *down.*	(= sooth *her*—separable)
I tried to *calm down.*	(= return to mental calm—inseparable)
Ben tried to *break* <u>the problem</u> *down.*	(= divide into manageable sections—separable)
The old car finally *broke down.*	(= machine stopped working—inseparable)
Mary *looked* <u>the unknown word</u> *up.*	(= check reference source—separable)
Mary heard a noise and *looked up.*	(= raise eyes—inseparable)

B

ENGLISH VERB PATTERNS

Introduction: The Way Tenses Are Formed

Regular Verb, Active Form: *ask*

Auxiliary Verbs
  be
  do
  have

Passive Voice
  ask—regular verb, passive form: (*to*) *be asked*
  give—irregular verb, passive form: (*to*) *be given*

Regular Verbs 84–115

Irregular Verbs 116–217

Modals and "Semi-Modals" 219–251

Causative Verbs: *get, have, let, make* 252–261

Index of Verbs

Introduction:
The Way Tenses Are Formed

In Part B, we will give the conjugations for a large number of English verbs. To show the typical pattern of tenses for each *person*, the regular and active verb (*to*) *ask* and the auxiliaries *be*, *do*, and *have*, are shown with all persons (*I*, *you*, *he*, *we*, *they*, etc.), as are the passive forms of *ask*, and the irregular verb *give*. After that, only the simple present tense will list the forms for all persons. For other tenses, only the 1st person singular (*I*) will be listed because the other person forms—with the exception of the 3rd person (*he/she/it*), which adds *–s* or *–es*— have identical forms in almost all cases. Throughout, the negative of each tense is shown after the abbreviation **neg**.

As you probably know, when you look up a verb in the dictionary, it gives you first the simple form (infinitive without *to*), next the past tense, and finally the past participle—essential for forming all the perfect tenses (the pattern of the irregular verb (*to*) *go* is found as *go-went-gone*, for example).

Under the heading *These Verbs Follow the Same Pattern,* you will find some verbs that are conjugated identically (*grow* and *throw*, for example). Sometimes, though, even if the spelling pattern or pronunciation are similar (*break* and *make*, or *get* and *set)*, the conjugation pattern is completely different. In such cases, these dissimilar verbs are listed under the warning heading of *These Verbs Follow a Different Pattern.*

Regular verb, active form: *ask*

INFINITIVE/IMPERATIVE	**NEGATIVE**
(to) ask/Ask . . . !	(to) not ask/Don't ask . . . !
Present Participle	**Past Participle**
asking	asked
Neg. not asking	**Neg.** not asked

PRESENT TENSES

Simple Present Tense
I ask
you ask
he/she/it asks
we ask
you ask
they ask

Neg. don't/doesn't ask

Present Progressive
I am asking
you are asking
he/she/it is asking
we are asking
you are asking
they are asking

Neg. (am) not/aren't/isn't asking

Present Perfect
I have asked
you have asked
he/she/it has asked
we have asked
you have asked
they have asked

Neg. haven't/hasn't asked

Present Perfect Progressive
I have been asking
you have been asking
he/she/it has been asking
we have been asking
you have been asking
they have been asking

Neg. haven't/hasn't been asking

PAST TENSES

Simple Past Tense
I asked
you asked
he/she/it asked
we asked
you asked
they asked

Neg. didn't ask

Past Progressive
I was asking
you were asking
he/she/it was asking
we were asking
you were asking
they were asking

Neg. wasn't/weren't asking

Past Perfect
I had asked
you had asked
he/she/it had asked
we had asked
you had asked
they had asked

Neg. hadn't asked

Past Perfect Progressive
I had been asking
you had been asking
he/she/it had been asking
we had been asking
you had been asking
they had been asking

Neg. hadn't been asking

FUTURE TENSES

Simple Future Tense
I will ask
you will ask
he/she/it will ask
we will ask
you will ask
they will ask

Neg. won't ask

Future Progressive
I will be asking
you will be asking
he/she/it will be asking
we will be asking
you will be asking
they will be asking

Neg. won't be asking

Future Perfect
I will have asked
you will have asked
he/she/it will have asked
we will have asked
you will have asked
they will have asked

Neg. won't have asked

Immediate Future Tense
I am going to ask
you are going to ask
he/she/it is going to ask
we are going to ask
you are going to ask
they are going to ask

Neg. (am) not/aren't/isn't going to ask

Immediate Future Progressive
I am going to be asking
you are going to be asking
he/she/it is going to be asking
we are going to be asking
you are going to be asking
they are going to be asking

Neg. (am) not/aren't/isn't going to be asking

CONDITIONALS

Future Conditional
(If) I ask, . . . will . . .
(If) you ask, . . . will . . .
(If) he/she/it asks, . . . will . . .
(If) we ask, . . . will . . .
If) you ask, . . . will . . .
(If) they ask, . . . will . . .

Neg. (If) don't/doesn't ask, will . . .

Unreal Conditional-Progressive Form
(If) I were asking, . . . would . . .
(If) you were asking, . . . would . . .
(If) he/she/it were asking, . . . would . . .
(If) we were asking, . . . would . . .
(If) you were asking, . . . would . . .
(If) they were asking, . . . would . . .

Unreal Conditional
(If) I asked, . . . would . . .
(If) you asked, . . . would . . .
(If) he/she/it asked, . . . would . . .
(If) we asked, . . . would . . .
((If) you asked, . . . would . . .
(If) they asked, . . . would . . .

Neg. (If) didn't ask, . . . would . . .

Past Conditional
(If) I had asked, . . . would have
(+ past participle)
(If) you had asked, . . . would have
(+ past participle)
(If) he/she/it had asked, . . . would have
(+ past participle)

Neg. (If) <u>weren't</u> ask<u>ing</u>, . . . <u>would</u> . . .

Past Conditional-Progressive Form
(If) I <u>had been</u> ask<u>ing</u>, . . . <u>would have</u>
(+ past participle)
(If) you <u>had been</u> ask<u>ing</u>, . . . <u>would have</u>
(+ past participle)
(If) he/she/it <u>had been</u> ask<u>ing</u>, . . . <u>would</u>
<u>have</u> (+ past participle)
(If) we <u>had been</u> ask<u>ing</u>, . . . <u>would have</u>
(+ past participle)
(If) you <u>had been</u> ask<u>ing</u>, . . . <u>would have</u>
(+ past participle)
(If) they <u>had been</u> ask<u>ing</u>, . . . <u>would have</u>
(+ past participle)

Neg. (If) I <u>hadn't been</u> ask<u>ing</u>, . . . <u>would</u>
<u>have</u> (+ past participle)

(If) we <u>had</u> ask<u>ed</u>, . . . <u>would have</u>
(+ past participle)
(If) you <u>had</u> ask<u>ed</u>, . . . <u>would have</u>
(+ past participle)
(If) they <u>had</u> ask<u>ed</u>, . . . <u>would have</u>
(+ past participle)

Neg. (If) I <u>hadn't</u> ask<u>ed</u>, . . . <u>would have</u>
(+ past participle)

These Verbs Follow the Same Pattern
check
greet
help
jump
walk

"It never hurts *to ask*."

"May I *ask* you a question?" "*Don't ask* me now—I've got to finish this report
before 3:00."

"We *asked* you to give us a report by Thursday."

The authorities *have asked* all noncitizens to register with their consulates.

Betty *had asked* all her friends to the party, but only a few came.

"He *would have asked* your permission last week, but you were out."

"*If I asked* you to work late on Friday, would you (do it)?"	Use of this conditional indicates the speaker (1) thinks agreement is
The minister *will be asking* for contributions after the service.	*unlikely*, or (2) thinks the request is unreasonable—otherwise the future conditional would be used.

"Charles *would have been asking* me to marry him any minute if his mother hadn't
come downstairs just then."

Auxiliary Verbs

Irregular verb, auxiliary and full verb: *be*

INFINITIVE/IMPERATIVE	*NEGATIVE*
(to) be/Be . . . !	(to) <u>not</u> be/<u>Don't</u> be . . . !
Present Participle	***Past Participle***
be<u>ing</u>	be<u>en</u>
Neg. <u>not</u> being	***Neg.*** <u>not</u> been

PRESENT TENSES

Simple Present Tense
I <u>am</u>
you <u>are</u>
he/she/it <u>is</u>
we <u>are</u>
you <u>are</u>
they <u>are</u>

Neg. (<u>am</u>) <u>not</u>/<u>aren't</u>/<u>isn't</u>

Present Progressive
I <u>am</u> be<u>ing</u>
you <u>are</u> be<u>ing</u>
he/she/it <u>is</u> be<u>ing</u>
we <u>are</u> be<u>ing</u>
you <u>are</u> be<u>ing</u>
they <u>are</u> be<u>ing</u>

Neg. (<u>am</u>) <u>not</u>/<u>aren't</u>/<u>isn't</u> be<u>ing</u>

Present Perfect
I <u>have</u> be<u>en</u>
you <u>have</u> be<u>en</u>
he/she/it <u>has</u> be<u>en</u>
we <u>have</u> be<u>en</u>

you <u>have</u> be<u>en</u>
they <u>have</u> be<u>en</u>

Neg. <u>haven't</u>/<u>hasn't</u> be<u>en</u>

PAST TENSES

Simple Past Tense
I <u>was</u>
you <u>were</u>
he/she/it <u>was</u>
we <u>were</u>
you <u>were</u>
they <u>were</u>

Neg. <u>wasn't</u>/<u>weren't</u>

Past Progressive
I <u>was</u> be<u>ing</u>
you <u>were</u> be<u>ing</u>
he/she/it <u>was</u> be<u>ing</u>
we <u>were</u> be<u>ing</u>
you <u>were</u> be<u>ing</u>
they <u>were</u> be<u>ing</u>

Neg. <u>wasn't</u>/<u>weren't</u> be<u>ing</u>

Past Perfect
I <u>had</u> be<u>en</u>
you <u>had</u> be<u>en</u>
he/she/it <u>had</u> be<u>en</u>
we <u>had</u> be<u>en</u>
you <u>had</u> be<u>en</u>
they <u>had</u> be<u>en</u>

Neg. <u>hadn't</u> be<u>en</u>

Past Perfect Progressive
I <u>had</u> be<u>en</u> be<u>ing</u>
you <u>had</u> be<u>en</u> be<u>ing</u>
he/she/it <u>had</u> be<u>en</u> be<u>ing</u>
we <u>had</u> be<u>en</u> be<u>ing</u>
you <u>had</u> be<u>en</u> be<u>ing</u>
they <u>had</u> be<u>en</u> be<u>ing</u>

Neg. <u>hadn't</u> be<u>en</u> be<u>ing</u>

FUTURE TENSES

Simple Future Tense
I will be
you will be
he/she/it will be
we will be
you will be
they will be

Neg. won't be

Future Progressive*
I will be being
you will be being
he/she/it will be being
we will be being
you will be being
they will be being

Neg. won't be being

Future Perfect
I will have been
you will have been
he/she/it will have been
we will have been
you will have been
they will have been

Neg. won't have been

Immediate Future Tense
I am going to be
you are going to be
he/she/it is going to be
we are going to be
you are going to be
they are going to be

Neg. (am) not/aren't/isn't going to be

Immediate Future Progressive
I am going to be being
you are going to be being
he/she/it is going to be being
we are going to be being
you are going to be being
they are going to be being

Neg. (am) not/aren't/isn't going to be being

CONDITIONALS

Future Conditional
(If) I am, . . . will . . .
(If) you are, . . . will . . .
(If) he/she/it is, . . . will . . .
(If) we are, . . . will . . .
(If) you are, . . . will . . .
(If) they are, . . . will . . .

Neg. (If) (am) not/aren't/isn't, . . . will . . .
(If) am/are/is, . . . won't . . .

Unreal Conditional
(If) I were, . . . would . . .
(If) you were, . . . would . . .
(If) he/she/it were, . . . would . . .
(If) we were, . . . would . . .
(If) you were, . . . would . . .
(If) they were, . . . would . . .

Neg. (If) weren't, . . . would . . .
(If) were, . . . wouldn't . . .

Note: *Not frequently used with *be* except in the passive voice.

Unreal Conditional-Progressive Form
(If) I were being, . . . would . . .
(If) you were being, . . . would . . .
(If) he/she/it were being, . . . would . . .
(If) we were being, . . . would . . .
(If) you were being, . . . would . . .
(If) they were being, . . . would . . .

Neg. (If) weren't being, . . . would . . . (If) were being, . . . wouldn't . . .

Past Conditional—Progressive Form
(If) I had been being, . . . would have . . . (+ past participle)
(If) you had been being, . . . would have . . . (+ past participle)
(If) he/she/it had been being, . . . would have . . . (+ past participle)
(If) we had been being, . . . would have . . . (+ past participle)

Past Conditional
(If) I had been, . . . would have . . . (+ past participle)
(If) you had been, . . . would have . . . (+ past participle)
(If) he/she/it had been, . . . would have . . . (+ past participle)
(If) we had been, . . . would have . . . (+ past participle)
(If) you had been, . . . would have . . . (+ past participle)
(If) they had been, . . . would have . . . (+ past participle)

Neg. (If) hadn't been, . . . would have . . . (+ past participle)
(If) had been, . . . wouldn't have . . . (+ past participle)

(If) you had been being, . . . would have . . . (+ past participle)
(If) they had been being, . . . would have . . . (+ past participle)

Neg. (If) I hadn't been being, . . . would have . . . (+ past participle)
(If) I had been being, . . . wouldn't have . . . (+ past participle)

Notes: *Be* is used as an auxiliary (+ full verb, simple form) for yes/no questions in these tenses:

present progressive   (simple present form)
present perfect progressive   (past participle—after *have*)
past progressive   (simple past form)
past perfect progressive   (past participle—after *have*)
simple future   (simple present—only with *going to* form)
future progressive   (simple form after *will*; simple present after *going to* form)
future perfect   (past participle—after both *will* and *have*)
unreal conditional progressive   (subjunctive form)
past conditional progressive   (past participle—after *have*)
the passive voice   (all forms)

"How *are* you?"

"I *am* fine. I *would be* much better, but the children *are being* very difficult."

Using *would* in this case implies the unreal conditional (I would be much better, *if* the children *weren't being* so difficult).

Margaret *is* tired.

"Who *are* those people?"

"Don't *be* so curious!"

They said last summer that it *would be* a cold winter this year.

"*Are* you *going to be* on vacation during the audit?"

Colin's daughter *was* born on New Year's Eve. I wonder how old she *will be* on January 1st?

Andrew tried *to be* patient, but the neighbors *were* so noisy that he went next door and told them *to be* quiet.

It *would have been* a nice day, if the sun *had been* shining.

"*Are* you sure this *is* the restaurant the guidebook said *would be* so hard to get into? There *aren't* more than three couples here."

"They *were* probably *being* kind. This place *is* only for tourists."

If I thought Harold *were being* truly serious about quitting his job, I *'d be* more worried than I *have been*.

Irregular verb; emphatic verb; auxiliary and full verb: *do*

QUESTIONS

Used as an auxiliary (+ full verb, simple form) for yes/no questions in these tenses:
simple present	(simple present)
simple past	(simple past form)

INFINITIVE/IMPERATIVE	*NEGATIVE*
(to) do/Do . . . !	(to) not do/Don't do . . . !

Present Participle	***Past Participle***
doing	done

Neg. not doing	***Neg.*** not done

PRESENT TENSES

Simple Present Tense
I do
you do
he/she/it does
we do
you do
they do

Neg. don't/doesn't do

Present Progressive
I am doing
you are doing
he/she/it is doing
we are doing
you are doing
they are doing

Neg. (am) not/aren't/isn't doing

Present Perfect
I have done
you have done
he/she/it has done
we have done
you have done
they have done

Neg. haven't/hasn't done

Present Perfect Progressive
I have been doing
you have been doing
he/she/it has been doing
we have been doing
you have been doing
they have been doing

Neg. haven't/hasn't been doing

PAST TENSES

Simple Past Tense
I did
you did
he/she/it did
we did
you did
they did

Neg. didn't do

Past Progressive
I was doing
you were doing
he/she/it was doing
we were doing
you were doing
they were doing

Neg. wasn't/weren't doing

Past Perfect
I had done
you had done
he/she/it had done
we had done
you had done
they had done

Neg. hadn't done

Past Perfect Progressive
I had been doing
you had been doing
he/she/it had been doing
we had been doing
you had been doing
they had been doing

Neg. hadn't been doing

FUTURE TENSES

Simple Future Tense
I will do
you will do
he/she/it will do
we will do
you will do
they will do

Neg. won't do

Immediate Future Tense
I am going to do
you are going to do
he/she/it is going to do
we are going to do
you are going to do
they are going to do

Neg. (am) not/aren't/isn't going to do

Future Progressive
I will be doing
you will be doing
he/she/it will be doing
we will be doing
you will be doing
they will be doing

Neg. won't be doing

Immediate Future Progressive
I am going to be doing
you are going to be doing
he/she/it is going to be doing
we are going to be doing
you are going to be doing
they are going to be doing

Neg. (am) not/aren't/isn't going to be doing

Future Perfect
I will have done
you will have done
he/she/it will have done
we will have done
you will have done
they will have done

Neg. won't have done

CONDITIONALS

Future Conditional
(If) I do, . . . will . . .
(If) you do, . . . will . . .
(If) he/she/it does, . . . will . . .
(If) we do, . . . will . . .
(If) you do, . . . will . . .
(If) they do, . . . will . . .

Neg. (If) don't/doesn't do, . . . will . . .

Unreal Conditional
(If) I did, . . . would . . .
(If) you did, . . . would . . .
(If) he/she/it did, . . . would . . .
(If) we did, . . . would . . .
(If) you did, . . . would . . .
(If) they did, . . . would . . .

Neg. (If) didn't do, . . . would . . .

Unreal Conditional—Progressive Form
(If) I <u>were</u> do<u>ing</u>, . . . <u>would</u> . . .
(If) you <u>were</u> doing, . . . <u>would</u> . . .
(If) he/she/it <u>were</u> doing, . . . <u>would</u> . . .
(If) we <u>were</u> doing, . . . <u>would</u> . . .
(If) you <u>were</u> doing, . . . <u>would</u> . . .
(If) they <u>were</u> doing, . . . <u>would</u> . . .

Past Conditional
(If) I <u>had</u> do<u>ne</u>, . . . <u>would have</u>
(+ past participle)
(If) you <u>had</u> done, . . . <u>would have</u>
(+ past participle)
(If) he/she/it <u>had</u> do<u>ne</u>, . . . <u>would have</u>
(+ past participle)
(If) we <u>had</u> done, . . . <u>would have</u>
(+ past participle)
(If) you <u>had</u> done, . . . <u>would have</u>
(+ past participle)
(If) they <u>had</u> done, . . . <u>would have</u>
(+ past participle)

Neg. (If) <u>weren't</u> doing, . . . <u>would</u> . . .

Neg. (If) I <u>hadn't</u> do<u>ne</u>, . . . <u>would have</u>
(+ past participle)

Past Conditional—Progressive Form
(If) I <u>had been</u> do<u>ing</u>, . . . <u>would have</u> (+ past participle)
(If) you <u>had been</u> doing, . . . <u>would have</u> (+ past participle)
(If) he/she/it <u>had been</u> doing, . . . <u>would have</u> (+ past participle)
(If) we <u>had been</u> doing, . . . <u>would have</u> (+ past participle)
(If) you <u>had been</u> doing, . . . <u>would have</u> (+ past participle)
(If) they <u>had been</u> doing, . . . <u>would have</u> (+ past participle)

Neg. (If) I <u>hadn't been</u> doing, . . . <u>would have</u> (+ past participle)

"*Don't do* that to the cat, Sammy!"—
"What *did* I *do*?"

"What *does* Mike *do*?"—"He's an engineer."
(= what is his profession? Compare with next example)

"What *is* Mike *doing*?"—"He's over at the building site, I think."
(= what are his actions at the moment)

"How *are* your stocks *doing* these days?"—"They're *not doing* well at all. They *didn't do* very well in the two previous quarters, either."

"Sally still works downtown, *doesn't* she?"—"*Does* she? I thought she *was going to do* that summer session in Maine."

"*Did* you go to that new musical at the Lyceum?"—"No, I *didn't dare*. *I've done* some major damage to my savings since all that Christmas shopping we *did* last month."

"Marie *would have done* the dishes, but she *didn't* want to spoil her new manicure."
(= wash the dishes; do the washing up)

"*Do* come to the party, Kris! We *'d* all *be* so disappointed *if* you *didn't* (come)."

(= *Please* come) This use of *do* is emphatic—a sort of verbal italics. Although widely used in both American and British English, it is especially popular in Britain, where it is preferred to *please* when urging the listener to do something.

"That *does* it! If Terry *doesn't* start *doing* his share of the work, I'm quitting."

(= I have had enough of this [situation]; this [latest thing] is too much for me to accept.)

"He'll soon *be done helping* his wife with the new baby."

Irregular verb; emphatic verb; auxiliary and full verb: *have*

INFINITIVE/IMPERATIVE	**NEGATIVE**
(to) have/Have . . . !	(to) not have/Don't have . . . !
Present Participle	**Past Participle**
having	had
Neg. not having	**Neg.** not had

PRESENT TENSES

Simple Present Tense
I have
you have
he/she/it has
we have
you have
they have

Neg. don't/doesn't have*

In Britain, the following form is more popular:
I've got   we've got
you've got   you've got
he's/she's/it's got   they've got

Neg. haven't/hasn't got

Present Progressive
I am having
you are having
he/she/it is having
we are having
you are having
they are having

Neg. (am) not/aren't/isn't having

Present Perfect
I have had
you have had
he/she/it has had
we have had
you have had
they have had

Neg. haven't/hasn't had

Present Perfect Progressive
I have been having
you have been having
he/she/it has been having
we have been having
you have been having
they have been having

Neg. haven't/hasn't been having

PAST TENSES

Simple Past Tense
I had
you had
he/she/it had
we had
you had
they had

Neg. didn't have

Past Progressive
I was having
you were having
he/she/it was having
we were having
you were having
they were having

Neg. wasn't/weren't having

Note: *Only in the sense of possess; auxiliary's negative form is *haven't/hasn't*.

In Britain, the following form is more popular (only in the sense of *possess*):
I'd got
you'd got
he'd/she'd/it had got
we'd got
you'd got
they'd got

Neg. hadn't got

Past Perfect
I had had
you had had
he/she/it had had
we had had
you had had
they had had

Neg. hadn't had

Past Perfect Progressive
I had been having
you had been having
he/she/it had been having
we had been having
you had been having
they had been having

Neg. hadn't been having

FUTURE TENSES

Simple Future Tense
I will have
you will have
he/she/it will have
we will have
you will have
they will have

Neg. won't have

Immediate Future Tense
I am going to have
you are going to have
he/she/it is going to have
we are going to have
you are going to have
they are going to have

Neg. (am) not/aren't/isn't going to have

Future Progressive
I will be having
you will be having
he/she/it will be having
we will be having
you will be having
they will be having

Neg. won't be having

Immediate Future Progressive
I am going to be having
you are going to be having
he/she/it is going to be having
we are going to be having
you are going to be having
they are going to be having

Neg. (am) not/aren't/isn't going to be having

Future Perfect
I will have had
you will have had
he/she/it will have had
we will have had
you will have had
they will have had

Neg. won't have had

CONDITIONALS

Future Conditional
(If) I have, . . . will . . .
(If) you have, . . . will . . .
(If) he/she/it has, . . . will . . .
(If) we have, . . . will . . .
(If) you have, . . . will . . .
(If) they have, . . . will . . .

Neg. (If) don't/doesn't have, . . . will . . .

Unreal Conditional—Progressive Form
(If) I were having, . . . would . . .
(If) you were having, . . . would . . .
(If) he/she/it were having, . . . would . . .
(If) we were having, . . . would . . .
(If) you were having, . . . would . . .
(If) they were having, . . . would . . .

Neg. (If) weren't having, . . . would . . .

Unreal Conditional
(If) I had, . . . would . . .
(If) you had, . . . would . . .
(If) he/she/it had, . . . would . . .
(If) we had, . . . would . . .
(If) you had, . . . would . . .
(If) they had, . . . would . . .

Neg. (If) didn't have, . . . would . . .

Past Conditional
(If) I had had, . . . would have
(+ past participle)
(If) you had had, . . . would have
(+ past participle)
(If) he/she/it had had, . . . would have
(+ past participle)
(If) we had had, . . . would have
(+ past participle)
(If) you had had, . . . would have
(+ past participle)
(If) they had had, . . . would have
(+ past participle)

Neg. (If) I hadn't had, . . . would have
(+ past participle)

Past Conditional—Progressive Form
(If) I had been having, . . . would have (+ past participle)
(If) you had been having, . . . would have (+ past participle)
(If) he/she/it had been having, . . . would have (+ past participle)
(If) we had been having, . . . would have (+ past participle)
(If) you had been having, . . . would have (+ past participle)
(If) they had been having, . . . would have (+ past participle)

Neg. (If) I hadn't been having, . . . would have (+ past participle)

Have is used as an auxiliary (+ full verb and present or past participle) for yes/no questions in these tenses:

present perfect	(simple present form)
present perfect progressive	(simple present—before *be*)
past perfect	(simple past form)
past perfect progressive	(simple past form—before *be*)
future perfect	(simple present—after *will*)
past conditional	(simple past form—before *be*)
past conditional progressive	(simple past form—before *be*)

I *had* two cars up until this spring, but one of them *was having* engine trouble, so I gave it to my brother.

(1 = possess; 2 = experiencing)

"Do you *have* time for lunch today, Bob?"—"I *have* time for a quick sandwich. I *have* a client coming in at 2:00."

(3 = expect)

One of my kids *had to have* five fillings when I took him to the dentist.

The *had to* in *had to have* is the past tense of the modal meaning *must*; the *have* is an idiomatic usage meaning *get* or *receive.*

We *haven't* finished paying for the car yet—and we bought it last year.

(= true auxiliary usage)

The Mortons *are having* some friends over for dinner on Saturday.

"*Haven't* you *had* Kathy's famous roast duck?"—"No, but I *had* heard she was a great cook."

The company *would have had* huge profits this year if there *hadn't* been that slump in October.

Passive Voice

Regular verb, passive form: be asked

QUESTIONS

For yes/no questions, see auxiliary *be*

INFINITIVE/IMPERATIVE	*NEGATIVE*
(to) be asked/Ask!	(to) not be asked/Don't ask!
Present Participle	*Past Participle*
being asked	been asked
Neg. not being asked	*Neg.* not been asked

PRESENT TENSES

Simple Present Tense
I am asked
you are asked
he/she/it is asked
we are asked
you are asked
they are asked

Neg. (am) not/aren't/isn't asked

Present Progressive
I am being asked
you are being asked
he/she/it is being asked
we are being asked
you are being asked
they are being asked

Neg. (am) not/aren't/isn't being asked

Present Perfect
I have been asked
you have been asked
he/she/it has been asked
we have been asked
you have been asked
they have been asked

Neg. haven't/hasn't been asked

PAST TENSES

Simple Past Tense
I was asked
you were asked
he/she/it was asked
we were asked
you were asked
they were asked

Neg. wasn't/weren't asked

Past Progressive
I was being asked
you were being asked
he/she/it was being asked
we were being asked
you were being asked
they were being asked

Neg. wasn't/weren't being asked

Past Perfect
I had been asked
you had been asked
he/she/it had been asked
we had been asked

you had been asked
they had been asked

Neg. hadn't been asked

FUTURE TENSES

Simple Future Tense
I will be asked
you will be asked
he/she/it will be asked
we will be asked
you will be asked
they will be asked

Neg. won't be asked

Future Perfect
I will have been asked
you will have been asked
he/she/it will have been asked
we will have been asked
you will have been asked
they will have been asked

Neg. won't have been asked

Immediate Future Tense
I am going to be asked
you are going to be asked
he/she/it is going to be asked
we are going to be asked
you are going to be asked
they are going to be asked

Neg. (am) not/aren't/isn't going to be asked

CONDITIONALS

Unreal Conditional—Progressive Form
(If) I were being asked, . . . would . . .
(If) you were being asked, . . . would . . .
(If) he/she/it were being asked, . . . would . . .
(If) we were being asked, . . . would . . .
(If) you were being asked, . . . would . . .
(If) they were being asked, . . . would . . .

Neg. (If) weren't being asked, . . . would . . .

Unreal Conditional
(If) I were asked, . . . would . . .
(If) you were asked, . . . would . . .
(If) he/she/it were asked, . . . would . . .
(If) we were asked, . . . would . . .
(If) you were asked, . . . would . . .
(If) they were asked, . . . would . . .

Neg. (If) weren't asked, . . . would . . .

Past Conditional
(If) I had been asked, . . . would have (+ past participle)
(If) you had been asked, . . . would have (+ past participle)
(If) he/she/it had been asked, . . . would have (+ past participle)
(If) we had been asked, . . . would have (+ past participle)
(If) you had been asked, . . . would have (+ past participle)
(If) they had been asked, . . . would have (+ past participle)

Neg. (If) I hadn't been asked, . . . would have (+ past participle)

Ursula *is* often *asked* why she moved back to Germany.
Joanna *will be asked* some difficult questions on the exam.
Film stars *are* always *being asked* for their autographs.

My brother *has* frequently *been asked* if he's a professional football player.

Why *has* George *been asked* to give a speech at the China Institute, when Paula's Chinese is so much more fluent?

If I *were asked* what I'd most like to change about my life, it would be my . . .

COMPLETE CONJUGATIONS   be given

Regular verb, passive form: be given

QUESTIONS

For yes/no questions, see auxiliary *be*.

INFINITIVE/IMPERATIVE	***NEGATIVE***
(to) be given/Give . . . !	(to) not be given/Don't give . . . !
Present Participle	***Past Participle***
being given	been given
Neg. not being given	***Neg.*** not been given

PRESENT TENSES

Simple Present Tense
I am given
you are given
he/she/it is given
we are given
you are given
they are given

Neg. (am) not/aren't/isn't given

Present Progressive
I am being given
you are being given
he/she/it is being given
we are being given
you are being given
they are being given

Neg. (am) not/aren't/isn't being given

Present Perfect
I have been given
you have been given
he/she/it has been given
we have been given
you have been given
they have been given

Neg. haven't/hasn't been given

PAST TENSES

Simple Past Tense
I was given
you were given
he/she/it was given
we were given
you were given
they were given

Neg. wasn't/weren't given

Past Progressive
I was being given
you were being given
he/she/it was being given
we were being given
you were being given
they were being given

Neg. wasn't/weren't being given

Past Perfect
I had been given
you had been given
he/she/it had been given
we had been given

you had been given
they had been given

Neg. hadn't been given

FUTURE TENSES

Simple Future Tense
I <u>will</u> be given
you <u>will</u> be given
he/she/it <u>will</u> be given
we <u>will</u> be given
you <u>will</u> be given
they <u>will</u> be given

Neg. <u>won't</u> be given

Future Perfect
I <u>will</u> <u>have</u> be<u>en</u> given
you <u>will</u> <u>have</u> be<u>en</u> given
he/she/it <u>will</u> <u>have</u> be<u>en</u> given
we <u>will</u> <u>have</u> be<u>en</u> given
you <u>will</u> <u>have</u> be<u>en</u> given
they <u>will</u> <u>have</u> be<u>en</u> given

Neg. <u>won't</u> <u>have</u> been given

Immediate Future Tense
I <u>am</u> <u>going to</u> be given
you <u>are</u> <u>going to</u> be given
he/she/it <u>is</u> <u>going to</u> be given
we <u>are</u> <u>going to</u> be given
you <u>are</u> <u>going to</u> be given
they <u>are</u> <u>going to</u> be given

Neg. (<u>am</u>) <u>not</u>/<u>aren't</u>/<u>isn't</u> <u>going to</u> be given

CONDITIONALS

Unreal Conditional—Progressive Form
(<u>If</u>) I <u>were</u> being given, . . . <u>would</u> . . .
(<u>If</u>) you <u>were</u> being given, . . . <u>would</u> . . .
(<u>If</u>) he/she/it <u>were</u> being given, . . . <u>would</u> . . .
(<u>If</u>) we <u>were</u> being given, . . . <u>would</u> . . .
(<u>If</u>) you <u>were</u> being given, . . . <u>would</u> . . .
(<u>If</u>) they <u>were</u> being given, . . . <u>would</u> . . .

Neg. (<u>If</u>) <u>weren't</u> being given, . . . <u>would</u> . . .

Unreal Conditional
(<u>If</u>) I <u>were</u> given, . . . <u>would</u> . . .
(<u>If</u>) you <u>were</u> given, . . . <u>would</u> . . .
(<u>If</u>) he/she/it <u>were</u> given, . . . <u>would</u> . . .
(<u>If</u>) we <u>were</u> given, . . . <u>would</u> . . .
(<u>If</u>) you <u>were</u> given, . . . <u>would</u> . . .
(<u>If</u>) they <u>were</u> given, . . . <u>would</u> . . .

Neg. (<u>If</u>) <u>weren't</u> given, . . . <u>would</u> . . .

Past Conditional
(<u>If</u>) I <u>had</u> be<u>en</u> given, . . . <u>would have</u> (+ past participle)
(<u>If</u>) you <u>had</u> be<u>en</u> given, . . . <u>would have</u> (+ past participle)
(<u>If</u>) he/she/it <u>had</u> be<u>en</u> given, . . . <u>would have</u> (+ past participle)
(<u>If</u>) we <u>had</u> be<u>en</u> given, . . . <u>would have</u> (+ past participle)
(<u>If</u>) you <u>had</u> be<u>en</u> given, . . . <u>would have</u> (+ past participle)
(<u>If</u>) they <u>had</u> be<u>en</u> given, . . . <u>would have</u> (+ past participle)

Neg. (<u>If</u>) I <u>hadn't</u> be<u>en</u> given, . . . <u>would have</u> (+ past participle)

Mother *is being given* so many lovely presents for her fiftieth birthday.

So far, she *has* already *been given* a silver teapot and a silk scarf.

Johnny *was given* one last chance to stop drinking by the judge—he *'d* already *been given* several suspended sentences.   (*one last chance* = one more chance, but the last one)

Aren't the Oscars *given* out in March?

Sarah *was given* plenty of love and affection as a child, so why is she so cold and selfish?

Regular Verbs

Regular verb, active form: *beg*

INFINITIVE/IMPERATIVE	***NEGATIVE***
(to) beg/Beg . . . !	(to) not beg/Don't beg . . . !
Present Participle*	***Past Participle****
begging	begged
Neg. not begging	***Neg.*** not begged

PRESENT TENSES

Simple Present Tense
I beg
you beg
he/she/it begs
we beg
you beg
they beg

Neg. don't/doesn't beg

Present Perfect
I have begged

Neg. haven't/hasn't begged

Present Progressive
I am begging
you are begging
he/she/it is begging
we are begging
you are begging
they are begging

Neg. (am) not/aren't/isn't begging

PAST TENSES

Simple Past Tense
I begged

Neg. didn't beg

Past Perfect
I had begged

Neg. hadn't begged

Past Progressive
I was begging

Neg. wasn't/weren't begging

Past Perfect Progressive
I had been begging

Neg. hadn't been begging

FUTURE TENSES

Simple Future Tense
I will beg

Neg. won't beg

Future Progressive
I will be begging

Neg. won't be begging

Immediate Future Tense
I am going to beg

Neg. (am) not/aren't/isn't going to beg

Immediate Future Progressive
I am going to be begging

Neg. (am) not/aren't/isn't going to be begging

Note: *Spelling change: Verbs ending in a single -*g* following a single vowel double the -*g* before -*ing* and -*ed*.

84

Future Perfect
I will have begged

Neg. won't have begged

CONDITIONALS

Future Conditional
(If) I beg, . . . will . . .

Neg. (If) don't/doesn't beg, . . . will . . .
(If) beg, . . . won't . . .

Unreal Conditional—Progressive Form
(If) I were begging, . . . would . . .

Neg. (If) weren't begging, . . . would . . .
(If) were begging, . . . wouldn't . . .

Unreal Conditional
(If) I begged, . . . would . . .

Neg. (If) didn't beg, . . . would . . .
(If) begged, . . . wouldn't . . .

Past Conditional
(If) I had begged, . . . would have . . .
(+ past participle)

Neg. (If) hadn't begged, . . . would have . . . (+ past participle)
(If) had begged, . . . wouldn't have (+ past participle)

Past Conditional—Progressive Form
(If) I had been begging, . . . would have . . . (+ past participle)

Neg. (If) hadn't been begging, . . . would have . . . (+ past participle)
(If) had been begging, . . . wouldn't have . . . (+ past participle)

These Verbs Follow the Same Pattern

bat (i.e., in baseball or cricket)	panic
clap (= applaud)	prod (= urge)
compel (= force)	rub
drag (= pull after)	shop
drop	stab
hug	stop
jog	submit (= offer for approval)
lag (behind)	

I had to *beg* the bank to extend the loan.	The verb is in simple form because it comes after a modal (*have to*).
Stop *begging*, Kenny! I said no!	
I'm not too proud to *beg*.	
I *beg* your pardon.	This is a set expression of semi-formal apology.
Helen *has been begging* me to show her my wedding dress.	

Regular verb, active form: *belong*

INFINITIVE/IMPERATIVE	*NEGATIVE*
(to) belong/belong . . . !	(to) not belong/Don't belong . . . !

PRESENT TENSES

Simple Present Tense	*Present Progressive*
I belong	I <u>am</u> belong<u>ing</u>
you belong	you <u>are</u> belong<u>ing</u>
he/she/it belong<u>s</u>	he/she/it <u>is</u> belong<u>ing</u>
we belong	we <u>are</u> belong<u>ing</u>
you belong	you <u>are</u> belong<u>ing</u>
they belong	they <u>are</u> belong<u>ing</u>

Neg. <u>don't</u>/<u>doesn't</u> belong

Present Perfect
I <u>have</u> belong<u>ed</u>

Neg. <u>haven't</u>/<u>hasn't</u> belong<u>ed</u>

PAST TENSES

Simple Past Tense	*Past Perfect*
I belong<u>ed</u>	I <u>had</u> belong<u>ed</u>
Neg. <u>didn't</u> belong	*Neg.* <u>hadn't</u> belong<u>ed</u>

FUTURE TENSES

Simple Future Tense	*Immediate Future Tense*
I <u>will</u> belong	I <u>am going to</u> belong
Neg. <u>won't</u> belong	*Neg.* (am) <u>not</u>/<u>aren't</u>/<u>isn't going to</u> belong

Future Perfect
I <u>will have</u> belong<u>ed</u>

Neg. <u>won't have</u> belong<u>ed</u>

CONDITIONALS

Present Participle	*Past Participle*
belong<u>ing</u>	belong<u>ed</u>
Neg. <u>not</u> belonging	*Neg.* <u>not</u> belong<u>ed</u>

Future Conditional	*Unreal Conditional*
(<u>If</u>) I belong, . . . <u>will</u> . . .	(<u>If</u>) I belong<u>ed</u>, . . . <u>would</u> . . .
Neg. (<u>If</u>) <u>don't</u>/<u>doesn't</u> belong, . . . <u>will</u> . . .	*Neg.* (<u>If</u>) <u>didn't</u> belong, . . . <u>would</u> . . .
(<u>If</u>) belong, . . . <u>won't</u> . . .	(<u>If</u>) belong<u>ed</u>, . . . <u>wouldn't</u> . . .

Past Conditional
(If) I had belonged, . . . would have . . .
(+ past participle)

Neg. (If) hadn't belonged, . . . would have . . . (+ past participle)
(If) had belonged, . . . wouldn't have . . . (+ past participle)

Mr. Wentworth *belongs* to several professional associations.	(= be a member of)
Many people *belong* to the local golf club, but I don't.	
We really feel as if we *belong* in this community.	(= fit in/be a part of)
Margaret never really *belonged* in this company.	
With your abilities, Tim, I think you really *belong* in marketing, not R & D.	(= deserve to be/be suited to)

No drunken driver *belongs* behind the wheel of a car!

Those scissors *belong* in the drawer, not in the sink.

Regular verb, active form: *call*

INFINITIVE/IMPERATIVE	**NEGATIVE**
(to) call/Call . . . !	(to) not call/Don't call . . . !

PRESENT TENSES

Simple Present Tense
I call
you call
he/she/it calls
we call
you call
they call

Neg. don't/doesn't call

Present Perfect
I have called

Neg. haven't/hasn't called

Present Progressive
I am calling

Neg. (am) not/aren't/isn't calling

PAST TENSES

Simple Past Tense
I called

Neg. didn't call

Past Perfect
I had called

Neg. hadn't called

Past Progressive
I was calling

Neg. wasn't/weren't calling

Past Perfect Progressive
I had been calling

Neg. hadn't been calling

FUTURE TENSES

Simple Future Tense
I will call

Neg. won't call

Future Progressive
I will be calling

Neg. won't be calling

Future Perfect
I will have called

Neg. won't have called

Immediate Future Tense
I am going to call

Neg. (am) not/aren't/isn't going to call

Immediate Future Progressive
I am going to be calling

Neg. (am) not/aren't/isn't going to be calling

CONDITIONALS

Present Participle
calling

Neg. not calling

Past Participle
called

Neg. not called

Future Conditional
(If) I call, . . . will . . .

Neg. (If) don't/doesn't call, . . . will . . .
(If) call, . . . won't . . .

Unreal Conditional—Progressive Form
(If) I were calling, . . . would . . .

Neg. (If) weren't calling, . . . would . . .
(If) were calling, . . . wouldn't . . .

Past Conditional—Progressive Form
(If) I had been calling, . . . would have . . .
(+ past participle)

Neg. (If) hadn't been calling, . . . would
have . . . (+ past participle)
(If) had been calling, . . . wouldn't
have . . . (+ past participle)

Unreal Conditional
(If) I called, . . . would . . .

Neg. (If) didn't call, . . . would . . .
(If) called, . . . wouldn't . . .

Past Conditional
(If) I had called, . . . would have . . .
(+ past participle)

Neg. (If) hadn't called, . . . would have . . .
(+ past participle)
(If) had called, . . . wouldn't have . . .
(+ past participle)

These Verbs Follow the Same Pattern
pull
recall   (= remember)
stall   (= motor doesn't start/postpone or
          delay an action)

Call is a component of many phrasal verbs (see Part A, Section 12 Phrasal
Verbs, page 52): *call on, call off, call up, call for, call into*, etc. These all
have quite different meanings, but are all conjugated the same way. *Don't
call* me William, just *call* me Bill.

Were you *calling* me?	(= voice)
I've *been calling* Gloria for hours—is something wrong with her phone?	(= telephone)
We'*ll call* you when dinner is ready.	(= voice)
Will you *call* me with the results, Doctor?	(= telephone)
The boss *called* Mark into his office the other day.	Often used when a superior talks to an employee privately, especially for the purpose of criticism.

Regular verb, active form: *carry*

INFINITIVE/IMPERATIVE	***NEGATIVE***
(to) carry/Carry . . . !	(to) not carry/Don't carry . . . !
Present Participle	***Past Participle****
carry<u>ing</u>	carr<u>ied</u>
Neg. <u>not</u> carry<u>ing</u>	***Neg.*** <u>not</u> carr<u>ied</u>

PRESENT TENSES

Simple Present Tense*
I carry
you carry
he/she/it carr<u>ies</u>
we carry
you carry
they carry

Neg. <u>don't</u>/<u>doesn't</u> carry

Present Progressive
I <u>am</u> carry<u>ing</u>

Neg. (<u>am</u>) <u>not</u>/<u>aren't</u>/<u>isn't</u> carry<u>ing</u>

Present Perfect
I <u>have</u> carr<u>ied</u>

Neg. <u>haven't</u>/<u>hasn't</u> carr<u>ied</u>

PAST TENSES

Simple Past Tense
I carr<u>ied</u>

Neg. <u>didn't</u> carry

Past Perfect
I <u>had</u> carr<u>ied</u>

Neg. <u>hadn't</u> carr<u>ied</u>

Past Progressive
I <u>was</u> carry<u>ing</u>

Neg. <u>wasn't</u>/<u>weren't</u> carry<u>ing</u>

Past Perfect Progressive
I <u>had</u> <u>been</u> carry<u>ing</u>

Neg. <u>hadn't</u> <u>been</u> carry<u>ing</u>

FUTURE TENSES

Simple Future Tense
I <u>will</u> carry

Neg. <u>won't</u> carry

Future Progressive
I <u>will</u> <u>be</u> carry<u>ing</u>

Neg. <u>won't</u> <u>be</u> carry<u>ing</u>

Future Perfect
I <u>will</u> <u>have</u> carr<u>ied</u>

Neg. <u>won't</u> <u>have</u> carr<u>ied</u>

Immediate Future Tense
I <u>am</u> <u>going</u> <u>to</u> carry

Neg. (<u>am</u>) <u>not</u>/<u>aren't</u>/<u>isn't</u> <u>going</u> <u>to</u> carry

Immediate Future Progressive
I <u>am</u> <u>going</u> <u>to</u> <u>be</u> carry<u>ing</u>

Neg. (<u>am</u>) <u>not</u>/<u>aren't</u>/<u>isn't</u> <u>going</u> <u>to</u> <u>be</u> carry<u>ing</u>

Note: *Spelling change: Verbs ending in *-y* following one or more consonants change the *-y* to *ie* in the 3rd person, simple present tense, and to *-i* in all *-ed* tenses.

CONDITIONALS

Future Conditional
(If) I carry, . . . will . . .

Neg. (If) don't/doesn't carry, . . . will . . .
(If) carry, . . . won't . . .

Unreal Conditional—Progressive Form
(If) I were carrying, . . . would . . .

Neg. (If) weren't carrying, . . . would . . .
(If) were carrying, . . . wouldn't . . .

Past Conditional—Progressive Form
(If) I had been carrying, . . . would
have . . . (+ past participle)

Neg. (If) hadn't been carrying, . . . would
have . . . (+ past participle)
(If) had been carrying, . . . wouldn't
have . . . (+ past participle)

Unreal Conditional
(If) I carried, . . . would . . .

Neg. (If) didn't carry, . . . would . . .
(If) carried, . . . wouldn't . . .

Past Conditional
(If) I had carried, . . . would have . . .
(+ past participle)

Neg. (If) hadn't carried, . . . would
have . . . (+ past participle)
(If) had carried, . . . wouldn't have . . .
(+ past participle)

These Verbs Follow the Same Pattern
apply (to/for)
cry
hurry
marry
rely (on) (= depend on/count on)
study
supply
try

These Verbs Follow a Different Pattern
pay   stay
play   stray
pray   toy (with)
prey (on)

Tom had *to carry* his luggage all the way to the bus.	
Excuse me, *do* you *carry* Excelsior brand canned milk?	(= store usually sells)
The soprano's voice *carried* to the top of the opera house.	(= sound reaches)
Kathy *has carried* her diet much too far.	(= do to an extreme degree)
All the newspapers and TV stations *carried* the story.	(= media write/talk about)

Regular verb, active form: *change*

INFINITIVE/IMPERATIVE	NEGATIVE
(to) change/Change . . .!	(to) not change/Don't change . . .!
Present Participle*	**Past Participle***
changing	changed
Neg. not changing	**Neg.** not changed

PRESENT TENSES

Simple Present Tense
I change
you change
he/she/it changes
we change
you change
they change

Neg. don't/doesn't change

Present Perfect
I have changed

Neg. haven't/hasn't changed

Present Progressive
I am changing

Neg. (am) not/aren't/isn't changing

PAST TENSES

Simple Past Tense
I changed

Neg. didn't change

Past Perfect
I had changed

Neg. hadn't changed

Past Progressive
I was changing

Neg. wasn't/weren't changing

Past Perfect Progressive
I had been changing

Neg. hadn't been changing

FUTURE TENSES

Simple Future Tense
I will change

Neg. won't change

Future Progressive
I will be changing

Neg. won't be changing

Future Perfect
I will have changed

Neg. won't have changed

Immediate Future Tense
I am going to change

Neg. (am) not/aren't/isn't going to change

Immediate Future Progressive
I am going to be changing

Neg. (am) not/aren't/isn't going to be changing

Note: *Spelling change: Regular verbs ending in -e following a consonant drop the -e before -ing endings and add -d for -ed endings.

CONDITIONALS

Future Conditional
(If) I change, . . . will . . .

Neg. (If) don't/doesn't change, . . . will . . .
(If) change, . . . won't . . .

Unreal Conditional—Progressive Form
(If) I were changing, . . . would . . .

Neg. (If) weren't changing, . . . would . . .
(If) were changing, . . . wouldn't . . .

Past Conditional—Progressive Form
(If) I had been changing, . . . would
have . . . (+ past participle)

Neg. (If) hadn't been changing, . . . would
have . . . (+ past participle)
(If) had been changing, . . . wouldn't have
. . . (+ past participle)

Unreal Conditional
(If) I changed, . . . would . . .

Neg. (If) didn't change, . . . would . . .
(If) changed, . . . wouldn't . . .

Past Conditional
(If) I had changed, . . . would have . . .
(+ past participle)

Neg. (If) hadn't changed, . . . would
have . . . (+ past participle)
(If) had changed, . . . wouldn't have . . .
(+ past participle)

These Verbs Follow the Same Pattern
arrange
exchange
range

Change your clothes before dinner!

The weather *is* really *changing*, isn't it?

Has Nancy *changed* a lot since college?

Carl *was changing* lanes when the truck hit him.

Times *change*, and we have to *change* with them.

We *had* already *changed* our marketing strategy by the time the new Board was appointed.

If I *change* my hairstyle, *will* my face look thinner?

Regular verb, active form: *die*

INFINITIVE/IMPERATIVE	***NEGATIVE***
(to) die/Die . . . !	(to) not die/Don't die . . . !
Present Participle*	***Past Participle****
dying	died
Neg. not dying	***Neg.*** not died

PRESENT TENSES

Simple Present Tense
I die
you die
he/she/it dies
we die
you die
they die

Neg. don't/doesn't die

Present Progressive
I am dying

Neg. (am) not/aren't/isn't dying

Present Perfect
I have died

Neg. haven't/hasn't died

PAST TENSES

Simple Past Tense
I died

Neg. didn't die

Past Perfect
I had died

Neg. hadn't died

Past Progressive
I was dying

Neg. wasn't/weren't dying

Past Perfect Progressive
I had been dying

Neg. hadn't been dying

FUTURE TENSES

Simple Future Tense
I will die

Neg. won't die

Future Progressive
I will be dying

Neg. won't be dying

Immediate Future Tense
I am going to die

Neg. (am) not/aren't/isn't going to die

Immediate Future Progressive
I am going to be dying

Neg. (am) not/aren't/isn't going to be
dying

Note: *Spelling change: Verbs ending in *-ie* change the *-ie* to *-y* in all *-ing* tenses.

Future Perfect
I will have died

Neg. won't have died

CONDITIONALS

Future Conditional
(If) I die, . . . will . . .

Neg. (If) don't/doesn't die, . . . will . . .
(If) die, . . . won't . . .

Unreal Conditional—Progressive Form
(If) I were dying, . . . would . . .

Neg. (If) weren't dying, . . . would . . .
(If) were dying, . . . wouldn't . . .

Past Conditional—Progressive Form
(If) I had been dying, . . . would have . . .
(+ past participle)

Neg. (If) hadn't been dying, . . . would have . . . (+ past participle)
(If) had been dying, . . . wouldn't have . . .
(+ past participle)

Unreal Conditional
(If) I died, . . . would . . .

Neg. (If) didn't die, . . . would . . .
(If) died, . . . wouldn't . . .

Past Conditional
(If) I had died, . . . would have . . .
(+ past participle)

Neg. (If) hadn't died, . . . would have . . .
(+ past participle)
(If) had died, . . . wouldn't have . . .
(+ past participle)

These Verbs Follow the Same Pattern
tie
rely (on)
vie

I laughed so hard I almost *died*.

That man doesn't deserve *to die* for an accidental shooting.

What should I do about my lawn—all the grass *is dying*.

Many kinds of wildlife *have died* out   (*have died* out = become extinct)
because of pollution.

Too many people *die* in car accidents because they don't use seat belts.

My mother said, "You don't *die* from a broken heart."

I'*m dying* to get these tight shoes off!   (= figurative use—can't wait.)

finish   REGULAR VERBS

Regular verb, active form: *finish*

INFINITIVE/IMPERATIVE	*NEGATIVE*
(to) finish/Finish . . . !	(to) not finish/Don't finish . . . !
Present Participle	*Past Participle*
finish<u>ing</u>	finish<u>ed</u>
Neg. <u>not</u> finish<u>ing</u>	*Neg.* <u>not</u> finish<u>ed</u>

PRESENT TENSES

Simple Present Tense*
I finish
you finish
he/she/it finish<u>es</u>
we finish
you finish
they finish

Neg. <u>don't</u>/<u>doesn't</u> finish

Present Progressive
I <u>am</u> finish<u>ing</u>

Neg. (<u>am</u>) <u>not</u>/<u>aren't</u>/<u>isn't</u> finish<u>ing</u>

Present Perfect
I <u>have</u> finish<u>ed</u>

Neg. <u>haven't</u>/<u>hasn't</u> finish<u>ed</u>

PAST TENSES

Simple Past Tense
I finish<u>ed</u>

Neg. <u>didn't</u> finish

Past Perfect
I <u>had</u> finish<u>ed</u>

Neg. <u>hadn't</u> finish<u>ed</u>

Past Progressive
I <u>was</u> finish<u>ing</u>

Neg. <u>wasn't</u>/<u>weren't</u> finish<u>ing</u>

Past Perfect Progressive
I <u>had</u> <u>been</u> finish<u>ing</u>

Neg. <u>hadn't</u> <u>been</u> finish<u>ing</u>

FUTURE TENSES

Simple Future Tense
I <u>will</u> finish

Neg. <u>won't</u> finish

Future Progressive
I <u>will</u> <u>be</u> finish<u>ing</u>

Neg. <u>won't</u> <u>be</u> finish<u>ing</u>

Future Perfect
I <u>will</u> <u>have</u> finish<u>ed</u>

Neg. <u>won't</u> <u>have</u> finish<u>ed</u>

Immediate Future Tense
I <u>am</u> <u>going</u> <u>to</u> finish

Neg. (<u>am</u>) <u>not</u>/<u>aren't</u>/<u>isn't</u> <u>going</u> <u>to</u> finish

Immediate Future Progressive
I <u>am</u> <u>going</u> <u>to</u> <u>be</u> finish<u>ing</u>

Neg. (<u>am</u>) <u>not</u>/<u>aren't</u>/<u>isn't</u> <u>going</u> <u>to</u> <u>be</u> finish<u>ing</u>

Note: *Spelling change: Verbs ending in *-sh*, *-ch*, *-ss*, *-x*, and *-o* form the 3rd person singular with *-es* instead of *-s*.

CONDITIONALS

Future Conditional
(If) I finish, . . . will . . .

Neg. (If) don't/doesn't finish, . . . will . . .
(If) finish, . . . won't . . .

Unreal Conditional—Progressive Form
(If) I were finishing, . . . would . . .

Neg. (If) weren't finishing, . . . would . . .
(If) were finishing, . . . wouldn't . . .

Past Conditional—Progressive Form
(If) I had been finishing, . . . would
have . . . (+ past participle)

Neg. (If) hadn't been finishing, . . . would
have . . . (+ past participle)
(If) had been finishing, . . . wouldn't
have . . . (+ past participle)

Unreal Conditional
(If) I finished, . . . would . . .

Neg. (If) didn't finish, . . . would . . .
(If) finished, . . . wouldn't . . .

Past Conditional
(If) I had finished, . . . would have . . .
(+ past participle)

Neg. (If) hadn't finished, . . . would
have . . . (+ past participle)
(If) had finished, . . . wouldn't have . . .
(+ past participle)

These Verbs Follow the Same Pattern
approach (= come close to)
crush
do
furnish (= decorate empty room)
go
kiss
miss
punish
push
touch
vanish (= emphatic word for disappear)

When *are* you *going to finish* your homework?
Have you and George *finished* redecorating yet?
I *was* just *finishing* dinner when you called.
Henry *has finished* college.
The film *finishes* at 7:00.
If the mechanic *had finished* working on the car today, he *would have* called.
Kelly claims *to be finished* with Len   (= finish permanently)
once and for all.

Regular verb, active form: *free*

INFINITIVE/IMPERATIVE	*NEGATIVE*
(to) free/Free . . . !	(to) not free/Don't free . . . !
Present Participle	*Past Participle**
free<u>ing</u>	free<u>d</u>
Neg. <u>not</u> free<u>ing</u>	*Neg.* <u>not</u> free<u>d</u>

PRESENT TENSES

Simple Present Tense
I free
you free
he/she/it free<u>s</u>
we free
you free
they free

Neg. <u>don't/doesn't</u> free

Present Progressive
I <u>am</u> free<u>ing</u>

Present Perfect
I <u>have</u> free<u>d</u>

Neg. <u>haven't/hasn't</u> free<u>d</u>

Neg. (<u>am</u>) <u>not/aren't/isn't</u> free<u>ing</u>

PAST TENSES

Simple Past Tense
I free<u>d</u>

Neg. <u>didn't</u> free

Past Perfect
I <u>had</u> free<u>d</u>

Neg. <u>hadn't</u> free<u>d</u>

Past Progressive
I <u>was</u> free<u>ing</u>

Neg. <u>wasn't/weren't</u> free<u>ing</u>

Past Perfect Progressive
I <u>had been</u> free<u>ing</u>

Neg. <u>hadn't been</u> free<u>ing</u>

FUTURE TENSES

Simple Future Tense
I <u>will</u> free

Neg. <u>won't</u> free

Future Progressive
I <u>will be</u> free<u>ing</u>

Neg. <u>won't be</u> free<u>ing</u>

Immediate Future Tense
I <u>am going to</u> free

Neg. (<u>am</u>) <u>not/aren't/isn't</u> <u>going to</u> free

Immediate Future Progressive
I <u>am going to be</u> free<u>ing</u>

Neg. (<u>am</u>) <u>not/aren't/isn't</u> <u>going to be</u> free<u>ing</u>

Note: *Spelling change: Verbs ending in -*ee* add only -*d* for the -*ed* ending.

Future Perfect
I will have freed

Neg. won't have freed

CONDITIONALS

Future Conditional
(If) I free, . . . will . . .

Neg. (If) don't/doesn't free, . . . will . . .
(If) free, . . . won't . . .

Unreal Conditional—Progressive Form
(If) I were freeing, . . . would . . .

Neg. (If) weren't freeing, . . . would . . .
(If) were freeing, . . . wouldn't . . .

Past Conditional—Progressive Form
(If) I had been freeing, . . . would have . . .
(+ past participle)

Neg. (If) hadn't been freeing, . . . would
have . . . (+ past participle)
(If) had been freeing, . . . wouldn't
have . . . (+ past participle)

Unreal Conditional
(If) I freed, . . . would . . .

Neg. (If) didn't free, . . . would . . .
(If) freed, . . . wouldn't . . .

Past Conditional
(If) I had freed, . . . would have . . .
(+ past participle)

Neg. (If) hadn't freed, . . . would have . . .
(+ past participle)
(If) had freed, . . . wouldn't have . . .
(+ past participle)

These Verbs Follow the Same Pattern
agree
disagree
flee
guarantee

The warden agreed *to free* the prisoners.
Reporters claimed the suspect should *have been freed* immediately.
Lincoln is remembered because he *freed* the slaves.
We've decided that *we'll free* this baby hawk in the spring.
If you *free* the puppy, ho'*ll* starve.

Regular verb, active form: *help*

INFINITIVE/IMPERATIVE	*NEGATIVE*
(to) help/Help . . . !	(to) not help/Don't help . . . !

PRESENT TENSES

Simple Present Tense
I help
you help
he/she/it helps
we help
you help
they help

Neg. don't/doesn't help

Present Progressive
I am helping

Neg. (am) not/aren't/isn't helping

Present Perfect
I have helped

Neg. haven't/hasn't helped

PAST TENSES

Simple Past Tense
I helped

Neg. didn't help

Past Perfect
I had helped

Neg. hadn't helped

Past Progressive
I was helping

Neg. wasn't/weren't helping

Past Perfect Progressive
I had been helping

Neg. hadn't been helping

FUTURE TENSES

Simple Future Tense
I will help

Neg. won't help

Future Progressive
I will be helping

Neg. won't be helping

Future Perfect
I will have helped

Neg. won't have helped

Immediate Future Tense
I am going to help

Neg. (am) not/aren't/isn't going to help

Immediate Future Progressive
I am going to be helping

Neg. (am) not/aren't/isn't going to be helping

CONDITIONALS

Present Participle
helping

Neg. not helping

Past Participle
helped

Neg. not helped

Future Conditional
(If) I help, . . . will . . .

Neg. (If) don't/doesn't help, . . . will . . .
(If) help, . . . won't . . .

Unreal Conditional—Progressive Form
(If) I were helping, . . . would . . .

Neg. (If) weren't helping, . . . would . . .
(If) were helping, . . . wouldn't . . .

Past Conditional—Progressive Form
(If) I had been helping, . . . would have . . . (+ past participle)

Neg. (If) hadn't been helping, . . . would have . . . (+ past participle)
(If) had been helping, . . . wouldn't
have . . . (+ past participle)

Unreal Conditional
(If) I helped, . . . would . . .

Neg. (If) didn't help, . . . would . . .
(If) helped, . . . wouldn't . . .

Past Conditional
(If) I had helped, . . . would have . . .
(+ past participle)

Neg. (If) hadn't helped, . . . would
have . . . (+ past participle)
(If) had helped, . . . wouldn't have . . .
(+ past participle)

Help! I can't swim!

Help me move this bookcase, would
you?

This medicine *isn't helping* my
headache at all.   (= make better)

If John *helps* himself first, then I'*ll
help* him, too.

It can't *be helped*—we'll have to sell   (= no other choice possible)
the other car.

Who *helped* themselves to the last   (= to take something—usually food—
piece of cake?   without asking permission first)

This organization *has been helping*
the community for over 40 years.

All the dark clothing in this shop *won't*   (= make a difference)
help—I've got to lose 10 pounds!

Regular verb, active form: *learn*

INFINITIVE/IMPERATIVE	***NEGATIVE***
(to) learn/Learn . . . !	(to) not learn/Don't learn . . . !
Present Participle	***Past Participle***
learning	learned
Neg. not learning	***Neg.*** not learned

PRESENT TENSES

Simple Present Tense
I learn
you learn
he/she/it learns
we learn
you learn
they learn

Neg. don't/doesn't learn

Present Perfect
I have learned

Neg. haven't/hasn't learned

Present Progressive
I am learning

Neg. (am) not/aren't/isn't learning

PAST TENSES

Simple Past Tense
I learned

Neg. didn't learn

Past Perfect
I had learned

Neg. hadn't learned

Past Progressive
I was learning

Neg. wasn't/weren't learning

Past Perfect Progressive
I had been learning

Neg. hadn't been learning

FUTURE TENSES

Simple Future Tense
I will learn

Neg. won't learn

Future Progressive
I will be learning

Neg. won't be learning

Future Perfect
I will have learned

Neg. won't have learned

Immediate Future Tense
I am going to learn

Neg. (am) not/aren't/isn't going to learn

Immediate Future Progressive
I am going to be learning

Neg. (am) not/aren't/isn't going to be learning

CONDITIONALS

Future Conditional
(If) I learn, . . . will . . .

Neg. (If) don't/doesn't learn, . . . will . . .
(If) learn, . . . won't . . .

Unreal Conditional—Progressive Form
(If) I were learning, . . . would . . .

Neg. (If) weren't learning, . . . would . . .
(If) were learning, . . . wouldn't . . .

Past Conditional—Progressive Form
(If) I had been learning, . . . would
have . . . (+ past participle)

Neg. (If) hadn't been learning, . . . would
have . . . (+ past participle)
(If) had been learning, . . . wouldn't
have . . . (+ past participle)

Unreal Conditional
(If) I learned, . . . would . . .

Neg. (If) didn't learn, . . . would . . .
(If) learned, . . . wouldn't . . .

Past Conditional
(If) I had learned, . . . would have . . .
(+ past participle)

Neg. (If) hadn't learned, . . . would
have . . . (+ past participle)
(If) had learned, . . . wouldn't have . . .
(+ past participle)

These Verbs Follow the Same Pattern
adjourn
burn
earn
turn

I have to *learn* this poem by heart.   (*by heart* = memorize)
We'*re learning* so much from this
course.

Helena *learned about* her husband's   (= find out)
accident on the evening news.

Live and *learn*!   (= experience teaches)

Joe just *learned* a quicker route to   *Learn* and *study* are not synonymous:
the office.   *study* = exposure to new information;
  learn = intellectually grasp the new
I'm no expert at this software pro-   information.
gram, but I'*m learning*.

Eddie *has learned* the dangers of   (*the hard way* = through painful experi-
smoking the hard way.   ence)

Regular verb, active form: *look*

INFINITIVE/IMPERATIVE	***NEGATIVE***
(to) look/Look . . . !	(to) not look/Don't look . . . !
Present Participle	***Past Participle***
look<u>ing</u>	look<u>ed</u>
Neg. <u>not</u> look<u>ing</u>	***Neg.*** <u>not</u> look<u>ed</u>

PRESENT TENSES

Simple Present Tense
I look
you look
he/she/it look<u>s</u>
we look
you look
they look

Neg. <u>don't</u>/<u>doesn't</u> look

Present Progressive
I <u>am</u> look<u>ing</u>

Neg. <u>(am)</u> <u>not</u>/<u>aren't</u>/<u>isn't</u> look<u>ing</u>

Present Perfect
I <u>have</u> look<u>ed</u>

Neg. <u>haven't</u>/<u>hasn't</u> look<u>ed</u>

PAST TENSES

Simple Past Tense
I look<u>ed</u>

Neg. <u>didn't</u> look

Past Perfect
I <u>had</u> look<u>ed</u>

Neg. <u>hadn't</u> look<u>ed</u>

Past Progressive
I <u>was</u> look<u>ing</u>

Neg. <u>wasn't</u>/<u>weren't</u> look<u>ing</u>

Past Perfect Progressive
I <u>had been</u> look<u>ing</u>

Neg. <u>hadn't been</u> look<u>ing</u>

FUTURE TENSES

Simple Future Tense
I <u>will</u> look

Neg. <u>won't</u> look

Future Progressive
I <u>will</u> <u>be</u> look<u>ing</u>

Neg. <u>won't</u> <u>be</u> look<u>ing</u>

Future Perfect
I <u>will</u> <u>have</u> look<u>ed</u>

Neg. <u>won't</u> <u>have</u> look<u>ed</u>

Immediate Future Tense
I <u>am going to</u> look

Neg. <u>(am)</u> <u>not</u>/<u>aren't</u>/<u>isn't</u> <u>going to</u> look

Immediate Future Progressive
I <u>am going to</u> <u>be</u> look<u>ing</u>

Neg. <u>(am)</u> <u>not</u>/<u>aren't</u>/<u>isn't</u> <u>going to</u> <u>be</u> look<u>ing</u>

CONDITIONALS

Future Conditional
(<u>If</u>) I look, . . . <u>will</u> . . .

Unreal Conditional
(<u>If</u>) I look<u>ed</u>, . . . <u>would</u> . . .

Neg. (If) <u>don't/doesn't</u> look, . . . <u>will</u> . . .
(If) look, . . . <u>won't</u> . . .

Unreal Conditional—Progressive Form
(If) I <u>were</u> looking, . . . would . . .

Neg. (If) <u>weren't</u> looking, . . . would . . .
(If) <u>were</u> looking, . . . <u>wouldn't</u> . . .

Past Conditional—Progressive Form
(If) I <u>had been</u> looking, . . . <u>would</u> <u>have</u> . . .
(+ past participle)

Neg. (If) <u>hadn't</u> <u>been</u> looking, . . . would
have . . . (+ past participle)
(If) <u>had been</u> looking, . . . <u>wouldn't</u>
have . . . (+ past participle)

Neg. (If) <u>didn't</u> look, . . . <u>would</u> . . .
(If) look<u>ed</u>, . . . <u>wouldn't</u> . . .

Past Conditional
(If) I <u>had</u> look<u>ed</u>, . . . would have . . .
(+ past participle)

Neg. (If) <u>hadn't</u> look<u>ed</u>, . . . <u>would</u>
<u>have</u> . . . (+ past participle)
(If) <u>had</u> look<u>ed</u>, . . . <u>wouldn't</u> have . . .
(+ past participle)

These Verbs Follow the Same Pattern
book (= reserve—restaurant table, travel
accommodations, etc.)
cook
hook (= catch a fish)

Look has two meanings: (1) to actively focus your eyes on someone/some-
thing; (2) to have the appearance of . . . If *look* is followed by *at* or most other
prepositions, it has the first meaning; if followed by *like* it has the second
meaning. When *look* is used alone, context gives the meaning. *Look* is not
synonymous with *see* or *watch*. *See* does not imply active focus on something
specific; *watch* implies looking at a moving object. Unlike *see* and *watch*, the
passive voice is seldom used with *look*.

Look at this article in the paper!	(meaning 1)
I'm *looking* for my glasses—have you seen them?	(meaning 1)
Don't *look* so sad.	(meaning 2)
I *was looking* through this magazine while waiting for you.	(meaning 1)
It *looks* like rain.	(= appearance of sky/clouds) (meaning 2)
Virginia *hasn't been looking* at all well lately.	(meaning 2)
If the traffic *looks* heavy, we'*ll* turn back.	(turn back = return to starting point) (meaning 2)

Regular verb, active form: *love*

INFINITIVE/IMPERATIVE	***NEGATIVE***
(to) love/Love . . . !	(to) not love/Don't love . . . !
Present Participle*	***Past Participle****
lov<u>ing</u>	lov<u>ed</u>
Neg. <u>not</u> lov<u>ing</u>	***Neg.*** <u>not</u> lov<u>ed</u>

PRESENT TENSES

Simple Present Tense
I love
you love
he/she/it love<u>s</u>
we love
you love
they love

Neg. <u>don't/doesn't</u> love

Present Perfect
I <u>have</u> lov<u>ed</u>

Neg. <u>haven't/hasn't</u> lov<u>ed</u>

Present Progressive[t]
I <u>am</u> lov<u>ing</u>

Neg. <u>(am) not/aren't/isn't</u> lov<u>ing</u>

PAST TENSES

Simple Past Tense
I lov<u>ed</u>

Neg. <u>didn't</u> love

Past Perfect
I <u>had</u> lov<u>ed</u>

Neg. <u>hadn't</u> lov<u>ed</u>

Past Progressive[t]
I <u>was</u> lov<u>ing</u>

Neg. <u>wasn't/weren't</u> lov<u>ing</u>

Past Perfect Progressive[t]
I <u>had been</u> lov<u>ing</u>

Neg. <u>hadn't been</u> lov<u>ing</u>

FUTURE TENSES

Simple Future Tense
I <u>will</u> love

Neg. <u>won't</u> love

Future Progressive[t]
I <u>will</u> <u>be</u> lov<u>ing</u>

Neg. <u>won't</u> <u>be</u> loving

Future Perfect
I <u>will</u> <u>have</u> lov<u>ed</u>

Neg. <u>won't</u> <u>have</u> lov<u>ed</u>

Immediate Future Tense
I <u>am going to</u> love

Neg. <u>(am) not/aren't/isn't going to</u> love

Immediate Future Progressive
I <u>am going to</u> <u>be</u> lov<u>ing</u>

Neg. <u>(am) not/aren't/isn't going to</u> <u>be</u> lov-<u>ing</u>

Note: *Spelling change: Regular verbs ending in -*e* following a consonant drop the -*e* before -*ing* endings and add -*d* for -*ed* endings.

CONDITIONALS

Future Conditional
(<u>If</u>) I love, . . . <u>will</u> . . .

Neg. (<u>If</u>) <u>don't</u>/<u>doesn't</u> love, . . . <u>will</u> . . .
(<u>If</u>) love, . . . <u>won't</u> . . .

Unreal Conditional—Progressive Form[f]
(<u>If</u>) I <u>were</u> lov<u>ing</u>, . . . <u>would</u> . . .

Neg. (<u>If</u>) <u>weren't</u> loving, . . . <u>would</u> . . .
(<u>If</u>) <u>were</u> loving, . . . <u>wouldn't</u> . . .

Past Conditional—Progressive Form[f]
(<u>If</u>) I <u>had been</u> lov<u>ing</u>, . . . <u>would have</u> . . .
(+ past participle)

Neg. (<u>If</u>) <u>hadn't been</u> loving, . . . <u>would</u>
<u>have</u> . . . (+ past participle)
(<u>If</u>) <u>had been</u> lov<u>ing</u>, . . . <u>wouldn't have</u> . . .
(+ past participle)

Unreal Conditional
(<u>If</u>) I lov<u>ed</u>, . . . <u>would</u> . . .

Neg. (<u>If</u>) <u>didn't</u> love, . . . <u>would</u> . . .
(<u>If</u>) lov<u>ed</u>, . . . <u>wouldn't</u> . . .

Past Conditional
(<u>If</u>) I <u>had</u> lov<u>ed</u>, . . . <u>would have</u> . . .
(+ past participle)

Neg. (<u>If</u>) <u>hadn't</u> loved, . . . <u>would have</u> . . .
(+ past participle)
(<u>If</u>) <u>had</u> lov<u>ed</u>, . . . <u>wouldn't have</u> . . .
(+ past participle)

These Verbs Follow the Same Pattern

admire	consume
advise	erase
base (on)	replace
browse	save
charge	

Note: [f]Because *love* is a state-of-being verb (see Part A, Section 4 *Something to Think About: State-of-Being Verbs*, page 10), it is not correctly used in a progressive sense. Any constructions using *be* + *loving* are not really a progressive tense, but a type of adjective called a *participial adjective* (a *loving* mother, the *crying* baby, a *helping* hand, the *rushing* traffic, etc.) that uses a verb's present participle to modify a noun. See Grammar Handbook for more detail.

Most Americans *love* ketchup with
their french fries, but Tim detests it.

I'*ve loved* Martha since we were in college.

Debbie *used to love* the ballet, but now she prefers opera.

It's Christine who *loves* ice cream, not me.

Don't you *love* this movie?

Paul just *loves* skiing.

If William *had loved* me as much as
he *loved* his job, we never *would*
have broken up.

(*detest* = emphatic form of *hate*)

By using this question form (*negative interrogative*), the speaker signals that he/she is expecting agreement.

(*break up* = end relationship/marriage)

Regular verb, active form: *miss*

INFINITIVE/IMPERATIVE	***NEGATIVE***
(to) miss/Miss . . . !	(to) not miss/Don't miss . . . !
Present Participle	***Past Participle***
missing	missed
Neg. not missing	***Neg.*** not missed

PRESENT TENSES

Simple Present Tense*
I miss
you miss
he/she/it misses
we miss
you miss
they miss

Neg. don't/doesn't miss

Present Progressive
I am missing

Neg. (am) not/aren't/isn't missing

Present Perfect
I have missed

Neg. haven't/hasn't missed

PAST TENSES

Simple Past Tense
I missed

Neg. didn't miss

Past Perfect
I had missed

Neg. hadn't missed

Past Progressive
I was missing

Neg. wasn't/weren't missing

Past Perfect Progressive
I had been missing

Neg. hadn't been missing

FUTURE TENSES

Simple Future Tense
I will miss

Neg. won't miss

Future Progressive
I will be missing

Neg. won't be missing

Future Perfect
I will have missed

Neg. won't have missed

Immediate Future Tense
I am going to miss

Neg. (am) not/aren't/isn't going to miss

Immediate Future Progressive
I am going to be missing

Neg. (am) not/aren't/isn't going to be missing

Note: *Spelling change: Verbs ending in *-sh*, *-ch*, *-ss*, *-x*, and *-o* form the 3rd person singular with *-es* instead of *-s*.

CONDITIONALS

Future Conditional
(If) I miss, . . . <u>will</u> . . .

Neg. (If) <u>don't</u>/<u>doesn't</u> miss, . . . <u>will</u> . . .
(If) miss, . . . <u>won't</u> . . .

Unreal Conditional—Progressive Form
(If) I <u>were</u> missing, . . . <u>would</u> . . .

Neg. (If) <u>weren't</u> missing, . . . <u>would</u> . . .
(If) <u>were</u> missing, . . . <u>wouldn't</u> . . .

Unreal Conditional
(If) I miss<u>ed</u>, . . . <u>would</u> . . .

Neg. (If) <u>didn't</u> miss, . . . <u>would</u> . . .
(If) miss<u>ed</u>, . . . <u>wouldn't</u> . . .

Past Conditional
(If) I <u>had</u> miss<u>ed</u>, . . . <u>would</u> <u>have</u> . . .
(+ past participle)

Neg. (If) <u>hadn't</u> missed, . . . <u>would</u> <u>have</u> . . .
(+ past participle)
(If) <u>had</u> miss<u>ed</u>, . . . <u>wouldn't</u> <u>have</u> . . .
(+ past participle)

Past Conditional—Progressive Form
(If) I <u>had been</u> missing, . . . <u>would</u> <u>have</u> . . . (+ past participle)

Neg. (If) <u>hadn't</u> <u>been</u> missing, . . . <u>would</u> <u>have</u> . . . (+ past participle)
(If) <u>had been</u> missing, . . . <u>wouldn't</u> <u>have</u> . . . (+ past participle)

These Verbs Follow the Same Pattern

crush
discuss (= talk about in conversation)
dismiss (= fire from job; give permission to leave (usually school or military)
dress
fix (= repair)

guess
kiss
mix
reminisce (= discuss old times)
watch

Miss has three meanings: (1) to feel the lack of someone or something that is absent; (2) to not be in time for something with a fixed starting time, such as a train departure or a meeting, or (3) to not take timely advantage of an opportunity.

Don't *miss* the new Jack Nicholson film—it's great!

I *wouldn't miss* it for the world   (= I will definitely be there)

Tell Jim he's *missing* a wonderful seminar.

We *missed* the plane by five minutes.

My mother died 20 years ago—and I still *miss* her.

Betty and Mark *are going to miss* their old house.

Henry *missed* his chance for promotion during the takeover.

If you don't hurry, we'*ll miss* the start of the game.

My wristwatch *has been missing* for a few days.

Regular verb, active form: *park*

INFINITIVE/IMPERATIVE	***NEGATIVE***
(to) park/Park . . . !	(to) not park/Don't park . . . !
Present Participle	***Past Participle***
parking	parked
Neg. not parking	***Neg.*** not parked

PRESENT TENSES

Simple Present Tense
I park
you park
he/she/it parks
we park
you park
they park

Neg. don't/doesn't park

Present Progressive
I am parking

Neg. (am) not/aren't/isn't parking

Present Perfect
I have parked

Neg. haven't/hasn't parked

PAST TENSES

Simple Past Tense
I parked

Neg. didn't park

Past Progressive
I was parking

Neg. wasn't/weren't parking

Past Perfect
I had parked

Neg. hadn't parked

Past Perfect Progressive
I had been parking

Neg. hadn't been parking

FUTURE TENSES

Simple Future Tense
I will park

Neg. won't park

Immediate Future Tense
I am going to park

Neg. (am) not/aren't/isn't going to park

Future Progressive
I will be parking

Neg. won't be parking

Immediate Future Progressive
I am going to be parking

Neg. (am) not/aren't/isn't going to be parking

Future Perfect
I will have parked

Neg. won't have parked

CONDITIONALS

Future Conditional
(If) I park, . . . will . . .

Neg. (If) don't/doesn't park, . . . will . . .
(If) park, . . . won't . . .

Unreal Conditional—Progressive Form
(If) I were parking, . . . would . . .

Neg. (If) weren't parking, . . . would . . .
(If) were parking, . . . wouldn't . . .

Past Conditional—Progressive Form
(If) I had been parking, . . . would
have . . . (+ past participle)

Neg. (If) hadn't been parking, . . . would
have . . . (+ past participle)
(If) had been parking, . . . wouldn't
have . . . (+ past participle)

Unreal Conditional
(If) I parked, . . . would . . .

Neg. (If) didn't park, . . . would . . .
(If) parked, . . . wouldn't . . .

Past Conditional
(If) I had parked, . . . would have . . .
(+ past participle)

Neg. (If) hadn't parked, . . . would
have . . . (+ past participle)
(If) had parked, . . . wouldn't have . . .
(+ past participle)

These Verbs Follow the Same Pattern
lack (= not have something necessary)
last
mark
pack
sort
work

This Verb Follows a Different Pattern
hurt

Trucks aren't allowed to *park* on this street.

George, *park* over there.

That delivery van always *parks* in front of our house.

Why *did* you *park* in the street?

Harriet *parked* in a no-parking zone.

Who *parked* in our driveway?

Sam's car *was parked* when the truck ran into it.

If you *hadn't parked* on the wrong side of the street, you *wouldn't have* been given
a ticket.

Regular verb, active form: *watch*

INFINITIVE/IMPERATIVE	NEGATIVE
(to) watch/Watch . . . !	(to) not watch/Don't watch . . . !
Present Participle	**Past Participle**
watching	watched
Neg. not watching	**Neg.** not watched

PRESENT TENSES

Simple Present Tense*
I watch
you watch
he/she/it watches
we watch
you watch
they watch

Neg. don't/doesn't watch

Present Progressive
I am watching

Neg. (am) not/aren't/isn't watching

Present Perfect
I have watched

Neg. haven't/hasn't watched

PAST TENSES

Simple Past Tense
I watched

Neg. didn't watch

Past Perfect
I had watched

Neg. hadn't watched

Past Progressive
I was watching

Neg. wasn't/weren't watching

Past Perfect Progressive
I had been watching

Neg. hadn't been watching

FUTURE TENSES

Simple Future Tense
I will watch

Neg. won't watch

Future Progressive
I will be watching

Neg. won't be watching

Immediate Future Tense
I am going to watch

Neg. (am) not/aren't/isn't going to watch

Immediate Future Progressive
I am going to be watching

Neg. (am) not/aren't/isn't going to be watching

Note: *Spelling change: Verbs ending in *-sh*, *-ch*, *-ss*, *-x*, and *-o* form the 3rd person singular with *-es* instead of *-s*.

Future Perfect
I will have watched

Neg. won't have watched

CONDITIONALS

Future Conditional
(If) I watch, . . . will . . .

Neg. (If) don't/doesn't watch, . . . will . . .
(If) watch, . . . won't . . .

Unreal Conditional—Progressive Form
(If) I were watching, . . . would . . .

Neg. (If) weren't watching, . . . would . . .
(If) were watching, . . . wouldn't . . .

Past Conditional—Progressive Form
(If) I had been watching, . . . would have . . . (+ past participle)

Neg. (If) hadn't been watching, . . . would have . . . (+ past participle)
(If) had been watching, . . . wouldn't have . . . (+ past participle)

Unreal Conditional
(If) I watched, . . . would . . .

Neg. (If) didn't watch, . . . would . . .
(If) watched, . . . wouldn't . . .

Past Conditional
(If) I had watched, . . . would have . . .
(+ past participle)

Neg. (If) hadn't watched, . . . would
have . . . (+ past participle)
(If) had watched, . . . wouldn't have . . .
(+ past participle)

Acme Products is a stock *to watch*.

I'll show you—*watch* me!

Watch your step!   (= be careful/look where you walk)

Watch it! This pan is hot.   (= be careful of . . .)

I like to *watch* these goldfish swimming.

Are you *watching* anything interesting?

Bill *has watched* Monday night football on TV every week for years.

Watch is not completely interchangeable with *see* or *look*. (See note under *look*, page 107.)

My boss *has been watching* me all morning.

If Bernie *had been watching* the traffic, he *could have* avoided that traffic jam.

Regular verb, active form: *work*

INFINITIVE/IMPERATIVE	NEGATIVE
(to) work/Work . . . !	(to) not work/Don't work . . . !
Present Participle	**Past Participle**
work<u>ing</u>	work<u>ed</u>
Neg. <u>not</u> work<u>ing</u>	**Neg.** <u>not</u> work<u>ed</u>

PRESENT TENSES

Simple Present Tense
I work
you work
he/she/it work<u>s</u>
we work
you work
they work

Neg. <u>don't/doesn't</u> work

Present Perfect
I <u>have</u> work<u>ed</u>

Neg. <u>haven't/hasn't</u> work<u>ed</u>

Present Progressive
I <u>am</u> work<u>ing</u>

Neg. (<u>am</u>) <u>not/aren't/isn't</u> work<u>ing</u>

PAST TENSES

Simple Past Tense
I work<u>ed</u>

Neg. <u>didn't</u> work

Past Perfect
I <u>had</u> work<u>ed</u>

Neg. <u>hadn't</u> work<u>ed</u>

Past Progressive
I <u>was</u> work<u>ing</u>

Neg. <u>wasn't/weren't</u> work<u>ing</u>

Past Perfect Progressive
I <u>had been</u> work<u>ing</u>

Neg. <u>hadn't been</u> work<u>ing</u>

FUTURE TENSES

Simple Future Tense
I <u>will</u> work

Neg. <u>won't</u> work

Future Progressive
I <u>will</u> <u>be</u> work<u>ing</u>

Neg. <u>won't</u> <u>be</u> work<u>ing</u>

Future Perfect
I <u>will</u> <u>have</u> work<u>ed</u>

Neg. <u>won't</u> <u>have</u> work<u>ed</u>

Immediate Future Tense
I <u>am going to</u> work

Neg. (<u>am</u>) <u>not/aren't/isn't</u> <u>going to</u> work

Immediate Future Progressive
I <u>am going to</u> <u>be</u> work<u>ing</u>

Neg. (<u>am</u>) <u>not/aren't/isn't</u> <u>going to</u> <u>be</u>
work<u>ing</u>

CONDITIONALS

Future Conditional
(<u>If</u>) I work, . . . <u>will</u> . . .

Neg. (<u>If</u>) <u>don't</u>/<u>doesn't</u> work, . . . <u>will</u> . . .
(<u>If</u>) I work, . . . <u>won't</u> . . .

Unreal Conditional—Progressive Form
(<u>If</u>) I <u>were</u> work<u>ing</u>, . . . <u>would</u> . . .

Neg. (<u>If</u>) <u>weren't</u> work<u>ing</u>, . . . <u>would</u> . . .
(<u>If</u>) I <u>were</u> work<u>ing</u>, . . . <u>wouldn't</u> . . .

Unreal Conditional
(<u>If</u>) I work<u>ed</u>, . . . <u>would</u> . . .

Neg. (<u>If</u>) <u>didn't</u> work, . . . <u>would</u> . . .
(<u>If</u>) work<u>ed</u>, . . . <u>wouldn't</u> . . .

Past Conditional
(<u>If</u>) I <u>had</u> work<u>ed</u>, . . . <u>would</u> <u>have</u> . . .
(+ past participle)

Neg. (<u>If</u>) <u>hadn't</u> work<u>ed</u>, . . . <u>would</u>
<u>have</u> . . . (+ past participle)
(<u>If</u>) <u>had</u> work<u>ed</u>, . . . <u>wouldn't</u> <u>have</u> . . .
(+ past participle)

Past Conditional—Progressive Form
(<u>If</u>) I <u>had been</u> work<u>ing</u>, . . . <u>would</u> <u>have</u> . . . (+ past participle)

Neg. (<u>If</u>) <u>hadn't</u> <u>been</u> work<u>ing</u>, . . . <u>would</u> <u>have</u> . . . (+ past participle)
(<u>If</u>) <u>had</u> <u>been</u> work<u>ing</u>, . . . <u>wouldn't</u> <u>have</u> . . . (+ past participle)

Work has two meanings: (1) to do a job; (2) for a device, machine, or plan to operate correctly.

Work quickly, but thoroughly!	(meaning 1)
Jim **works** for an accounting firm.	(*work for* = regular job) (meaning 1)
Anna **works** as a model.	(*work as* = profession—permanent or temporary) (meaning 1)
I'*m working* at the moment—may I call you back?	(meaning 1)
I'*ll be working* this Saturday until about 4:00.	(meaning 1)
Sally's idea was good, but it *doesn't work* in practice.	(meaning 2)
This watch *isn't working* properly.	(meaning 2)
My computer *hasn't been working* right since the blackout.	(meaning 2)

Irregular Verbs

In the following section, you will find complete conjugations for irregular verbs. Irregular verbs display their irregularity in two different ways: 1) their pattern of conjugation (1-2-3, 1-2-1, etc.), which is only half the story; and 2) the (usually vowel) changes the infinitive experiences in forming the simple past and past participle. The following guidelines aren't absolute rules, but they bring some order to a seemingly chaotic process.

pattern 1-1-1—no change in any of the forms

burst/burst/burst
cost/cost/cost
cut/cut/cut

hit/hit/hit
hurt/hurt/hurt
put/put/put

pattern 1-2-1—simple form changes in the simple past (usually through a vowel change), but reverts to (auxiliary *have*+) the identical simple form in the past participle/perfect tense-forms

become/became/become
come/came/come
run/ran/run

pattern 1-2-2—verbs that have identical simple past and past participle forms. This is the largest group of irregular verbs, and can be divided as follows:

group 1: verbs that have *–ee* in their simple form (or whose simple form is pronounced "ee," but not always spelled that way) change to a single, short *–e* sound in the simple past and past participle—usually ending in a hard final consonant, *-d, -t, or -pt*; this includes a small subgroup whose simple form long vowels also change to a short vowel in the simple past and past participle and end in a hard final consonant—usually *-t*

bleed/bled/bled
feed/fed/fed
feel/felt/felt
keep/kept/kept
lead/led/led

read/read/read*
sleep/slept/slept
sweep/swept/swept
lose/lost/lost (lose pronounced "looze")
shoot/shot/shot

exception: *beat*—pattern 1-1-2

group 2: verbs whose simple form ends in *–ch* or *–tch* (after a vowel— usually *–a*) change to *–ught* in the simple past and past participle; this includes a large subgroup whose simple form vowels (*-i* or *-u*) and remaining consonants also change to *-ought* in the simple past and past participle

catch/caught/caught
teach/taught/taught (drops *–e*)
bring/brought/brought

fight/fought/fought
think/thought/thought
buy/bought/bought

Note: *Although the irregular verb *read* looks like it belongs to the 1-1-1 pattern, it is actually a 1-2-2 pattern verb because the simple past and past participle are pronounced "*red*" not "*reed*."

group 3: verbs whose simple form ends in -*d* changes to -*t* in the simple past and past participle forms

bend/bent/bent
build/built/built
lend/lent/lent

send/sent/sent
spend/spent/spent

group 4: verbs whose simple form vowel (–*i* or –*a*) changes to –*u* in the simple past and past participle forms

dig/dug/dug
hang/hung/hung
swing/swung/swung

group 5: other pattern 1-2-2 verbs that go through similar vowel changes from simple form to past and past participle, but whose patterns are otherwise less easy to classify

sell/sold/sold
tell/told/told
find/found/found
hear/heard/heard (*hear* pronounced
"heer"/*heard* pronounced "hurd")
hold/held/held

say/said/said (*said* pronounced "sedd")
shake/shook/shook
stand/stood/stood
take/took/took
win/won/won

pattern 1-2-3—verbs whose simple form, past, and past participle forms are all slightly or substantially different from each other. Verbs with this pattern can be divided into two major groups: 1) those with a short –*i* sound in the simple form that changes to a short –*a* sound in the past, and a short –*u* sound in the past participle; and 2) typical of this group is that there is some vowel change from the simple form to the past, and that the past participle adds –*en* (or just –*n* for some verbs) to the simple form. In a third subgroup, the changes resemble one or both of the other groups, but don't follow a consistent pattern.

group 1:

begin/began/begun
drink/drank/drunk
ring/rang/rung

sing/sang/sung
sink/sank/sunk
swim/swam/swum

group 2:

eat/ate/eaten
fall/fell/fallen
forget/forgot/forgotten*
get/got/gotten*/**
give/gave/given

grow/grew/grown
know/knew/known
rise/rose/risen
see/saw/seen
throw/threw/thrown

group 3:

fly/flew/flown
lie/lay/lain
steal/stole/stolen

swear/swore/sworn
tear/tore/torn

Note: *Slight variation.
**British past participle is *got*.

Irregular verb, active form: *beat*

INFINITIVE/IMPERATIVE	**NEGATIVE**
(to) beat/Beat . . . !	(to) not beat/Don't beat . . . !
Present Participle	**Past Participle**
beating	beaten
Neg. not beating	**Neg.** not beaten

PRESENT TENSES

Simple Present Tense
I beat
you beat
he/she/it beats
we beat
you beat
they beat

Neg. don't/doesn't beat

Present Progressive
I am beating

Neg. (am) not/aren't/isn't beating

Present Perfect
I have beaten

Neg. haven't/hasn't beaten

PAST TENSES

Simple Past Tense
I beat

Neg. didn't beat

Past Perfect
I had beaten

Neg. hadn't beaten

Past Progressive
I was beating

Neg. wasn't/weren't beating

Past Perfect Progressive
I had been beating

Neg. hadn't been beating

FUTURE TENSES

Simple Future Tense
I will beat

Neg. won't beat

Future Progressive
I will be beating

Neg. won't be beating

Future Perfect
I will have beaten

Neg. won't have beaten

Immediate Future Tense
I am going to beat

Neg. (am) not/aren't/isn't going to beat

Immediate Future Progressive
I am going to be beating

Neg. (am) not/aren't/isn't going to be beating

CONDITIONALS

Future Conditional
(If) I beat, . . . will . . .

Neg. (If) don't/doesn't beat, . . . will . . .
(If) beat, . . . won't . . .

Unreal Conditional—Progressive Form
(If) I were beating, . . . would . . .

Neg. (If) weren't beating, . . . would . . .
were beating . . . wouldn't . . .

Unreal Conditional
(If) I beat, . . . would . . .

Neg. (If) didn't beat, . . . would . . .
(If) beat, . . . wouldn't . . .

Past Conditional
(If) I had beaten, . . . would have . . .
(+ past participle)

Neg. (If) hadn't beaten, . . . would have . . . (+ past participle)
(If) had beaten, . . . wouldn't have . . .
(+ past participle)

Past Conditional—Progressive Form
(If) I had been beating, . . . would have . . . (+ past participle)

Neg. (If) hadn't been beating, . . . would have . . . (+ past participle)
(If) had been beating, . . . wouldn't have . . . (+ past participle)

These Verbs Follow a Different Pattern
cheat	eat	heat	repeat
defeat	greet	meet	seat

Bill McDonald *is beating* Ted Allen in the primaries, and hopes *to beat* him in the November elections.

Continue *beating* the egg whites until they're stiff.

The reporters at The Chronicle *beat* the others to the story.

If we can *beat* the competition by launching our product first, we'*ll own* the market.

Johnny *has been beaten* up four times by that Harris boy!

Irregular verb, active form: *become*

INFINITIVE/IMPERATIVE	***NEGATIVE***
(to) become/Become . . . !	(to) not become/Don't become . . . !
Present Participle	***Past Participle***
becom<u>ing</u>	become
Neg. <u>not</u> becom<u>ing</u>	***Neg.*** <u>not</u> become

PRESENT TENSES

Simple Present Tense
I become
you become
he/she/it become<u>s</u>
we become
you become
they become

Neg. <u>don't</u>/<u>doesn't</u> become

Present Perfect
I <u>have</u> become

Neg. <u>haven't</u>/<u>hasn't</u> become

Present Progressive *[*†]
I <u>am</u> becom<u>ing</u>

Neg. (<u>am</u>) <u>not</u>/<u>aren't</u>/<u>isn't</u> becom<u>ing</u>

PAST TENSES

Simple Past Tense
I bec<u>a</u>me

Neg. <u>didn't</u> become

Past Perfect
I <u>had</u> become

Neg. <u>hadn't</u> become

Past Progressive [†]
I <u>was</u> becom<u>ing</u>

Neg. <u>wasn't</u>/<u>weren't</u> becom<u>ing</u>

Past Perfect Progressive [†]
I <u>had been</u> becom<u>ing</u>

Neg. <u>hadn't been</u> becom<u>ing</u>

FUTURE TENSES

Simple Future Tense
I <u>will</u> become

Neg. <u>won't</u> become

Future Progressive
I <u>will be</u> becom<u>ing</u>

Neg. <u>won't be</u> becom<u>ing</u>

Immediate Future Tense
I <u>am going to</u> become

Neg. (<u>am</u>) <u>not</u>/<u>aren't</u>/<u>isn't</u> <u>going to</u> become

Immediate Future Progressive
I <u>am going to be</u> becom<u>ing</u>

Neg. (<u>am</u>) <u>not</u>/<u>aren't</u>/<u>isn't</u> <u>going to</u> <u>be</u> becom<u>ing</u>

Note: *Spelling change: Verbs ending in -*e* following a consonant drop the -*e* before -*ing* endings.

120

Future Perfect
I will have become

Neg. won't have become

CONDITIONALS

Future Conditional
(If) I become, . . . will . . .

Neg. (If) don't/doesn't become, . . .
will . . . (If) become, . . . won't . . .

Unreal Conditional—Progressive Form[†]
(If) I were becoming, . . . would . . .

Neg. (If) weren't becoming, . . . would . . .
(If) were becoming, . . . wouldn't . . .

Unreal Conditional
(If) I became, . . . would . . .

Neg. (If) didn't become, . . . would . . .
(If) became, . . . wouldn't . . .

Past Conditional
(If) I had become, . . . would have . . .
(+ past participle)

Neg. (If) hadn't become, . . . would
have . . . (+ past participle)
(If) had become, . . . wouldn't have . . .
(+ past participle)

Past Conditional—Progressive Form[†]
(If) I had been becoming, . . . would have . . . (+ past participle)

Neg. (If) hadn't been becoming, . . . would have . . . (+ past participle)
(If) had been becoming, . . . wouldn't have . . . (+ past participle)

This Verb Follows the Same Pattern
come

Note: [†]Some constructions using *be* + *becoming* may not be a progressive tense, but a type of adjective called a *participial adjective* (your most *becoming* outfit, a *loving* mother, the *crying* baby, a *helping* hand, the *rushing* traffic, etc.) that uses a verb's present participle to modify a noun. In this sense, the meaning of *becoming* changes completely: it means "looks good" or "visually emphasizes something positive." See Grammar Handbook for more detail.

Ted wants to *become* a doctor when he grows up.

I'*m becoming* concerned about the drop in productivity.

Marge *was becoming* very forgetful before she got ill.

The old Collins mansion *is going to become* a restaurant.

What *has become* of Blanche since   (= what has happened to)
she left town?

Scott *had become* a bundle of nerves after he stopped smoking.

If Harry *had become* a farmer, he *would have* been a much happier man.

Irregular verb, active form: *begin*

INFINITIVE/IMPERATIVE	***NEGATIVE***
(to) begin/Begin . . . !	(to) not begin/Don't begin . . . !
Present Participle*	***Past Participle***
begin<u>ning</u>	beg<u>un</u>
Neg. <u>not</u> begin<u>ning</u>	***Neg.*** <u>not</u> beg<u>un</u>

PRESENT TENSES

Simple Present Tense
I begin
you begin
he/she/it begin<u>s</u>
we begin
you begin
they begin

Neg. <u>don't/doesn't</u> begin

Present Progressive
I <u>am</u> begin<u>ning</u>

Neg. <u>(am) not/aren't/isn't</u> begin<u>ning</u>

Present Perfect
I <u>have</u> beg<u>un</u>

Neg. <u>haven't/hasn't</u> beg<u>un</u>

PAST TENSES

Simple Past Tense
I beg<u>an</u>

Neg. <u>didn't</u> begin

Past Perfect
I <u>had</u> beg<u>un</u>

Neg. <u>hadn't</u> beg<u>un</u>

Past Progressive
I <u>was</u> begin<u>ning</u>

Neg. <u>wasn't/weren't</u> begin<u>ning</u>

Past Perfect Progressive
I <u>had been</u> begin<u>ning</u>

Neg. <u>hadn't been</u> begin<u>ning</u>

FUTURE TENSES

Simple Future Tense
I <u>will</u> begin

Neg. <u>won't</u> begin

Future Progressive
I <u>will be</u> begin<u>ning</u>

Neg. <u>won't be</u> begin<u>ning</u>

Immediate Future Tense
I <u>am going to</u> begin

Neg. <u>(am) not/aren't/isn't going to</u> begin

Immediate Future Progressive
I <u>am going to be</u> begin<u>ning</u>

Neg. <u>(am) not/aren't/isn't going to be</u> begin<u>ning</u>

Note: *Spelling change: Irregular verbs ending in a single consonant following a single vowel double the last consonant before *-ing*.

Future Perfect
I will have begun

Neg. won't have begun

CONDITIONALS

Future Conditional
(If) I begin, . . . will . . .

Neg. (If) don't/doesn't begin, . . . will . . .
(If) begin, . . . won't . . .

Unreal Conditional—Progressive Form
(If) I were beginning, . . . would . . .

Neg. (If) weren't beginning, . . . would . . .
(If) were beginning, . . . wouldn't . . .

Past Conditional—Progressive Form
(If) I had been beginning, . . . would have . . . (+ past participle)

Neg. (If) hadn't been beginning, . . . would have . . . (+ past participle)
(If) had been beginning, . . . wouldn't have . . . (+ past participle)

Unreal Conditional
(If) I began, . . . would . . .

Neg. (If) didn't begin, . . . would . . .
(If) began, . . . wouldn't . . .

Past Conditional
(If) I had begun, . . . would have . . . (+ past participle)

Neg. (If) hadn't begun, . . . would have . . . (+ past participle)
(If) had begun, . . . wouldn't have . . . (+ past participle)

These Verbs Follow the Same Pattern
drink	sink
ring	stink
sing	swim

These Verbs Follow a Different Pattern
sin
win

I'*m beginning* to understand.
I *was* just *beginning* to enjoy myself.
Joe *began* to feel ill.
The new management policies *will begin* on March 1.
I'*m going to begin* by redecorating the living room.
Quick, the film *has* just *begun*.
Everyone *had begun* eating long before Leslie and Phil arrived.
By Easter, Todd *will* probably *have begun* to walk.

Irregular verb, active form: *break*

INFINITIVE/IMPERATIVE	***NEGATIVE***
(to) break/Break . . . !	(to) not break/Don't break . . . !
Present Participle	***Past Participle***
breaking	broken
Neg. not breaking	***Neg.*** not broken

PRESENT TENSES

Simple Present Tense
I break
you break
he/she/it breaks
we break
you break
they break

Neg. don't/doesn't break

Present Progressive
I am breaking

Neg. (am) not/aren't/isn't breaking

Present Perfect
I have broken

Neg. haven't/hasn't broken

PAST TENSES

Simple Past Tense
I broke

Neg. didn't break

Past Perfect
I had broken

Neg. hadn't broken

Past Progressive
I was breaking

Neg. wasn't/weren't breaking

Past Perfect Progressive
I had been breaking

Neg. hadn't been breaking

FUTURE TENSES

Simple Future Tense
I will break

Neg. won't break

Future Progressive
I will be breaking

Neg. won't be breaking

Immediate Future Tense
I am going to break

Neg. (am) not/aren't/isn't going to break

Immediate Future Progressive
I am going to be breaking

Neg. (am) not/aren't/isn't going to be breaking

Future Perfect
I will have broken

Neg. won't have broken

CONDITIONALS

Future Conditional
(If) I break, . . . will . . .

Neg. (If) don't/doesn't break, . . . will . . .
(If) break, . . . won't . . .

Unreal Conditional-Progressive Form
(If) I were breaking, . . . would . . .

Neg. (If) weren't breaking, . . . would . . .
(If) were breaking, . . . wouldn't . . .

Past Conditional-Progressive Form
(If) I had been breaking, would have
(+ past participle)

Neg. (If) hadn't been breaking, would
have (+ past participle)
(If) had been breaking, wouldn't have
(+ past participle)

Unreal Conditional
(If) I broke, . . . would . . .

Neg. (If) didn't break, . . . would . . .
(If) broke, . . . wouldn't . . .

Past Conditional
(If) I had broken, . . . would have . . .
(+ past participle)

Neg. (If) hadn't broken, . . . would have . . .
(+ past participle)
(If) had broken, . . . wouldn't have . . .
(+ past participle)

These Verbs Follow the Same Pattern
speak*
wake (up)

These Verbs Follow a Different Pattern
make   leak
shake   take

Note: *Although *break* (pronounced "brake") and *speak* (pronounced "speek") follow the same conjugation patterns, they are pronounced differently in any tense that builds on the simple form (tenses based on the simple past and past participle are identical in pronunciation for both verbs).

Christine has managed *to break* Tommy of sucking his thumb.
(*break . . . of . . .* = train to end a bad habit)

It's *breaking* Barbara's heart to have to sell her home.

I hope you're *not going to break* your promise.

Paul and Tina *are breaking* up.
(*break up* = end relationship/divorce, etc.)

Burglars *broke* into my house last week, and now my neighbor's house *is being broken* into.
(*break into* = enter place by force)

All my best dishes *have been broken*.

The policeman was suspended because he *had broken* the rules.

After Carol *had broken* both her legs, she needed constant care.

Irregular verb, active form: *bring*

INFINITIVE/IMPERATIVE	***NEGATIVE***
(to) bring/Bring . . . !	(to) not bring/Don't bring . . . !
Present Participle	***Past Participle***
bring<u>ing</u>	br<u>ought</u>
Neg. <u>not</u> bring<u>ing</u>	***Neg.*** <u>not</u> br<u>ought</u>

PRESENT TENSES

Simple Present Tense
I bring
you bring
he/she/it bring<u>s</u>
we bring
you bring
they bring

Neg. <u>don't</u>/<u>doesn't</u> bring

Present Progressive
I <u>am</u> bring<u>ing</u>

Neg. (<u>am</u>) <u>not</u>/<u>aren't</u>/<u>isn't</u> bring<u>ing</u>

Present Perfect
I <u>have</u> br<u>ought</u>

Neg. <u>haven't</u>/<u>hasn't</u> br<u>ought</u>

PAST TENSES

Simple Past Tense
I br<u>ought</u>

Neg. <u>didn't</u> bring

Past Perfect
I <u>had</u> brought

Neg. <u>hadn't</u> br<u>ought</u>

Past Progressive
I <u>was</u> bring<u>ing</u>

Neg. <u>wasn't</u>/<u>weren't</u> bring<u>ing</u>

Past Perfect Progressive
I <u>had been</u> bring<u>ing</u>

Neg. <u>hadn't been</u> bring<u>ing</u>

FUTURE TENSES

Simple Future Tense
I <u>will</u> bring

Neg. <u>won't</u> bring

Future Progressive
I <u>will</u> <u>be</u> bring<u>ing</u>

Neg. <u>won't</u> <u>be</u> bring<u>ing</u>

Future Perfect
I <u>will</u> <u>have</u> br<u>ought</u>

Neg. <u>won't</u> <u>have</u> br<u>ought</u>

Immediate Future Tense
I <u>am going to</u> bring

Neg. (<u>am</u>) <u>not</u>/<u>aren't</u>/<u>isn't</u> <u>going to</u> bring

Immediate Future Progressive
I <u>am going to</u> <u>be</u> bring<u>ing</u>

Neg. (<u>am</u>) <u>not</u>/<u>aren't</u>/<u>isn't</u> <u>going to</u> <u>be</u> bring<u>ing</u>

CONDITIONALS

Future Conditional
(If) I bring, . . . will . . .

Neg. (If) don't/doesn't bring, . . . will . . .
(If) bring, . . . won't . . .

Unreal Conditional—Progressive Form
(If) I were bringing, . . . would . . .

Neg. (If) weren't bringing, . . . would . . .
(If) were bringing, . . . wouldn't . . .

Unreal Conditional
(If) I brought, . . . would . . .

Neg. (If) didn't bring, . . . would . . .
(If) brought, . . . wouldn't . . .

Past Conditional
(If) I had brought, . . . would have . . .
(+ past participle)

Neg. (If) hadn't brought, . . . would have . . . (+ past participle)
(If) had brought, . . . wouldn't have . . . (+ past participle)

Past Conditional—Progressive Form
(If) I had been bringing, . . . would have . . . (+ past participle)

Neg. (If) hadn't been bringing, . . . would have . . . (+ past participle)
(If) had been bringing, . . . wouldn't have . . . (+ past participle)

Bring your swimsuit with you.

Passengers aren't allowed to *bring* pets into the plane.

What should I *bring* to the party?

Is Frank *bringing* that boring woman with him again?

Forgive me for *bringing* up the subject, but you don't look well.   (*bring up* = start to talk about)

I'*ll bring* the dessert if you'*ll bring* the appetizers.

More details of the scandal *were being brought* out daily.   (*bring out/bring to light* = expose information, secrets, etc.)

Michael and Denise *have brought up* their children very well.   (bring up = train and teach one's children—not for animals)

If you *had brought* those reports, it *would have* helped us at the meeting.

Irregular verb, active form: *buy*

INFINITIVE/IMPERATIVE	**NEGATIVE**
(to) buy/Buy . . . !	(to) not buy/Don't buy . . . !
Present Participle	**Past Participle**
buying	bought
Neg. not buying	**Neg.** not bought

PRESENT TENSES

Simple Present Tense
I buy
you buy
he/she/it buys
we buy
you buy
they buy

Neg. don't/doesn't buy

Present Progressive
I am buying

Neg. (am) not/aren't/isn't buying

Present Perfect
I have bought

Neg. haven't/hasn't bought

PAST TENSES

Simple Past Tense
I bought

Neg. didn't buy

Past Progressive
I was buying

Neg. wasn't/weren't buying

Past Perfect
I had bought

Neg. hadn't bought

Past Perfect Progressive
I had been buying

Neg. hadn't been buying

FUTURE TENSES

Simple Future Tense
I will buy

Neg. won't buy

Immediate Future Tense
I am going to buy

Neg. (am) not/aren't/isn't going to buy

Future Progressive
I will be buying

Neg. won't be buying

Immediate Future Progressive
I am going to be buying

Neg. (am) not/aren't/isn't going to be buying

Future Perfect
I will have bought

Neg. won't have bought

CONDITIONALS

Future Conditional
(If) I buy, . . . will . . .

Neg. (If) don't/doesn't buy, . . . will . . .
(If) buy, . . . won't . . .

Unreal Conditional—Progressive Form
(If) I were buying, . . . would . . .

Neg. (If) weren't buying, . . . would . . .
(If) were buying, . . . wouldn't . . .

Past Conditional—Progressive Form
(If) I had been buying, . . . would have . . .
(+ past participle)

Neg. (If) hadn't been buying, . . . would
have . . . (+ past participle)
(If) had been buying, . . . wouldn't
have . . . (+ past participle)

Unreal Conditional
(If) I bought, . . . would . . .

Neg. (If) didn't buy, . . . would . . .
(If) bought, . . . wouldn't . . .

Past Conditional
(If) I had bought, . . . would have . . .
(+ past participle)

Neg. (If) hadn't bought, . . . would
have . . . (+ past participle)
(If) had bought, . . . wouldn't have . . .
(+ past participle)

These Verbs Follow the Same Pattern
bring
fight
seek (= literary variation of *look for*)
teach
think
catch*

Note: *Catch* adds *-ught* instead of *-ought* in the simple past and past participle, but otherwise follows the same conjugation patterns as *buy*.

Please *buy* some fruit while you're at the market.

Nora *is buying* a new dress for the reception.

Chris and Mike *are going to buy* a new house.

Marty *would* like to *buy* a sports car, but he'*ll* probably *buy* a van instead.

If you *buy* a new car, *will* you get the same make?

The company *had been bought* by a
conglomerate by the time my shares
were bought out.

(*buy out* = buy all of a part-owner's
share in a company, property, etc.)

Irregular verb, active form: *catch*

INFINITIVE/IMPERATIVE	*NEGATIVE*
(to) catch/Catch . . . !	(to) not catch/Don't catch . . . !
Present Participle	***Past Participle***
catching	caught
Neg. not catching	***Neg.*** not caught

PRESENT TENSES

Simple Present Tense*
I catch
you catch
he/she/it catches
we catch
you catch
they catch

Neg. don't/doesn't catch

Present Progressive
I am catching

Neg. (am) not/aren't/isn't catching

Present Perfect
I have caught

Neg. haven't/hasn't caught

PAST TENSES

Simple Past Tense
I caught

Neg. didn't catch

Past Perfect
I had caught

Neg. hadn't caught

Past Progressive
I was catching

Neg. wasn't/weren't catching

Past Perfect Progressive
I had been catching

Neg. hadn't been catching

FUTURE TENSES

Simple Future Tense
I am going to catch

Neg. I (am) not/aren't/isn't going to catch

Future Progressive
I will be catching

Neg. won't be catching

Future Perfect
I will have caught

Neg. won't have caught

Immediate Future Tense
I will catch

Neg. won't catch

Immediate Future Progressive
I am going to be catching

Neg. (am) not/aren't/isn't going to be catching

Note: *Spelling change: Verbs ending in *-sh, -ch, -ss, -x,* and *-o* form the 3rd person singular with *-es* instead of *-s*.

CONDITIONALS

Future Conditional
(If) I catch, . . . will . . .

Neg. (If) don't/doesn't catch, . . . will . . .
(If) catch, . . . won't . . .

Unreal Conditional—Progressive Form
(If) I were catching, . . . would . . .

Neg. (If) weren't catching, . . . would . . .
(If) were catching, . . . wouldn't . . .

Past Conditional—Progressive Form
(If) I had been catching, . . . would have . . .
(+ past participle)

Neg. (If) hadn't been catching, . . . would
have . . . (+ past participle)
(If) had been catching, . . . wouldn't
have . . . (+ past participle)

Unreal Conditional
(If) I caught, . . . would . . .

Neg. (If) didn't catch, . . . would . . .
(If) caught, . . . wouldn't . . .

Past Conditional
(If) I had caught, . . . would have . . .
(+ past participle)

Neg. (If) hadn't caught, . . . would
have . . . (+ past participle)
(If) had caught, . . . wouldn't have . . .
(+ past participle)

These Verbs Follow the Same Pattern
teach   fight*
bring*   think*
buy*

These Verbs Follow a Different Pattern
match   switch
scratch   touch
stretch   watch

Note: *These verbs add *ought* instead of just -*ught* in the simple past and past participle, but otherwise follow the same conjugation patterns as *catch*.

Catch the ball, Laddie!

Is that skin rash *catching*?   (= contagious)

It seems that Lewis *is catching* the same cold Janet *had caught* the week
before.

My father and I *caught* many trout in this river.

We *caught* sight of Lena leaving the   (*catch sight of* = notice accidentally)
store, but couldn't *catch* her attention
before she drove away.

I hope this fashion *won't catch* on the   (*catch on* = become popular)
way baseball caps did.

The thief *was* never *caught* by the police.

Walter *was catching* his breath at a   (*catch one's breath* = pause after
street corner when he saw the bank   exertion)
robbery.

Irregular verb, active form: *cut*

INFINITIVE/IMPERATIVE	**NEGATIVE**
(to) cut/Cut . . . !	(to) not cut/Don't cut . . . !
Present Participle*	**Past Participle**
cutting	cut
Neg. not cutting	**Neg.** not cut

PRESENT TENSES

Simple Present Tense
I cut
you cut
he/she/it cuts
we cut
you cut
they cut

Present Progressive
I am cutting

Neg. don't/doesn't cut

Neg. (am) not/aren't/isn't cutting

Present Perfect
I have cut

Neg. haven't/hasn't cut

PAST TENSES

Simple Past Tense
I cut

Past Progressive
I was cutting

Neg. didn't cut

Neg. wasn't/weren't cutting

Past Perfect
I had cut

Past Perfect Progressive
I had been cutting

Neg. hadn't cut

Neg. hadn't been cutting

FUTURE TENSES

Simple Future Tense
I will cut

Immediate Future Tense
I am going to cut

Neg. won't cut

Neg. (am) not/aren't/isn't going to cut

Future Progressive
I will be cutting

Immediate Future Progressive
I am going to be cutting

Neg. won't be cutting

Neg. (am) not/aren't/isn't going to be cutting

Future Perfect
I will have cut

Neg. won't have cut

Note: *Spelling change: Irregular verbs ending in a single consonant following a single vowel double the last consonant before -*ing*.

CONDITIONALS

Future Conditional
(If) I cut, . . . will . . .

Neg. (If) don't/doesn't cut, . . . will . . .
(If) cut, . . . won't . . .

Unreal Conditional—Progressive Form
(If) I were cutting, . . . would . . .

Neg. (If) weren't cutting, . . . would . . .
(If) were cutting, . . . wouldn't . . .

Unreal Conditional
(If) I cut, . . . would . . .

Neg. (If) didn't cut, . . . would . . .
(If) cut, . . . wouldn't . . .

Past Conditional
(If) I had cut, . . . would have . . .
(+ past participle)

Neg. (If) hadn't cut, . . . would have . . .
(+ past participle)
(If) had cut, . . . wouldn't have . . .
(+ past participle)

Past Conditional—Progressive Form
(If) I had been cutting, . . . would have . . . (+ past participle)

Neg. (If) hadn't been cutting, . . . would have . . . (+ past participle)
(If) had been cutting, . . . wouldn't have . . . (+ past participle)

These Verbs Follow the Same Pattern

bet	let
burst	put
cost	quit
hit	shut
hurt	spread

Cut has two meanings: (1) to slice with something sharp; (2) to reduce or decrease the amount of something.

Daniel *cut* his finger on a broken glass.

While the bride *was cutting* the wedding cake, the knife slipped.

The city *has cut* police benefits, but *hasn't cut* their hours.

This project *has been cutting* into my time with my family.   (*cut into* = decrease proportion of time, money, etc.)

The tailor *had* already *cut* the material by the time the shop opened.

The paper says that by the year 2020, cancer deaths *will have been cut* by two thirds.

Cut that out!   (= stop doing that!)

Let's *cut* through the woods—it's faster.   (= take a shorter route)

If they *cut* a new highway into these mountains, the environment *will* suffer.

Irregular verb, active form: *draw*

INFINITIVE/IMPERATIVE	*NEGATIVE*
(to) draw/Draw . . . !	(to) not draw/Don't draw . . . !
Present Participle	*Past Participle*
drawing	drawn
Neg. not drawing	*Neg.* not drawn

PRESENT TENSES

Simple Present Tense
I draw
you draw
he/she/it draws
we draw
you draw
they draw

Neg. don't/doesn't draw

Present Perfect
I have drawn

Neg. haven't/hasn't drawn

Present Progressive
I am drawing

Neg. (am) not/aren't/isn't drawing

PAST TENSES

Simple Past Tense
I drew

Neg. didn't draw

Past Perfect
I had drawn

Neg. hadn't drawn

Past Progressive
I was drawing

Neg. wasn't/weren't drawing

Past Perfect Progressive
I had been drawing

Neg. hadn't been drawing

FUTURE TENSES

Simple Future Tense
I will draw

Neg. won't draw

Future Progressive
I will be drawing

Neg. won't be drawing

Future Perfect
I will have drawn

Neg. won't have drawn

Immediate Future Tense
I am going to draw

Neg. (am) not/aren't/isn't going to draw

Immediate Future Progressive
I am going to be drawing

Neg. (am) not/aren't/isn't going to be drawing

CONDITIONALS

Future Conditional
(If) I draw, . . . will . . .

Neg. (If) don't/doesn't draw, . . . will . . .
(If) draw, . . . won't . . .

Unreal Conditional—Progressive Form
(If) I were drawing, . . . would . . .

Neg. (If) weren't drawing, . . . would . . .
(If) were drawing, . . . wouldn't . . .

Past Conditional—Progressive Form
(If) I had been drawing, . . . would
have . . . (+ past participle)

Neg. (If) hadn't been drawing, . . . would
have . . . (+ past participle)
(If) had been drawing, . . . wouldn't have
. . . (+ past participle)

Unreal Conditional
(If) I drew, . . . would . . .

Neg. (If) didn't draw, . . . would . . .
(If) drew, . . . wouldn't . . .

Past Conditional
(If) I had drawn, . . . would have . . .
(+ past participle)

Neg. (If) hadn't drawn, . . . would have . . .
(+ past participle)
(If) had drawn, . . . wouldn't have . . .
(+ past participle)

These Verbs Follow the Same Pattern

blow	throw
grow	withdraw
know	

These Verbs Follow a Different Pattern
saw (= cut with a saw)
thaw (= snow or ice melts)

Draw has three meanings: (1) to create a picture using something other than paints; (2) to pull something out—this meaning is usually slightly literary; (3) to gather together—people, things, or ideas.

Mike ca*n't draw* a straight line.

This accident *is drawing* a large crowd.

Who *drew* this on the wall?

What! Bill *drew* the winning number in the lottery?

I'*ll draw* you a map of the property.

The lawyers *had* already *drawn* up the contracts when the merger was canceled.

The professor *has drawn* his conclusions from various sources.

Irregular verb, active form: *drink*

INFINITIVE/IMPERATIVE	NEGATIVE
(to) drink/Drink . . . !	(to) not drink/Don't drink . . . !
Present Participle	**Past Participle**
drinking	drunk
Neg. not drinking	**Neg.** not drunk

PRESENT TENSES

Simple Present Tense
I drink
you drink
he/she/it drinks
we drink
you drink
they drink

Neg. don't/doesn't drink

Present Progressive
I am drinking

Neg. (am) not/aren't/isn't drinking

Present Perfect
I have drunk

Neg. haven't/hasn't drunk

PAST TENSES

Simple Past Tense
I drank

Neg. didn't drink

Past Perfect
I had drunk

Neg. hadn't drunk

Past Progressive
I was drinking

Neg. wasn't/weren't drinking

Past Perfect Progressive
I had been drinking

Neg. hadn't been drinking

FUTURE TENSES

Simple Future Tense
I will drink

Neg. won't drink

Future Progressive
I will be drinking

Neg. won't be drinking

Immediate Future Tense
I am going to drink

Neg. (am) not/aren't/isn't going to drink

Immediate Future Progressive
I am going to be drinking

Neg. (am) not/aren't/isn't going to be drinking

Future Perfect
I will have drunk

Neg. won't have drunk

CONDITIONALS

Future Conditional
(If) I drink, . . . will . . .

Neg. (If) don't/doesn't drink, . . . will . . .
(If) drink, . . . won't . . .

Unreal Conditional—Progressive Form
(If) I were drinking, . . . would . . .

Neg. (If) weren't drinking, . . . would . . .
(If) were drinking, . . . wouldn't . . .

Past Conditional—Progressive Form
(If) I had been drinking, . . . would have . . . (+ past participle)

Neg. (If) hadn't been drinking, . . . would have . . . (+ past participle)
(If) had been drinking, . . . wouldn't have . . . (+ past participle)

Unreal Conditional
(If) I drank, . . . would . . .

Neg. (If) didn't drink, . . . would . . .
(If) drank, . . . wouldn't . . .

Past Conditional
(If) I had drunk, . . . would have . . . (+ past participle)

Neg. (If) hadn't drunk, . . . would have . . . (+ past participle)
(If) had drunk, . . . wouldn't have . . . (+ past participle)

These Verbs Follow the Same Pattern
begin
sing
spring (= *jump*—for animals; for people only in classic writing or some idioms)
swim

These Verbs Follow a Different Pattern
link   sit   think

Do you like to *drink* coffee or tea?

Don't drink too much of this rum punch.

During dinner, we *were drinking* white wine with the fish, then switched to red with the meat.

I *haven't drunk* anything since lunch time.

If you *drink* that cocoa now, you *won't* be able to eat lunch.

Irregular verb, active form: *drive*

INFINITIVE/IMPERATIVE	*NEGATIVE*
(to) drive/Drive . . . !	(to) not drive/Don't drive . . . !
Present Participle*	*Past Participle*
driving	driven
Neg. not driving	*Neg.* not driven

PRESENT TENSES

Simple Present Tense
I drive
you drive
he/she/it drives
we drive
you drive
they drive

Neg. don't/doesn't drive

Present Perfect
I have driven

Neg. haven't/hasn't driven

Present Progressive
I am driving

Neg. (am) not/aren't/isn't driving

PAST TENSES

Simple Past Tense
I drove

Neg. didn't drive

Past Perfect
I had driven

Neg. hadn't driven

Past Progressive
I was driving

Neg. wasn't/weren't driving

Past Perfect Progressive
I had been driving

Neg. hadn't been driving

FUTURE TENSES

Simple Future Tense
I will drive

Neg. won't drive

Future Progressive
I will be driving

Neg. won't be driving

Immediate Future Tense
I am going to drive

Neg. (am) not/aren't/isn't going to drive

Immediate Future Progressive
I am going to be driving

Neg. (am) not/aren't/isn't going to be driving

Note: *Spelling change: Verbs ending in *-e* following a consonant drop the *-e* before *-ing* endings.

Future Perfect
I will have driven

Neg. won't have driven

CONDITIONALS

Future Conditional
(If) I drive, . . . will . . .

Neg. (If) don't/doesn't drive, . . . will . . .
(If) drive, . . . won't . . .

Unreal Conditional—Progressive Form
(If) I were driving, . . . would . . .

Neg. (If) weren't driving, . . . would . . .
(If) were driving, . . . wouldn't . . .

Past Conditional—Progressive Form
(If) I had been driving, . . . would have . . .
(+ past participle)

Neg. (If) hadn't been driving, . . . would
have . . . (+ past participle)
(If) had been driving, . . . wouldn't
have . . . (+ past participle)

Unreal Conditional
(If) I drove, . . . would . . .

Neg. (If) didn't drive, . . . would . . .
(If) drove, . . . wouldn't . . .

Past Conditional
(If) I had driven, . . . would have . . .
(+ past participle)

Neg. (If) hadn't driven, . . . would have . . .
(+ past participle)
(If) had driven, . . . wouldn't have . . .
(+ past participle)

These Verbs Follow the Same Pattern
arise
rise
strive (= try hard)

These Verbs Follow a Different Pattern
arrive
deprive (= force someone to be without)
derive (= develop from a source)
give
live

Do you drive?

What kind of car was he driving?

What are you driving at? (= what is the point of your conversation?)

Because of the snowstorm, the truck drove off the side of the road.

Phillip's habit of chewing his lip has been driving me crazy lately. (= strongly annoying)

Margaret's wild spending had driven her husband to the edge of bankruptcy.

If I drove an expensive car, people would charge me more.

Irregular verb, active form: *fall*

INFINITIVE/IMPERATIVE	NEGATIVE
(to) fall/Fall . . . !	(to) not fall/Don't fall . . . !
Present Participle	**Past Participle**
falling	fallen
Neg. not falling	**Neg.** not fallen

PRESENT TENSES

Simple Present Tense
I fall
you fall
he/she/it falls
we fall
you fall
they fall

Neg. don't/doesn't fall

Present Progressive
I am falling

Neg. (am) not/aren't/isn't falling

Present Perfect
I have fallen

Neg. haven't/hasn't fallen

PAST TENSES

Simple Past Tense
I fell

Neg. didn't fall

Past Progressive
I was falling

Neg. wasn't/weren't falling

Past Perfect
I had fallen

Neg. hadn't fallen

Past Perfect Progressive
I had been falling

Neg. hadn't been falling

FUTURE TENSES

Simple Future Tense
I will fall

Neg. won't fall

Immediate Future Tense
I am going to fall

Neg. (am) not/aren't/isn't going to fall

Future Progressive
I will be falling

Neg. won't be falling

Immediate Future Progressive
I am going to be falling

Neg. (am) not/aren't/isn't going to be falling

Future Perfect
I will have fallen

Neg. won't have fallen

CONDITIONALS

Future Conditional
(If) I fall, . . . will . . .

Neg. (If) don't/doesn't fall, . . . will . . .
(If) fall, . . . won't . . .

Unreal Conditional—Progressive Form
(If) I were falling, . . . would . . .

Neg. (If) weren't falling, . . . would . . .
(If) were falling, . . . wouldn't . . .

Past Conditional—Progressive Form
(If) I had been falling, . . . would have . . .
(+ past participle)

Neg. (If) hadn't been falling, . . . would
have . . . (+ past participle)
(If) had been falling, . . . wouldn't have . . .
(+ past participle)

Unreal Conditional
(If) I fell, . . . would . . .

Neg. (If) didn't fall, . . . would . . .
(If) fell, . . . wouldn't . . .

Past Conditional
(If) I had fallen, would have . . .
(+ past participle)

Neg. (If) hadn't fallen, . . . would have . . .
(+ past participle)
(If) had fallen, . . . wouldn't have . . .
(+ past participle)

These Verbs Follow a Different Pattern
call
forestall (= prevent—mostly literary)
install
recall (= remember)
stall (= deliberately delay)

Look! Snow *is falling*.

Sarah *is falling* further and further
behind with her work.

Be careful! You*'re going to fall* off
that ladder!

Mary *fell* and broke her arm.

The roof of that old house *has*
already *fallen* in and the fence *is*
falling down.

(*fall behind* – be late in completing
tasks)

(= fall from a high place)

(*fall in* = collapse inward or downward—
usually things; *fall down* = fall forward or
downward—things or people)

Irregular verb, active form: *feel*

INFINITIVE/IMPERATIVE	***NEGATIVE***
(to) feel/Feel . . . !	(to) not feel/Don't feel . . . !
Present Participle	***Past Participle***
feeling	felt
Neg. not feeling	***Neg.*** not felt

PRESENT TENSES

Simple Present Tense
I feel
you feel
he/she/it feels
we feel
you feel
they feel

Neg. don't/doesn't feel

Present Progressive
I am feeling

Neg. (am) not/aren't/isn't feeling

Present Perfect
I have felt

Neg. haven't/hasn't felt

PAST TENSES

Simple Past Tense
I felt

Neg. didn't feel

Past Perfect
I had felt

Neg. hadn't felt

Past Progressive
I was feeling

Neg. wasn't/weren't feeling

Past Perfect Progressive
I had been feeling

Neg. hadn't been feeling

FUTURE TENSES

Simple Future Tense
I will feel

Neg. won't feel

Future Progressive
I will be feeling

Neg. won't be feeling

Future Perfect
I will have felt

Neg. won't have felt

Immediate Future Tense
I am going to feel

Neg. (am) not/aren't/isn't going to feel

Immediate Future Progressive
I am going to be feeling

Neg. (am) not/aren't/isn't going to be feeling

CONDITIONALS

Future Conditional
(If) I feel, . . . will . . .

Neg. (If) don't/doesn't feel, . . . will . . .
(If) feel, . . . won't . . .

Unreal Conditional—Progressive Form
(If) I were feeling, . . . would . . .

Neg. (If) weren't feeling, . . . would . . .
(If) were feeling, . . . wouldn't . . .

Past Conditional—Progressive Form
(If) I had been feeling, . . . would have . . .
(+ past participle)

Neg. (If) hadn't been feeling, . . . would
have . . . (+ past participle)
(If) had been feeling, . . . wouldn't
have . . . (+ past participle)

Unreal Conditional
(If) I felt, . . . would . . .

Neg. (If) didn't feel, . . . would . . .
(If) felt, . . . wouldn't . . .

Past Conditional
(If) I had felt, . . . would have . . .
(+ past participle)

Neg. (If) hadn't felt, . . . would have . . .
(+ past participle)
(If) had felt, . . . wouldn't have . . .
(+ past participle)

These Verbs Follow the Same Pattern
feed
keep
lead (pronounced "leed")
leave
mean
read
sleep
sweep

Feel has several meanings: (1) to actively use the sense of touch; (2) to describe an overall physical, emotional, or intellectual condition; (3) to describe the effect *of something* on one's sense of touch—this meaning describes a state of being and cannot be used in a progressive form. (see Part A, Section 4 *Something to Think About: State-of-Being Verbs*, page 10)

Feel this fur—it *feels* just like velvet!	(meaning 1/meaning 3)
It's not your fault—*don't feel* guilty.	(meaning 2)
I'*m feeling* rather tired.	(meaning 2)
Joe *doesn't feel* like going to a New Year's party this year.	(*feel like* + -*ing* = be in the mood to . . .) (meaning 2)
Your forehead *feels* hot—*are* you *feeling* feverish?	(meaning 3/meaning 2)
They *felt* for the flashlight, but couldn't find it in the dark.	(meaning 1)

Irregular verb, active form: *find*

INFINITIVE/IMPERATIVE	NEGATIVE
(to) find/Find . . . !	(to) not find/Don't find . . . !
Present Participle	**Past Participle**
finding	found
Neg. not finding	**Neg.** not found

PRESENT TENSES

Simple Present Tense
I find
you find
he/she/it finds
we find
you find
they find

Neg. don't/doesn't find

Present Progressive
I am finding

Neg. (am) not/aren't/isn't finding

Present Perfect
I have found

Neg. haven't/hasn't found

PAST TENSES

Simple Past Tense
I found

Neg. didn't find

Past Perfect
I had found

Neg. hadn't found

Past Progressive
I was finding

Neg. wasn't/weren't finding

Past Perfect Progressive
I had been finding

Neg. hadn't been finding

FUTURE TENSES

Simple Future Tense
I will find

Neg. won't find

Future Progressive
I will be finding

Neg. won't be finding

Immediate Future Tense
I am going to find

Neg. (am) not/aren't/isn't going to find

Immediate Future Progressive
I am going to be finding

Neg. (am) not/aren't/isn't going to be finding

Future Perfect
I will have found

Neg. won't have found

CONDITIONALS

Future Conditional
(If) I find, . . . will . . .

Neg. (If) don't/doesn't find, . . . will . . .
(If) find, . . . won't . . .

Unreal Conditional—Progressive Form
(If) I were finding, . . . would . . .

Neg. (If) weren't finding, . . . would . . .
(If) were finding, . . . wouldn't . . .

Past Conditional—Progressive Form
(If) I had been finding, . . . would have . . .
(+ past participle)

Neg. (If) hadn't been finding, . . . would
have . . . (+ past participle)
(If) had been finding, . . . wouldn't
have . . . (+ past participle)

Unreal Conditional
(If) I found, . . . would . . .

Neg. (If) didn't find, . . . would . . .
(If) found, . . . wouldn't . . .

Past Conditional
(If) I had found, . . . would have . . .
(+ past participle)

Neg. (If) hadn't found, . . . would have . . .
(+ past participle)
(If) had found, . . . wouldn't have . . .
(+ past participle)

These Verbs Follow the Same Pattern
bind (= tie tightly)
grind
wind

This Verb Follows a Different Pattern
mind (= be bothered by . . . ; take care of)

Please *find* those estimates.
I can't *find* the cat anywhere.
Neil isn't here—he's out *finding* some firewood.
Helen *was finding* many errors as she checked the accounts.
Has Charles *found* an apartment yet?
I'm *going to find* out who owns that car.   (= discover information)
If you *find* my wallet, *will* you please let me know?

Irregular verb, active form: *get*

INFINITIVE/IMPERATIVE	***NEGATIVE***
(to) get/Get . . . !	(to) not get/Don't get . . . !
Present Participle*	***Past Participle***
getting	gotten
Neg. not getting	***Neg.*** not gotten

PRESENT TENSES

Simple Present Tense
I get
you get
he/she/it gets
we get
you get
they get

Neg. don't/doesn't get

Present Progressive
I am getting

Neg. (am) not/aren't/isn't getting

Present Perfect
I have gotten

Neg. haven't/hasn't gotten
In British usage, the past participle is *got*, not *gotten*.

PAST TENSES

Simple Past Tense
I got

Neg. didn't get

Past Perfect
I had gotten

Neg. hadn't gotten

Past Progressive
I was getting

Neg. wasn't/weren't getting

Past Perfect Progressive
I had been getting

Neg. hadn't been getting

FUTURE TENSES

Simple Future Tense
I will get

Neg. won't get

Future Progressive
I will be getting

Neg. won't be getting

Immediate Future Tense
I am going to get

Neg. (am) not/aren't/isn't going to get

Immediate Future Progressive
I am going to be getting

Neg. (am) not/aren't/isn't going to be getting

Note: *Spelling change: Irregular verbs ending in a single consonant following a single vowel double the last consonant before -ing.

Future Perfect
I will have gotten

Neg. won't have gotten

CONDITIONALS

Future Conditional
(If) I get, . . . will . . .

Neg. (If) don't/doesn't get, . . . will . . .
(If) get, . . . won't . . .

Unreal Conditional—Progressive Form
(If) I were getting, . . . would . . .

Neg. (If) weren't getting, . . . would . . .
(If) were getting, . . . wouldn't . . .

Past Conditional—Progressive Form
(If) I had been getting, . . . would have . . .
(+ past participle)

Neg. (If) hadn't been getting, . . . would
have . . . (+ past participle)
(If) had been getting, . . . wouldn't
have . . . (+ past participle)

Unreal Conditional
(If) I got, . . . would . . .

Neg. (If) didn't get, . . . would . . .
(If) got, . . . wouldn't . . .

Past Conditional
(If) I had gotten, . . . would have . . .
(+ past participle)

Neg. (If) hadn't gotten, . . . would have . . .
(+ past participle)
(If) had gotten, . . . wouldn't have . . .
(+ past participle)

These Verbs Follow the Same Pattern
forbid
forget

These Verbs Follow a Different Pattern
let
set

The usual meanings of *get* are to (1) acquire, (2) receive, or (3) find and buy, but English has hundreds of idiomatic uses of *get*, frequently as the verb half of numerous phrasal verbs.

Would you please *get* some coffee at the market?

I'*m getting* the meat out of the freezer now.

Phillip *gets* the newspaper on his way to work.

Todd *got* his wife a beautiful ring for her birthday.

Anne *is going to get* a second car.

Have you *gotten* your tax forms yet?

If I *got* a raise, we *could get* a bigger house.

Irregular verb, active form: *give*

INFINITIVE/IMPERATIVE	NEGATIVE
(to) give/Give . . . !	(to) not give/Don't give . . . !
Present Participle*	**Past Participle**
giving	given
Neg. not giving	**Neg.** not given

PRESENT TENSES

Simple Present Tense
I give
you give
he/she/it gives
we give
you give
they give

Neg. don't/doesn't give

Present Progressive
I am giving

Neg. (am) not/aren't/isn't giving

Present Perfect
I have given

Neg. haven't/hasn't given

PAST TENSES

Simple Past Tense
I gave

Neg. didn't give

Past Perfect
I had given

Neg. hadn't given

Past Progressive
I was giving

Neg. wasn't/weren't giving

Past Perfect Progressive
I had been giving

Neg. hadn't been giving

FUTURE TENSES

Simple Future Tense
I will give

Neg. won't give

Future Progressive
I will be giving

Neg. won't be giving

Immediate Future Tense
I am going to give

Neg. (am) not/aren't/isn't going to give

Immediate Future Progressive
I am going to be giving

Neg. (am) not/aren't/isn't going to be giving

Note: *Spelling change: Verbs ending in -*e* following a consonant drop the -*e* before -*ing* endings.

Future Perfect
I will have given

Neg. won't have given

CONDITIONALS

Future Conditional
(If) I give, will

Neg. (If) don't/doesn't give, . . . will . . .
(If) give, . . . won't . . .

Unreal Conditional—Progressive Form
(If) I were giving, . . . would . . .

Neg. (If) weren't giving, . . . would . . .
(If) were giving, . . . wouldn't . . .

Past Conditional—Progressive Form
(If) I had been giving, . . . would have . . .
(+ past participle)

Neg. (If) hadn't been giving, . . . would
have . . . (+ past participle)
(If) had been giving, . . . wouldn't have . . .
(+ past participle)

Unreal Conditional
(If) I gave, would

Neg. (If) didn't give, . . . would . . .
(If) gave, . . . wouldn't . . .

Past Conditional
(If) I had given, . . . would have . . .
(+ past participle)

Neg. (If) hadn't given, . . . would have . . .
(+ past participle)
(If) had given, . . . wouldn't have . . .
(+ past participle)

These Verbs Follow the Same Pattern
forgive ride
forbid rise

These Verbs Follow a Different Pattern
live
strive (for) (= try to achieve)

Give my best to your wife.
Harry *is giving* a speech on Labor Day.
This report *gives* the facts, but not the interpretations.
I'*m going to give* all my money to a charity when I die!
Larry's university *gave* him a first-rate education.
Mr. Hopkins *has given* his entire life to this cause.
If you *give* the cat all that ice cream, he'*ll* get sick.

Irregular verb, active form: *go*

INFINITIVE/IMPERATIVE	NEGATIVE
(to) go/Go . . . !	(to) not go/Don't go . . . !
Present Participle	**Past Participle**
going	gone
Neg. not going	**Neg.** not gone

PRESENT TENSES

Simple Present Tense*
I go
you go
he/she/it goes
we go
you go
they go

Neg. don't/doesn't go

Present Progressive
I am going

Neg. (am) not/aren't/isn't going

Present Perfect*
I have gone

Neg. haven't/hasn't gone

PAST TENSES

Simple Past Tense
I went

Neg. didn't go

Past Progressive
I was going

Neg. wasn't/weren't going

Past Perfect
I had gone

Neg. hadn't gone

Past Perfect Progressive
I had been going

Neg. hadn't been going

FUTURE TENSES

Simple Future Tense
I will go

Neg. won't go

Immediate Future Tense
I am going to go

Neg. (am) not/aren't/isn't going to go

Note: *Spelling change: Verbs ending in *-sh*, *-ch*, *-ss*, *-x*, and *-o* form the 3rd person singular with *-es* instead of *-s*.

Note: *Using *has/have gone* implies that the subject is still at a distance, whereas using *has/have been* (*be*) implies that the subject has returned.

Future Progressive
I will be going

Neg. won't be going

Future Perfect
I will have gone

Neg. won't have gone

Immediate Future Progressive
I am going to be going

Neg. (am) not/aren't/isn't going to be going

CONDITIONALS

Future Conditional
(If) I go, . . . will . . .

Neg. (If) don't/doesn't go, . . . will . . .
(If) go, . . . won't . . .

Unreal Conditional—Progressive Form
(If) I were going, . . . would . . .

Neg. (If) weren't going, . . . would . . .
(If) were going, . . . wouldn't . . .

Unreal Conditional
(If) I went, . . . would . . .

Neg. (If) didn't go, . . . would . . .
(If) went, . . . wouldn't . . .

Past Conditional
(If) I had gone, . . . would have . . .
(+ past participle)

Neg. (If) hadn't gone, . . . would have . . .
(+ past participle)
(If) had gone, . . . wouldn't have . . .
(+ past participle)

Past Conditional—Progressive Form
(If) I had been going, . . . would have . . . (+ past participle)

Neg. (If) hadn't been going, . . . would have . . . (+ past participle)
(If) had been going, . . . wouldn't have . . . (+ past participle)

Go on—say what you think! (*go on* = continue)

Tom *goes* to the gym on Tuesday and Thursday nights.

We'*re going* to Sardinia on our vacation.

They say Vicky *went* to Harvard, but I doubt it.

Dave *has* already *gone* into the meeting, but he'll call you before he *goes* home.

Paul's temperature *had gone* back to normal by the time the doctor saw him.

If the stock market *had gone* 100 points higher today, it *would have* broken all records.

Irregular verb, active form: *grow*

INFINITIVE/IMPERATIVE	NEGATIVE
(to) grow/Grow . . . !	(to) not grow/Don't grow . . . !
Present Participle	**Past Participle**
growing	grown
Neg. not growing	**Neg.** not grown

PRESENT TENSES

Simple Present Tense
I grow
you grow
he/she/it grows
we grow
you grow
they grow

Neg. don't/doesn't grow

Present Progressive
I am growing

Neg. (am) not/aren't/isn't growing

Present Perfect
I have grown

Neg. haven't/hasn't grown

PAST TENSES

Simple Past Tense
I grew

Neg. didn't grow

Past Perfect
I had grown

Neg. hadn't grown

Past Progressive
I was growing

Neg. wasn't/weren't growing

Past Perfect Progressive
I had been growing

Neg. hadn't been growing

FUTURE TENSES

Simple Future Tense
I will grow

Neg. won't grow

Future Progressive
I will be growing

Neg. won't be growing

Immediate Future Tense
I am going to grow

Neg. (am) not/aren't/isn't going to grow

Immediate Future Progressive
I am going to be growing

Neg. (am) not/aren't/isn't going to be growing

Future Perfect
I will have grown

Neg. won't have grown

CONDITIONALS

Future Conditional
(If) I grow, . . . will . . .

Neg. (If) don't/doesn't grow, . . . will . . .
(If) grow, . . . won't . . .

Unreal Conditional—Progressive Form
(If) I were growing, . . . would . . .

Neg. (If) weren't growing, . . . would . . .
(If) were growing, . . . wouldn't . . .

Past Conditional—Progressive Form
(If) I had been growing, . . . would have . . .
(+ past participle)

Neg. (If) hadn't been growing, . . . would
have . . . (+ past participle)
(If) had been growing, . . . wouldn't
have . . . (+ past participle)

Unreal Conditional
(If) I grew, . . . would . . .

Neg. (If) didn't grow, . . . would . . .
(If) grew, . . . wouldn't . . .

Past Conditional
(If) I had grown, . . . would have . . .
(+ past participle)

Neg. (If) hadn't grown, . . . would have . . .
(+ past participle)
(If) had grown, . . . wouldn't have . . .
(+ past participle)

These Verbs Follow the Same Pattern
blow
know
throw

These Verbs Follow a Different Pattern
tow (= pull or drag something behind)
sew
sow (= plant seeds)

My hair seems to *grow* faster in hot weather.

We're *growing* two kinds of corn in the garden this year.

The expenses just *grow* and *grow* !

Chris *was growing* quite heavy before he fell in love.

I'm not sure if peonies *will grow* in Florida—they're *not going to grow* as well as in a cooler climate.

Kyle *has grown* so tall in just six months.

Dad *has been growing* more and more forgetful lately—I'm worried.

If this corporation's debts *grow* any larger, we'*ll* have to shut down.

Irregular verb, active form: *hear*

INFINITIVE/IMPERATIVE	*NEGATIVE*
(to) hear/Hear . . . !	(to) not hear/Don't hear . . . !
Present Participle	*Past Participle*
hearing	heard
Neg. not hearing	*Neg.* not heard

PRESENT TENSES

Simple Present Tense
I hear
you hear
he/she/it hears
we hear
you hear
they hear

Neg. don't/doesn't hear

Present Progressive
I am hearing

Neg. (am) not/aren't/isn't hearing

Present Perfect
I have heard

Neg. haven't/hasn't heard

PAST TENSES

Simple Past Tense
I heard

Neg. didn't hear

Past Progressive
I was hearing

Neg. wasn't/weren't hearing

Past Perfect
I had heard

Neg. hadn't heard

Past Perfect Progressive
I had been hearing

Neg. hadn't been hearing

FUTURE TENSES

Simple Future Tense
I will hear

Neg. won't hear

Immediate Future Tense
I am going to hear

Neg. (am) not/aren't/isn't going to hear

Future Progressive
I will be hearing

Neg. won't be hearing

Immediate Future Progressive
I am going to be hearing

Neg. (am) not/aren't/isn't going to be hearing

Future Perfect
I <u>will</u> <u>have</u> hear<u>d</u>

Neg. <u>won't</u> <u>have</u> heard

CONDITIONALS

Future Conditional
(<u>If</u>) I hear, . . . <u>will</u> . . .

Neg. (<u>If</u>) <u>don't/doesn't</u> hear, . . . <u>will</u> . . .
(<u>If</u>) hear, . . . <u>won't</u> . . .

Unreal Conditional—Progressive Form
(<u>If</u>) I <u>were</u> hear<u>ing</u>, . . . <u>would</u> . . .

Neg. (<u>If</u>) <u>weren't</u> hear<u>ing</u>, . . . <u>would</u> . . .
(<u>If</u>) <u>were</u> hear<u>ing</u>, . . . <u>wouldn't</u> . . .

Past Conditional—Progressive Form
(<u>If</u>) I <u>had</u> <u>been</u> hear<u>ing</u>, . . . <u>would</u> <u>have</u> . . .
(+ past participle)

Neg. (<u>If</u>) <u>hadn't</u> <u>been</u> hear<u>ing</u>, . . . <u>would</u>
<u>have</u> . . . (+ past participle)
(If) <u>had</u> <u>been</u> hear<u>ing</u>, . . . <u>wouldn't</u> <u>have</u> . . .
(+ past participle)

Unreal Conditional
(<u>If</u>) I heard, . . . <u>would</u> . . .

Neg. (<u>If</u>) <u>didn't</u> hear, . . . <u>would</u> . . .
(<u>If</u>) hear<u>d</u>, . . . <u>wouldn't</u> . . .

Past Conditional
(<u>If</u>) I <u>had</u> heard, . . . <u>would</u> <u>have</u> . . .
(+ past participle)

Neg. (<u>If</u>) <u>hadn't</u> hear<u>d</u>, . . . <u>would</u> <u>have</u> . . .
(+ past participle)
(<u>If</u>) <u>had</u> heard, . . . <u>wouldn't</u> <u>have</u> . . .
(+ past participle)

These Verbs Follow the Same Pattern
mishear
overhear

These Verbs Follow a Different Pattern
bear (= carry something—usually literary/historic)
fear
swear
tear
wear

Do you *hear* that noise?
Didn't you *hear* what I said—no candy!
Joan of Arc said she *heard* the voices of angels.
I*'ve heard* that the company is being sold.
Margaret *hadn't heard* from her sister in years, when one day she called.
If Claire *hadn't heard* Bobby crying, we *would have had* a major fire.

Irregular verb, active form: *hold*

INFINITIVE/IMPERATIVE	***NEGATIVE***
(to) hold/Hold . . . !	(to) not hold/Don't hold . . . !
Present Participle	***Past Participle***
hold<u>ing</u>	h<u>e</u>ld
Neg. <u>not</u> hold<u>ing</u>	***Neg.*** <u>not</u> h<u>e</u>ld

PRESENT TENSES

Simple Present Tense
I hold
you hold
he/she/it hold<u>s</u>
we hold
you hold
they hold

Neg. <u>don't/doesn't</u> hold

Present Progressive
I <u>am</u> holding

Neg. (<u>am</u>) <u>not/aren't/isn't</u> holding

Present Perfect
I <u>have</u> h<u>e</u>ld

Neg. <u>haven't/hasn't</u> held

PAST TENSES

Simple Past Tense
I h<u>e</u>ld

Neg. <u>didn't</u> hold

Past Perfect
I <u>had</u> held

Neg. <u>hadn't</u> held

Past Progressive
I <u>was</u> holding

Neg. <u>wasn't/weren't</u> holding

Past Perfect Progressive
I <u>had</u> <u>been</u> holding

Neg. <u>hadn't</u> <u>been</u> holding

FUTURE TENSES

Simple Future Tense
I <u>will</u> hold

Neg. <u>won't</u> hold

Future Progressive
I <u>will</u> <u>be</u> holding

Neg. <u>won't</u> <u>be</u> holding

Future Perfect
I <u>will</u> <u>have</u> held

Neg. <u>won't</u> <u>have</u> held

Immediate Future Tense
I <u>am going to</u> hold

Neg. (<u>am</u>) <u>not/aren't/isn't</u> <u>going to</u> hold

Immediate Future Progressive
I <u>am going to</u> <u>be</u> holding

Neg. (<u>am</u>) <u>not/aren't/isn't</u> <u>going to</u> <u>be</u> holding

CONDITIONALS

Future Conditional
(If) I hold, . . . will . . .

Neg. (If) don't/doesn't hold, . . . will . . .
(If) hold, . . . won't . . .

Unreal Conditional—Progressive Form
(If) I were holding, . . . would . . .

Neg. (If) weren't holding, . . . would . . .
(If) were holding, . . . wouldn't . . .

Unreal Conditional
(If) I held, . . . would . . .

Neg. (If) didn't hold, . . . would . . .
(If) held, . . . wouldn't . . .

Past Conditional
(If) I had held, . . . would have . . .
(+ past participle)

Neg. (If) hadn't held, . . . would have . . .
(+ past participle)
(If) had held, . . . wouldn't have . . .
(+ past participle)

Past Conditional—Progressive Form
(If) I had been holding, . . . would have . . . (+ past participle)

Neg. (If) hadn't been holding, . . . would have . . . (+ past participle)
(If) had been holding, . . . wouldn't have . . . (+ past participle)

These Verbs Follow the Same Pattern
uphold   withhold

These Verbs Follow a Different Pattern
fold   scold

Hold has several meanings: (1) to grip something—usually with hands;
(2) to wait or keep something in reserve; (3) to host a large gathering—
party, funeral, conference, etc.

Hold the phone a minute!	(= asking caller to wait) (meaning 2)
Hold that thought while I go and check on something.	(= don't forget that idea) (meaning 2)
We*'re holding* the annual Christmas party at a Chinese restaurant this year.	(meaning 3)
The mugger *held* a knife to Bruce's throat.	(meaning 1)
Haven't you ever *held* a pair of chopsticks before?	(meaning 1)
We*'ve been holding* that book for you since September.	(meaning 2)
If the wedding *isn't held* in a church, *will* I still have to wear white?	(meaning 3)

Irregular verb, active form: *keep*

INFINITIVE/IMPERATIVE	NEGATIVE
(to) keep/Keep . . . !	(to) not keep/Don't keep . . . !
Present Participle	**Past Participle**
keeping	kept
Neg. not keeping	**Neg.** not kept

PRESENT TENSES

Simple Present Tense
I keep
you keep
he/she/it keeps
we keep
you keep
they keep

Neg. don't/doesn't keep

Present Progressive
I am keeping

Neg. (am) not/aren't/isn't keeping

Present Perfect
I have kept

Neg. haven't/hasn't kept

PAST TENSES

Simple Past Tense
I kept

Neg. didn't keep

Past Progressive
I was keeping

Neg. wasn't/weren't keeping

Past Perfect
I had kept

Neg. hadn't kept

Past Perfect Progressive
I had been keeping

Neg. hadn't been keeping

FUTURE TENSES

Simple Future Tense
I will keep

Neg. won't keep

Immediate Future Tense
I am going to keep

Neg. (am) not/aren't/isn't going to keep

Future Progressive
I will be keeping

Neg. won't be keeping

Immediate Future Progressive
I am going to be keeping

Neg. (am) not/aren't/isn't going to be keeping

Future Perfect
I will have kept

Neg. won't have kept

CONDITIONALS

Future Conditional
(If) I keep, . . . will . . .

Neg. (If) don't/doesn't keep, . . . will . . .
(If) keep, . . . won't . . .

Unreal Conditional—Progressive Form
(If) I were keeping, . . . would . . .

Neg. (If) weren't keeping, . . . would . . .
(If) were keeping, . . . wouldn't . . .

Unreal Conditional
(If) I kept, . . . would . . .

Neg. (If) didn't keep, . . . would . . .
(If) kept, . . . wouldn't . . .

Past Conditional
(If) I had kept, would have . . .
(+ past participle)

Neg. (If) hadn't kept, would have . . .
(+ past participle)
(If) had kept, wouldn't have . . .
(+ past participle)

Past Conditional—Progressive Form
(If) I had been keeping, . . . would have . . . (+ past participle)

Neg. (If) hadn't been keeping, . . . would have . . . (+ past participle)
(If) had been keeping, . . . wouldn't have . . . (+ past participle)

These Verbs Follow the Same Pattern

creep (= crawl)
feel
kneel (= rest on one's knees—for prayer, etc.)

meet
sleep
sweep (= clean with broom)

These Verbs Follow a Different Pattern

need
reap (= gather harvest—literary or biblical)

seek

Keep has several meanings: (1) to retain/withhold/reserve; (2) to own pets; (3) to continue doing something.

Keep the change!	(set expression when giving a tip by leaving one's change when paying) (meaning 1)
Don't keep singing that song!	(meaning 3)
It's so hard *to keep* up appearances on a pension.	(*keep up* = maintain established level) (meaning 3)
We're not allowed to *keep* pets in this apartment.	(meaning 2)
Mark *kept* every theater program he ever got.	(meaning 1)
Meetings *have kept* Tom at the office past 6:00 every night this week.	(meaning 3)
Eva *has been keeping* busy since retiring.	(meaning 3)

Irregular verb, active form: *know*

INFINITIVE/IMPERATIVE	***NEGATIVE***
(to) know/Know . . . !	(to) not know/Don't know . . . !
Present Participle	***Past Participle***
know<u>ing</u>	know<u>n</u>
Neg. <u>not</u> know<u>ing</u>	***Neg.*** <u>not</u> know<u>n</u>

PRESENT TENSES

Simple Present Tense
I know
you know
he/she/it know<u>s</u>
we know
you know
they know

Neg. <u>don't</u>/<u>doesn't</u> know

Present Perfect
I <u>have</u> know<u>n</u>

Neg. <u>haven't</u>/<u>hasn't</u> known

Present Progressive
I <u>am</u> knowing

Neg. (<u>am</u>) <u>not</u>/<u>aren't</u>/<u>isn't</u> knowing

PAST TENSES

Simple Past Tense
I kn<u>e</u>w

Neg. <u>didn't</u> know

Past Perfect
I <u>had</u> know<u>n</u>

Neg. <u>hadn't</u> know<u>n</u>

Past Progressive
I <u>was</u> knowing

Neg. <u>wasn't</u>/<u>weren't</u> knowing

Past Perfect Progressive
I <u>had</u> <u>been</u> knowing

Neg. <u>hadn't</u> <u>been</u> knowing

FUTURE TENSES

Simple Future Tense
I <u>will</u> know

Neg. <u>won't</u> know

Future Progressive
I <u>will</u> <u>be</u> knowing

Neg. <u>won't</u> <u>be</u> knowing

Immediate Future Tense
I <u>am</u> <u>going</u> <u>to</u> know

Neg. (<u>am</u>) <u>not</u>/<u>aren't</u>/<u>isn't</u> <u>going</u> <u>to</u> know

Immediate Future Progressive
I <u>am</u> <u>going</u> <u>to</u> <u>be</u> knowing

Neg. (<u>am</u>) <u>not</u>/<u>aren't</u>/<u>isn't</u> <u>going</u> <u>to</u> <u>be</u> knowing

Future Perfect
I will have known

Neg. won't have known

CONDITIONALS

Future Conditional
(If) I know, . . . will . . .

Neg. (If) don't/doesn't know, . . . will . . .
(If) know, . . . won't . . .

Unreal Conditional—Progressive Form
(If) I were knowing, . . . would . . .

Neg. (If) weren't knowing, . . . would . . .
(If) were knowing, . . . wouldn't . . .

Past Conditional—Progressive Form
(If) I had been knowing, . . . would
have . . . (+ past participle)

Neg. (If) hadn't been knowing, . . . would
have . . . (+ past participle)
(If) had been knowing, . . . wouldn't
have . . . (+ past participle)

Unreal Conditional
(If) I knew, . . . would . . .

Neg. (If) didn't know, . . . would . . .
(If) knew, . . . wouldn't . . .

Past Conditional
(If) I had known, . . . would have . . .
(+ past participle)

Neg. (If) hadn't known, . . . would have . . .
(+ past participle)
(If) had known, . . . wouldn't have . . .
(+ past participle)

These Verbs Follow the Same Pattern
blow
grow
throw

These Verbs Follow a Different Pattern
sew
sow
tow

I **don't know** what to do about this problem.

Jill **knows** every inch of this city by now.

Bruce **knows** how to speak Mandarin.

You **should have known** the shops   (*should have known* = it's logical
would be closed today.   for_to know that_)

Phil **knew** he should stop smoking, but couldn't (do it).

We **haven't known** Jerry for very long, but I **knew** his sister at college.

Irregular verb, active form: *lay*

INFINITIVE/IMPERATIVE	*NEGATIVE*
(to) lay/Lay . . . !	(to) not lay/Don't lay . . . !
Present Participle	*Past Participle*
lay<u>ing</u>	l<u>aid</u>
Neg. <u>not</u> lay<u>ing</u>	*Neg.* <u>not</u> l<u>aid</u>

PRESENT TENSES

Simple Present Tense
I lay
you lay
he/she/it lay<u>s</u>
we lay
you lay
they lay

Neg. <u>don't/doesn't</u> lay

Present Perfect
I <u>have</u> l<u>aid</u>

Neg. <u>haven't/hasn't</u> l<u>aid</u>

Present Progressive
I <u>am</u> lay<u>ing</u>

Neg. <u>(am)</u> <u>not/aren't/isn't</u> lay<u>ing</u>

PAST TENSES

Simple Past Tense
I l<u>aid</u>

Neg. <u>didn't</u> lay

Past Perfect
I <u>had</u> l<u>aid</u>

Neg. <u>hadn't</u> l<u>aid</u>

Past Progressive
I <u>was</u> lay<u>ing</u>

Neg. <u>wasn't/weren't</u> lay<u>ing</u>

Past Perfect Progressive
I <u>had</u> <u>been</u> lay<u>ing</u>

Neg. <u>hadn't</u> <u>been</u> lay<u>ing</u>

FUTURE TENSES

Simple Future Tense
I <u>will</u> lay

Neg. <u>won't</u> lay

Future Progressive
I <u>will</u> <u>be</u> lay<u>ing</u>

Neg. <u>won't</u> <u>be</u> lay<u>ing</u>

Immediate Future Tense
I <u>am</u> <u>going</u> <u>to</u> lay

Neg. <u>(am)</u> <u>not/aren't/isn't</u> <u>going</u> <u>to</u> lay

Immediate Future Progressive
I <u>am</u> <u>going</u> <u>to</u> <u>be</u> lay<u>ing</u>

Neg. <u>(am)</u> <u>not/aren't/isn't</u> <u>going</u> <u>to</u> <u>be</u> lay<u>ing</u>

Future Perfect
I will have laid

Neg. won't have laid

CONDITIONALS

Future Conditional
(If) I lay, . . . will . . .

Neg. (If) don't/doesn't lay, . . . will . . .
(If) lay, . . . won't . . .

Unreal Conditional—Progressive Form
(If) I were laying, . . . would . . .

Neg. (If) weren't laying, . . . would . . .
(If) were laying, . . . wouldn't . . .

Unreal Conditional
(If) I laid, . . . would . . .

Neg. (If) didn't lay, . . . would . . .
(If) laid, . . . wouldn't . . .

Past Conditional
(If) I had laid, . . . would have . . .
(+ past participle)

Neg. (If) hadn't laid, . . . would have . . .
(+ past participle)
(If) had laid, . . . wouldn't have . . .
(+ past participle)

Past Conditional—Progressive Form
(If) I had been laying, . . . would have . . . (+ past participle)

Neg. (If) hadn't been laying, . . . would have . . . (+ past participle)
(If) had been laying, . . . wouldn't have . . . (+ past participle)

These Verbs Follow the Same Pattern
pay
say

These Verbs Follow a Different Pattern
delay   pray
play   stay

Lay is often confused with **lie**. **Lay**, however, is a transitive verb—it needs a direct object to make sense, whereas **lie** is intransitive. See note under entry for **lie**.

Just **lay** the dry cleaning on the bed.

The nurse **laid** the baby in the new mother's arms.

Henry **laid** newspaper over the furniture before painting the ceiling.

We**'ve** already **laid** the groundwork for our new marketing strategy.   (*lay the groundwork for . . .* = make the preparations/create the foundation for . . . usually conceptual, not physical)

If you **hadn't laid** the quilt in the sun, it **wouldn't have** faded.

Irregular verb, active form: *lead*

INFINITIVE/IMPERATIVE	*NEGATIVE*
(to) lead/Lead . . . !	(to) not lead/Don't lead . . . !
Present Participle	*Past Participle*
leading	
Neg. not leading	*Neg.* not led

PRESENT TENSES

Simple Present Tense
I lead
you lead
he/she/it leads
we lead
you lead
they lead

Neg. don't/doesn't lead

Present Progressive
I am leading

Neg. (am) not/aren't/isn't leading

Present Perfect
I have led

Neg. haven't/hasn't led

PAST TENSES

Simple Past Tense
I led

Neg. didn't lead

Past Perfect
I had led

Neg. hadn't led

Past Progressive
I was leading

Neg. wasn't/weren't leading

Past Perfect Progressive
I had been leading

Neg. hadn't been leading

FUTURE TENSES

Simple Future Tense
I will lead

Neg. won't lead

Future Progressive
I will be leading

Neg. won't be leading

Immediate Future Tense
I am going to lead

Neg. (am) not/aren't/isn't going to lead

Immediate Future Progressive
I am going to be leading

Neg. (am) not/aren't/isn't going to be leading

Future Perfect
I will have led

Neg. won't have led

CONDITIONALS

Future Conditional
(If) I lead, . . . will . . .

Neg. (If) don't/doesn't lead, . . . will . . .
(If) lead, . . . won't . . .

Unreal Conditional—Progressive Form
(If) I were leading, . . . would . . .

Neg. (If) weren't leading, . . . would . . .
(If) were leading, . . . wouldn't . . .

Past Conditional—Progressive Form
(If) I had been leading, . . . would have . . .
(+ past participle)

Neg. (If) hadn't been leading, . . . would
have . . . (+ past participle)
(If) had been leading, . . . wouldn't
have . . . (+ past participle)

Unreal Conditional
(If) I led, . . . would . . .

Neg. (If) didn't lead, . . . would . . .
(If) led, . . . wouldn't . . .

Past Conditional
(If) I had led, . . . would have . . .
(+ past participle)

Neg. (If) hadn't led, . . . would have . . .
(+ past participle)
(If) had led, . . . wouldn't have . . .
(+ past participle)

These Verbs Follow the Same Pattern
bleed
feed
speed

These Verbs Follow a Different Pattern
beat
knead (= handle bread dough)
need
seed

Lead the way!   (= go first)
We're *leading* in the polls.
This road *leads* to Watsonville.
The home team *is leading* the visitors by a score of 8 to 2.
The guide *led* the tourists through the palace.
Ann *has led* an interesting life.

Irregular verb, active form: *leave*

INFINITIVE/IMPERATIVE	**NEGATIVE**
(to) leave/Leave . . . !	(to) not leave/Don't leave . . . !
Present Participle*	**Past Participle**
leaving	left
Neg. not leaving	**Neg.** not left

PRESENT TENSES

Simple Present Tense
I leave
you leave
he/she/it leaves
we leave
you leave
they leave

Neg. don't/doesn't leave

Present Perfect
I have left

Neg. haven't/hasn't left

Present Progressive
I am leaving

Neg. (am) not/aren't/isn't leaving

PAST TENSES

Simple Past Tense
I left

Neg. didn't leave

Past Perfect
I had left

Neg. hadn't left

Past Progressive
I was leaving

Neg. wasn't/weren't leaving

Past Perfect Progressive
I had been leaving

Neg. hadn't been leaving

FUTURE TENSES

Simple Future Tense
I will leave

Neg. won't leave

Future Progressive
I will be leaving

Neg. won't be leaving

Immediate Future Tense
I am going to leave

Neg. (am) not/aren't/isn't going to leave

Immediate Future Progressive
I am going to be leaving

Neg. (am) not/aren't/isn't going to be leaving

Note: *Spelling change: Verbs ending in *-e* following a consonant drop the *-e* before *-ing* endings.

Future Perfect
I will have left

Neg. won't have left

CONDITIONALS

Future Conditional
(If) I leave, . . . will . . .

Neg. (If) don't/doesn't leave, . . . will . . .
(If) leave, . . . won't . . .

Unreal Conditional—Progressive Form
(If) I were leaving, . . . would . . .

Neg. (If) weren't leaving, . . . would . . .
(If) were leaving, . . . wouldn't . . .

Past Conditional—Progressive Form
(If) I had been leaving, . . . would have . . .
(+ past participle)

Neg. (If) hadn't been leaving, . . . would have . . . (+ past participle)
(If) had been leaving, . . . wouldn't have . . .
(+ past participle)

Unreal Conditional
(If) I left, . . . would . . .

Neg. (If) didn't leave, . . . would . . .
(If) left, . . . wouldn't . . .

Past Conditional
(If) I had left, . . . would have . . .
(+ past participle)

Neg. (If) hadn't left, . . . would have . . .
(+ past participle)
(If) had left, . . . wouldn't have . . .
(+ past participle)

These Verbs Follow the Same Pattern
leap (= jump)
mean

These Verbs Follow a Different Pattern
believe
grieve (= strong sorrow over loss, death, etc.)
retrieve

Leave me alone!   (= don't bother me—very strong, possibly rude)

Don't leave the lights on when you come upstairs.

Dennis **is leaving** the company.

My flight **leaves** at 9:00 A.M.

That **leaves** me $3.00 until the bank opens.

It began to rain just as I **was leaving** the house.

Wendy's father **left** her a lot of money   (= give after death)

If I **had left** the chicken on the table, the dog **would have** eaten it.

Irregular verb, active form: *lie*

INFINITIVE/IMPERATIVE	***NEGATIVE***
(to) lie/Lie . . . !	(to) not lie/Don't lie . . . !
Present Participle *	***Past Participle***
lying	lain
Neg. not lying	***Neg.*** not lain

PRESENT TENSES

Simple Present Tense
I lie
you lie
he/she/it lies
we lie
you lie
they lie

Neg. don't/doesn't lie

Present Progressive
I am lying

Neg. (am) not/aren't/isn't lying

Present Perfect
I have lain

Neg. haven't/hasn't lain

PAST TENSES

Simple Past Tense
I lay

Neg. didn't lay

Past Perfect
I had lain

Neg. hadn't lain

Past Progressive
I was lying

Neg. wasn't/weren't lying

Past Perfect Progressive
I had been lying

Neg. hadn't been lying

FUTURE TENSES

Simple Future Tense
I will lie

Neg. won't lie

Future Progressive
I will be lying

Neg. won't be lying

Immediate Future Tense
I am going to lie

Neg. (am) not/aren't/isn't going to lie

Immediate Future Progressive
I am going to be lying

Neg. (am) not/aren't/isn't going to be lying

Note: *Spelling change: Verbs ending in *-ie* change the *-ie* to *-y* in all *-ing* tenses.

Future Perfect
I will have lain

Neg. won't have lain

CONDITIONALS

Future Conditional
(If) I lie, . . . will . . .

Neg. (If) don't/doesn't lie, . . . will . . .
(If) lie, . . . won't . . .

Unreal Conditional—Progressive Form
(If) I were lying, . . . would . . .

Neg. (If) weren't lying, . . . would . . .
(If) were lying, . . . wouldn't . . .

Unreal Conditional
(If) I lay, . . . would . . .

Neg. (If) didn't lie, . . . would . . .
(If) lay, . . . wouldn't . . .

Past Conditional
(If) I had lain, . . . would have . . .
(+ past participle)

Neg. (If) hadn't lain, . . . would have . . .
(+ past participle)
(If) had lain, . . . wouldn't have . . .
(+ past participle)

Past Conditional—Progressive Form
(If) I had been lying, . . . would have . . . (+ past participle)

Neg. (If) hadn't been lying, would have . . . (+ past participle)
(If) had been lying, . . . wouldn't have . . . (+ past participle)

These Verbs Follow a Different Pattern
comply (= follow rules; agree to request)
deny   supply
die   lie
rely (= depend on)

This Verb Follows the Same Pattern
underlie

Lie (= body position) causes some problems on two levels. People tend to confuse it with *lay* (= place flat). And because the present participle is *lying*, there is also fear of confusing it with *telling a lie* (the two concepts are spelled and conjugated differently).

Lie down, Rover!

Gene *lies* on his right side until he falls asleep.

My hair never *lies* flat after I wash it.

I'*m lying* on the beach in Acapulco, writing this postcard . . .

We'*re* just *going to lie* in bed until noon this Sunday.

I *lie* awake for hours if I drink coffee   (*lie awake* = lie in bed unable to sleep)
at night.

Irregular verb, active form: *light*

INFINITIVE/IMPERATIVE	NEGATIVE
(to) light/Light . . . !	(to) not light/Don't light . . . !
Present Participle	**Past Participle**
lighting	lit
Neg. not lighting	**Neg.** not lit

PRESENT TENSES

Simple Present Tense
I light
you light
he/she/it lights
we light
you light
they light

Neg. don't/doesn't light

Present Progressive
I am lighting

Neg. (am) not/aren't/isn't lighting

Present Perfect
I have lit

Neg. haven't/hasn't lit

PAST TENSES

Simple Past Tense*
I lit

Neg. didn't light

Past Progressive
I was lighting

Neg. wasn't/weren't lighting

Past Perfect
I had lit

Neg. hadn't lit

Past Perfect Progressive
I had been lighting

Neg. hadn't been lighting

FUTURE TENSES

Simple Future Tense
I will light

Neg. won't light

Immediate Future Tense
I am going to light

Neg. (am) not/aren't/isn't going to light

Future Progressive
I will be lighting

Neg. won't be lighting

Immediate Future Progressive
I am going to be lighting

Neg. (am) not/aren't/isn't going to be lighting

Note: *Lighted* is a nonstandard variant form in the simple past, but *lit* is the only generally accepted past participle.

Future Perfect
I will have lit

Neg. won't have lit

CONDITIONALS

Future Conditional
(If) I light, . . . will . . .

Neg. (If) don't/doesn't light, . . . will . . .
(If) light, . . . won't . . .

Unreal Conditional—Progressive Form
(If) I were lighting, . . . would . . .

Neg. (If) weren't lighting, . . . would . . .
(If) were lighting, . . . wouldn't . . .

Past Conditional—Progressive Form
(If) I had been lighting, . . . would
have . . . (+ past participle)

Neg. (If) hadn't been lighting, . . . would
have . . . (+ past participle)
(If) had been lighting, . . . wouldn't
have . . . (+ past participle)

Unreal Conditional
(If) I lit, . . . would . . .

Neg. (If) didn't light, . . . would . . .
(If) lit, . . . wouldn't . . .

Past Conditional
(If) I had lit, . . . would have . . .
(+ past participle)

Neg. (If) hadn't lit, . . . would have . . .
(+ past participle)
(If) had lit, . . . wouldn't have . . .
(+ past participle)

These Verbs Follow the Same Pattern
alight
relight (= light again)

These Verbs Follow a Different Pattern
delight (in)
fight

The kids can't wait to *light* the
Christmas tree.

(*can't wait to* . . . = be eager to . . .)

Bobby *was* just *lighting* a cigarette when I caught him.

I'*ll light* the candles and you pour the wine.

It was so cold last night that we *lit* a fire.

Have you *lit* the barbecue yet?

If Joe had remembered to *light* the furnace, the water pipes wouldn't
have frozen.

Irregular verb, active form: *lose*

INFINITIVE/IMPERATIVE	NEGATIVE
(to) lose/Lose . . . !	(to) not lose/Don't lose . . . !
Present Participle*	**Past Participle**
losing	lost
Neg. not losing	**Neg.** not lost

PRESENT TENSES

Simple Present Tense
I lose
you lose
he/she/it loses
we lose
you lose
they lose

Neg. don't/doesn't lose

Present Progressive
I am losing

Neg. (am) not/aren't/isn't losing

Present Perfect
I have lost

Neg. haven't/hasn't lost

PAST TENSES

Simple Past Tense
I lost

Neg. didn't lose

Past Perfect
I had lost

Neg. hadn't lost

Past Progressive
I was losing

Neg. wasn't/weren't losing

Past Perfect Progressive
I had been losing

Neg. hadn't been losing

FUTURE TENSES

Simple Future Tense
I will lose

Neg. won't lose

Future Progressive
I will be losing

Neg. won't be losing

Immediate Future Tense
I am going to lose

Neg. (am) not/aren't/isn't going to lose

Immediate Future Progressive
I am going to be losing

Neg. (am) not/aren't/isn't going to be losing

Note: *Spelling change: Verbs ending in *-e* following a consonant drop the *-e* before *-ing* endings.

Future Perfect
I will have lost

Neg. won't have lost

CONDITIONALS

Future Conditional
(If) I lose, . . . will . . .

Neg. (If) don't/doesn't lose, . . . will . . .
(If) lose, . . . won't . . .

Unreal Conditional—Progressive Form
(If) I were losing, . . . would . . .

Neg. (If) weren't losing, . . . would . . .
(If) were losing, . . . wouldn't . . .

Past Conditional—Progressive Form
(If) I had been losing, . . . would have . . .
(+ past participle)

Neg. (If) hadn't been losing, . . . would
have . . . (+ past participle)
(If) had been losing, . . . wouldn't have . . .
(+ past participle)

Unreal Conditional
(If) I lost, . . . would . . .

Neg. (If) didn't lose, . . . would . . .
(If) lost, . . . wouldn't . . .

Past Conditional
(If) I had lost, . . . would have . . .
(+ past participle)

Neg. (If) hadn't lost, . . . would have . . .
(+ past participle)
(If) had lost, . . . wouldn't have . . .
(+ past participle)

These Verbs Follow a Different Pattern
abuse
close
dose (= administer medicine or other treatment)

Be careful not to confuse *lose* (= misplace) with *loose* (= set free-verb; not tight-adj.), either in spelling or in meaning.

The doctor told Ellen *to lose* weight.

I've *lost* my glasses.

Mother *is losing* her accent after 20 years in this country.

Robert *was losing* interest in his work until his promotion.   (*lose interest in* = become bored by)

The company *lost* money on the project in Boston.

Have you *lost* your mind?   (= that's crazy behavior/a crazy idea, etc.)

Irregular verb, active form: *make*

INFINITIVE/IMPERATIVE	**NEGATIVE**
(to) make/Make . . . !	(to) not make/Don't make . . . !
Present Participle*	**Past Participle**
making	made
Neg. not making	**Neg.** not made

PRESENT TENSES

Simple Present Tense
I make
you make
he/she/it makes
we make
you make
they make

Present Progressive
I am making

Neg. don't/doesn't make

Neg. (am) not/aren't/isn't making

Present Perfect
I have made

Neg. haven't/hasn't made

PAST TENSES

Simple Past Tense
I made

Past Progressive
I was making

Neg. didn't make

Neg. wasn't/weren't making

Past Perfect
I had made

Past Perfect Progressive
I had been making

Neg. hadn't made

Neg. hadn't been making

FUTURE TENSES

Simple Future Tense
I will make

Immediate Future Tense
I am going to make

Neg. won't make

Neg. (am) not/aren't/isn't going to make

Future Progressive
I will be making

Immediate Future Progressive
I am going to be making

Neg. won't be making

Neg. (am) not/aren't/isn't going to be
making

Note: *Spelling change: Verbs ending in -*e* following a consonant drop the -*e* before -*ing* endings.

Future Perfect
I will have made

Neg. won't have made

CONDITIONALS

Future Conditional
(If) I make, . . . will . . .

Neg. (If) don't/doesn't make, . . . will . . .
(If) make, . . . won't . . .

Unreal Conditional—Progressive Form
(If) I were making, . . . would . . .

Neg. (If) weren't making, . . . would . . .
(If) were making, . . . wouldn't . . .

Past Conditional—Progressive Form
(If) I had been making, . . . would have . . .
(+ past participle)

Neg. (If) hadn't been making, . . . would
have . . . (+ past participle)
(If) had been making, . . . wouldn't have . . .
(+ past participle)

Unreal Conditional
(If) I made, . . . would . . .

Neg. (If) didn't make, . . . would . . .
(If) made, . . . wouldn't . . .

Past Conditional
(If) I had made, . . . would have . . .
(+ past participle)

Neg. (If) hadn't made, . . . would have . . .
(+ past participle)
(If) had made, . . . wouldn't have . . .
(+ past participle)

This Verb Follows the Same Pattern
remake

These Verbs Follow a Different Pattern
bake
take
wake

Would you *make* me a drink, please?
Nancy *is making* plans for her honeymoon.
I *make* dolls for a living.
Who *made* this beautiful vase?
What time *did* you *make* the appointment for?
Tim *made* quite a bit of money from those stocks he bought.
I*'ve made* my son a delicious cake for his birthday.
If you *had made* a lot of money, *would* it *have made* you happier?

Irregular verb, active form: *mean*

INFINITIVE/IMPERATIVE	***NEGATIVE***
(to) mean/Mean . . . !	(to) not mean/Don't mean . . . !
Present Participle	***Past Participle***
meaning	meant
Neg. not meaning	***Neg.*** not meant

PRESENT TENSES

Simple Present Tense
I mean
you mean
he/she/it means
we mean
you mean
they mean

Neg. don't/doesn't mean

Present Progressive
I am meaning

Neg. (am) not/aren't/isn't meaning

Present Perfect
I have meant

Neg. haven't/hasn't meant

PAST TENSES

Simple Past Tense
I meant

Neg. didn't mean

Past Perfect
I had meant

Neg. hadn't meant

Past Progressive
I was meaning

Neg. wasn't/weren't meaning

Past Perfect Progressive
I had been meaning

Neg. hadn't been meaning

FUTURE TENSES

Simple Future Tense
I will mean

Neg. won't mean

Future Progressive
I will be meaning

Neg. won't be meaning

Immediate Future Tense
I am going to mean

Neg. (am) not/aren't/isn't going to mean

Immediate Future Progressive
I am going to be meaning

Neg. (am) not/aren't/isn't going to be meaning

Future Perfect
I will have meant

Neg. won't have meant

CONDITIONALS

Future Conditional
(If) I mean, . . . will . . .

Neg. (If) don't/doesn't mean, . . . will . . .
(If) mean, . . . won't . . .

Unreal Conditional—Progressive Form
(If) I were meaning, . . . would . . .

Neg. (If) weren't meaning, . . . would . . .
(If) were meaning, . . . wouldn't . . .

Past Conditional—Progressive Form
(If) I had been meaning, . . . would
have . . . (+ past participle)

Neg. (If) hadn't been meaning, . . . would
have . . . (+ past participle)
(If) had been meaning, . . . wouldn't
have . . . (+ past participle)

Unreal Conditional
(If) I meant, . . . would . . .

Neg. (If) didn't mean, . . . would . . .
(If) meant, . . . wouldn't . . .

Past Conditional
(If) I had meant, . . . would have . . .
(+ past participle)

Neg. (If) hadn't meant, . . . would have . . .
(+ past participle)
(If) had meant, . . . wouldn't have . . .
(+ past participle)

This Verb Follows the Same Pattern
lean (/on)

These Verbs Follow a Different Pattern
clean
demean (= humiliate)

Really? You *don't mean* it!   (exclamation of disbelief)
What *did* she really *mean* by that remark?
Clark's doctor told him the chest pains *meant* no more cigars.
Inheriting that money *will mean* an Ivy League university education for Paula.
The poor sales *have meant* some layoffs at the company.
Don, I'*ve been meaning* to call you . . .
**If it *means* so much to you, we'*ll* go   (. . . *means so much* = . . . is
to the opera.**   important)

Irregular verb, active form: *meet*

INFINITIVE/IMPERATIVE	*NEGATIVE*
(to) meet/Meet . . . !	(to) not meet/Don't meet . . . !
Present Participle	*Past Participle*
meeting	met
Neg. not meeting	*Neg.* not met

PRESENT TENSES

Simple Present Tense
I meet
you meet
he/she/it meets
we meet
you meet
they meet

Neg. don't/doesn't meet

Present Perfect
I have met

Neg. haven't/hasn't met

Present Progressive
I am meeting

Neg. (am) not/aren't/isn't meeting

PAST TENSES

Simple Past Tense
I met

Neg. didn't meet

Past Perfect
I had met

Neg. hadn't met

Past Progressive
I was meeting

Neg. wasn't/weren't meeting

Past Perfect Progressive
I had been meeting

Neg. hadn't been meeting

FUTURE TENSES

Simple Future Tense
I will meet

Neg. won't meet

Future Progressive
I will be meeting

Neg. won't be meeting

Immediate Future Tense
I am going to meet

Neg. (am) not/aren't/isn't going to meet

Immediate Future Progressive
I am going to be meeting

Neg. (am) not/aren't/isn't going to be meeting

Future Perfect
I will have met

Neg. won't have met

CONDITIONALS

Future Conditional
(If) I meet, . . . will . . .

Neg. (If) don't/doesn't meet, . . . will . . .
(If) meet, . . . won't . . .

Unreal Conditional—Progressive Form
(If) I were meeting, . . . would . . .

Neg. (If) weren't meeting, . . . would . . .
(If) were meeting, . . . wouldn't . . .

Unreal Conditional
(If) I met, . . . would . . .

Neg. (If) didn't meet, . . . would . . .
(If) met, . . . wouldn't . . .

Past Conditional
(If) I had met, . . . would have . . .
(+ past participle)

Neg. (If) hadn't met, . . . would have . . .
(+ past participle)
(If) had met, . . . wouldn't have . . .
(+ past participle)

Past Conditional—Progressive Form
(If) I had been meeting, . . . would
have . . . (+ past participle)

These Verbs Follow a Different Pattern
greet
treat

Neg. (If) hadn't been meeting, . . . would have . . . (+ past participle)
(If) had been meeting, . . . wouldn't have . . . (+ past participle)

Meet me at the library.
I'd like you *to meet* Professor Stone.   (form of introduction)
I can't talk—I'm *meeting* my boss at 3:00.
Who *was* Andy *meeting* at the café?
Will you *be meeting* Mr. Hanson's plane?
Tina accidentally *met* her old college roommate yesterday.
We *haven't met*, but I've heard so much about you.

Irregular verb, active form: *pay*

INFINITIVE/IMPERATIVE	*NEGATIVE*
(to) pay/Pay . . . !	(to) not pay/Don't pay . . . !
Present Participle	*Past Participle*
pay<u>ing</u>	pa<u>id</u>
Neg. <u>not</u> pay<u>ing</u>	*Neg.* <u>not</u> pa<u>id</u>

PRESENT TENSES

Simple Present Tense
I pay
you pay
he/she/it pay<u>s</u>
we pay
you pay
they pay

Neg. <u>don't</u>/<u>doesn't</u> pay

Present Perfect
I <u>have</u> pa<u>id</u>

Neg. <u>haven't</u>/<u>hasn't</u> pa<u>id</u>

Present Progressive
I <u>am</u> pay<u>ing</u>

Neg. (<u>am</u>) <u>not</u>/<u>aren't</u>/<u>isn't</u> pay<u>ing</u>

PAST TENSES

Simple Past Tense
I pa<u>id</u>

Neg. <u>didn't</u> pay

Past Perfect
I <u>had</u> pa<u>id</u>

Neg. <u>hadn't</u> pa<u>id</u>

Past Progressive
I <u>was</u> pay<u>ing</u>

Neg. <u>wasn't</u>/<u>weren't</u> pay<u>ing</u>

Past Perfect Progressive
I <u>had</u> <u>been</u> pay<u>ing</u>

Neg. <u>hadn't</u> <u>been</u> pay<u>ing</u>

FUTURE TENSES

Simple Future Tense
I <u>will</u> pay

Neg. <u>won't</u> pay

Future Progressive
I <u>will</u> <u>be</u> pay<u>ing</u>

Neg. <u>won't</u> <u>be</u> pay<u>ing</u>

Immediate Future Tense
I <u>am</u> <u>going</u> <u>to</u> pay

Neg. (<u>am</u>) <u>not</u>/<u>aren't</u>/<u>isn't</u> <u>going</u> <u>to</u> pay

Immediate Future Progressive
I <u>am</u> <u>going</u> <u>to</u> <u>be</u> pay<u>ing</u>

Neg. (<u>am</u>) <u>not</u>/<u>aren't</u>/<u>isn't</u> <u>going</u> <u>to</u> <u>be</u> pay<u>ing</u>

Future Perfect
I will have paid

Neg. won't have paid

CONDITIONALS

Future Conditional
(If) I pay, . . . will . . .

Neg. (If) don't/doesn't pay, . . . will . . .
(If) pay, . . . won't . . .

Unreal Conditional—Progressive Form
(If) I were paying, . . . would . . .

Neg. (If) weren't paying, . . . would . . .
(If) were paying, . . . wouldn't . . .

Past Conditional—Progressive Form
(If) I had been paying, . . . would have . . .
(+ past participle)

Neg. (If) hadn't been paying, . . . would
have . . . (+ past participle)
(If) had been paying, . . . wouldn't
have . . . (+ past participle)

Unreal Conditional
(If) I paid, . . . would . . .

Neg. (If) didn't pay, . . . would . . .
(If) paid, . . . wouldn't . . .

Past Conditional
(II) I had paid, . . . would have . . .
(+ past participle)

Neg. (If) hadn't paid, . . . would have . . .
(+ past participle)
(If) had paid, . . . wouldn't have . . .
(+ past participle)

These Verbs Follow the Same Pattern
lay   say
overpay   underpay
repay

This Verb Follows a Different Pattern
sway

Pay, of course, means to give money in exchange for goods and services, but it also often means an emotional or figurative form of "payment," such as a reward or punishment.

May I *pay* with a $100 bill?

Richard always *pays* for everything in cash.

Who'*s paying* for lunch?

When the boss comes back, you'*ll pay* for this.

The Williamses *haven't* yet *paid* for most of their furniture.

If you *pay* with that credit card, we'*ll* have to add 2% to the price.

Irregular verb, active form: *put*

INFINITIVE/IMPERATIVE	NEGATIVE
(to) put/Put . . . !	(to) not put/Don't put . . . !
Present Participle*	**Past Participle**
putting	put
Neg. not putting	**Neg.** not put

PRESENT TENSES

Simple Present Tense
I put
you put
he/she/it puts
we put
you put
they put

Neg. don't/doesn't put

Present Progressive
I am putting

Neg. (am) not/aren't/isn't putting

Present Perfect
I have put

Neg. haven't/hasn't put

PAST TENSES

Simple Past Tense
I put

Neg. didn't put

Past Perfect
I had put

Neg. hadn't put

Past Progressive
I was putting

Neg. wasn't/weren't putting

Past Perfect Progressive
I had been putting

Neg. hadn't been putting

FUTURE TENSES

Simple Future Tense
I will put

Neg. won't put

Future Progressive
I will be putting

Neg. won't be putting

Immediate Future Tense
I am going to put

Neg. (am) not/aren't/isn't going to put

Immediate Future Progressive
I am going to be putting

Neg. (am) not/aren't/isn't going to be putting

Note: *Spelling change: Irregular verbs ending in a single consonant following a single vowel double the last consonant before *-ing*.

Future Perfect
I will have put

Neg. won't have put

CONDITIONALS

Future Conditional
(If) I put, . . . will . . .

Neg. (If) don't/doesn't put, . . . will . . .
(If) put, . . . won't . . .

Unreal Conditional—Progressive Form
(If) I were putting, . . . would . . .

Neg. (If) weren't putting, . . . would . . .
(If) were putting, . . . wouldn't . . .

Unreal Conditional
(If) I put, . . . would . . .

Neg. (If) didn't put, . . . would . . .
(If) put, . . . wouldn't . . .

Past Conditional
(If) I had put, . . . would have . . .
(+ past participle)

Neg. (If) hadn't put, . . . would have . . .
(+ past participle)
(If) had put, . . . wouldn't have . . .
(+ past participle)

Past Conditional—Progressive Form
(If) I had been putting, . . . would have . . . (+ past participle)

Neg. (If) hadn't been putting, . . . would have . . . (+ past participle)
(If) had been putting, . . . wouldn't have . . . (+ past participle)

These Verbs Follow the Same Pattern

bet	hit	let	set
cost	hurt	quit	shut
cut			

These Verbs Follow a Different Pattern
putt (= hit golf ball)   shout   sprout

Put the box on the steps, please.
What *did* you *put* in this stew—it's delicious!
Let's *put* things in perspective.   (= evaluate a situation objectively)
A promotion? I'*ll put* some   (*fridge* – refrigerator)
champagne in the fridge.
If I had to *put* up with your boss every   (*put up with* = endure)
day, I'*d* quit.

Irregular verb, active form: *read*

INFINITIVE/IMPERATIVE	***NEGATIVE***
(to) read/Read . . . !	(to) not read/Don't read . . . !
Present Participle	***Past Participle***
reading	read
Neg. not reading	***Neg.*** not read

PRESENT TENSES

Simple Present Tense
I read
you read
he/she/it reads
we read
you read
they read

Neg. don't/doesn't read

Present Progressive
I am reading

Neg. (am) not/aren't/isn't reading

Present Perfect
I have read

Neg. haven't/hasn't read

PAST TENSES

Simple Past Tense*
I read

Neg. didn't read

Past Perfect
I had read

Neg. hadn't read

Past Progressive
I was reading

Neg. wasn't/weren't reading

Past Perfect Progressive
I had been reading

Neg. hadn't been reading

FUTURE TENSES

Simple Future Tense
I will read

Neg. won't read

Future Progressive
I will be reading

Neg. won't be reading

Immediate Future Tense
I am going to read

Neg. (am) not/aren't/isn't going to read

Immediate Future Progressive
I am going to be reading

Neg. (am) not/aren't/isn't going to be reading

Note: *Both the simple past and past participle forms are pronounced "red," whereas the simple form is pronounced "reed."

Future Perfect
I will have read

Neg. won't have read

CONDITIONALS

Future Conditional
(If) I read, . . . will . . .

Neg. (If) don't/doesn't read, . . . will . . .
(If) read, . . . won't . . .

Unreal Conditional—Progressive Form
(If) I were reading, . . . would . . .

Neg. (If) weren't reading, . . . would . . .
(If) were reading, . . . wouldn't . . .

Past Conditional—Progressive Form
(If) I had been reading, . . . would
have . . . (+ past participle)

Neg. (If) hadn't been reading, . . . would
have . . . (+ past participle)
(If) had been reading, . . . wouldn't
have . . . (+ past participle)

Unreal Conditional
(If) I read, . . . would . . .

Neg. (If) didn't read, . . . would . . .
(If) read, . . . wouldn't . . .

Past Conditional
(If) I had read, . . . would have . . .
(+ past participle)

Neg. (If) hadn't read, . . . would have . . .
(+ past participle)
(If) had read, . . . wouldn't have . . .
(+ past participle)

These Verbs Follow the Same Pattern

bleed	leave
feed	mean
lead	

These Verbs Follow a Different Pattern
free
heed (= listen to/follow—usually advice,
warnings, etc.)
need

It used to be important for students *to read* the classics.

Will you *be reading* any books on your vacation?

The teacher *read* aloud from the book.   (*read aloud* = read using one's voice)

Shall I *read* Timmy a bedtime story?

Have you *read* the newspaper yet?

If management *doesn't read* my reports, why *should* I write them?

This book *has been read* by more people than you can count.

Irregular verb, active form: *ride*

INFINITIVE/IMPERATIVE	***NEGATIVE***
(to) ride/Ride . . . !	(to) not ride/Don't ride . . . !
Present Participle*	***Past Participle***
riding	ridden
Neg. not riding	**Neg.** not ridden

PRESENT TENSES

Simple Present Tense
I ride
you ride
he/she/it rides
we ride
you ride
they ride

Neg. don't/doesn't ride

Present Perfect
I have ridden

Neg. haven't/hasn't ridden

Present Progressive
I am riding

Neg. (am) not/aren't/isn't riding

PAST TENSES

Simple Past Tense
I rode

Neg. didn't ride

Past Perfect
I had ridden

Neg. hadn't ridden

Past Progressive
I was riding

Neg. wasn't/weren't riding

Past Perfect Progressive
I had been riding

Neg. hadn't been riding

FUTURE TENSES

Simple Future Tense
I will ride

Neg. won't ride

Future Progressive
I will be riding

Neg. won't be riding

Immediate Future Tense
I am going to ride

Neg. (am) not/aren't/isn't going to ride

Immediate Future Progressive
I am going to be riding

Neg. (am) not/aren't/isn't going to be riding

Note: *Spelling change: Verbs ending in -*e* following a consonant drop the -*e* before -*ing* endings.

Future Perfect
I will have ridden

Neg. won't have ridden

CONDITIONALS

Future Conditional
(If) I ride, . . . will . . .

Neg. (If) don't/doesn't ride, . . . will . . .
(If) ride, . . . won't . . .

Unreal Conditional—Progressive Form
(If) I were riding, . . . would . . .

Neg. (If) weren't riding, . . . would . . .
(If) were riding, . . . wouldn't . . .

Past Conditional—Progressive Form
(If) I had been riding, . . . would have . . .
(+ past participle)

Neg. (If) hadn't been riding, . . . would
have . . . (+ past participle)
(If) had been riding, . . . wouldn't have . . .
(+ past participle)

Unreal Conditional
(If) I rode, . . . would . . .

Neg. (If) didn't ride, . . . would . . .
(If) rode, . . . wouldn't . . .

Past Conditional
(If) I had ridden, . . . would have . . .
(+ past participle)

Neg. (If) hadn't ridden, . . . would have . . .
(+ past participle)
(If) had ridden, . . . wouldn't have . . .
(+ past participle)

These Verbs Follow the Same Pattern
drive
rise
strive (= try to reach an objective)
write

These Verbs Follow a Different Pattern
dial
slide

Patricia *rides* the bus to work.
Look at the surfer *ride* that wave . . . !
Tony *is going to ride* in the parade.
Mother once *rode* the Orient Express to Istanbul.
The president *rode* up in the elevator with me.
Have you ever *ridden* in a wagon?
Adam *hasn't ridden* a horse since he was a teenager.

Irregular verb, active form: *run*

INFINITIVE/IMPERATIVE	***NEGATIVE***
(to) run/Run . . . !	(to) not run/Don't run . . . !
Present Participle*	***Past Participle***
run<u>ning</u>	run
Neg. <u>not</u> run<u>ning</u>	***Neg.*** <u>not</u> run

PRESENT TENSES

Simple Present Tense
I run
you run
he/she/it run<u>s</u>
we run
you run
they run

Neg. <u>don't/doesn't</u> run

Present Progressive
I <u>am</u> run<u>ning</u>

Neg. <u>(am) not/aren't/isn't</u> run<u>ning</u>

Present Perfect
I <u>have</u> run

Neg. <u>haven't/hasn't</u> run

PAST TENSES

Simple Past Tense
I r<u>a</u>n

Neg. <u>didn't</u> run

Past Perfect
I <u>had</u> run

Neg. <u>hadn't</u> run

Past Progressive
I <u>was</u> run<u>ning</u>

Neg. <u>wasn't/weren't</u> run<u>ning</u>

Past Perfect Progressive
I <u>had</u> <u>been</u> run<u>ning</u>

Neg. <u>hadn't</u> <u>been</u> run<u>ning</u>

FUTURE TENSES

Simple Future Tense
I <u>will</u> run

Neg. <u>won't</u> run

Future Progressive
I <u>will</u> <u>be</u> run<u>ning</u>

Neg. <u>won't</u> <u>be</u> run<u>ning</u>

Immediate Future Tense
I <u>am going</u> <u>to</u> run

Neg. <u>(am) not/aren't/isn't</u> <u>going</u> <u>to</u> run

Immediate Future Progressive
I <u>am going</u> <u>to</u> <u>be</u> run<u>ning</u>

Neg. <u>(am) not/aren't/isn't</u> <u>going</u> <u>to</u> <u>be</u> run<u>ning</u>

Note: *Spelling change: Irregular verbs ending in a single consonant following a single vowel double the last consonant before -*ing*.

Future Perfect
I will have run

Neg. won't have run

CONDITIONALS

Future Conditional
(If) I run, . . . will . . .

Neg. (If) don't/doesn't run, . . . will . . .
(If) run, . . . won't . . .

Unreal Conditional—Progressive Form
(If) I were running, . . . would . . .

Neg. (If) weren't running, . . . would . . .
(If) were running, . . . wouldn't . . .

Past Conditional—Progressive Form
(If) I had been running, . . . would
have . . . (+ past participle)

Neg. (If) hadn't been running, . . . would have . . . (+ past participle)
(If) had been running, . . . wouldn't have . . . (+ past participle)

Unreal Conditional
(If) I ran, . . . would . . .

Neg. (If) didn't run, . . . would . . .
(If) ran, . . . wouldn't . . .

Past Conditional
(If) I had run, . . . would have . . .
(+ past participle)

Neg. (If) hadn't run, . . . would have . . .
(+ past participle)
(If) had run, . . . wouldn't have . . .
(+ past participle)

These Verbs Follow the Same Pattern
overrun
rerun

Run has several meanings, in addition to many combinations as a phrasal verb. The main ones are (1) to move quickly on foot; (2) to function—usually for machines and mechanisms; (3) to operate a business or control an organization; (4) to campaign for a political office; (5) the forward movement of water in a river or stream.

Please *run* to the store for some milk.

Hurry up! We'*re running* late.	(*running late* = not keeping on schedule)
The kids *were* already *running* around at 6:00 A.M.	
This car *runs* beautifully.	(= functions; moves)
They say the Governor *is going to run* for President.	(= try to be elected)
I'*ve run* into this problem before.	(*run into* = experience a situation)

Irregular verb, active form: *say*

INFINITIVE/IMPERATIVE	NEGATIVE
(to) say/Say . . . !	(to) not say/Don't say . . . !
Present Participle	**Past Participle**
saying	said
Neg. not saying	**Neg.** not said

PRESENT TENSES

Simple Present Tense
I say
you say
he/she/it says*
we say
you say
they say

Neg. don't/doesn't say

Present Progressive
I am saying

Neg. (am) not/aren't/isn't saying

Present Perfect†
I have said

Neg. haven't/hasn't said

PAST TENSES

Simple Past Tense
I said

Neg. didn't say

Past Perfect
I had said

Neg. hadn't said

Past Progressive
I was saying

Neg. wasn't/weren't saying

Past Perfect Progressive
I had been saying

Neg. hadn't been saying

FUTURE TENSES

Simple Future Tense
I will say

Neg. won't say

Future Progressive
I will be saying

Neg. won't be saying

Immediate Future Tense
I am going to say

Neg. (am) not/aren't/isn't going to say

Immediate Future Progressive
I am going to be saying

Neg. (am) not/aren't/isn't going to be saying

Note: *Pronounced "sez" only in 3rd person.
†Pronounced "sedd" for all persons in all tenses using simple past and past participle.

Future Perfect
I will have said

Neg. won't have said

CONDITIONALS

Future Conditional
(If) I say, . . . will . . .

Neg. (If) don't/doesn't say, . . . will . . .
(If) say, . . . won't . . .

Unreal Conditional—Progressive Form
(If) I were saying, . . . would . . .

Neg. (If) weren't saying, . . . would . . .
(If) were saying, . . . wouldn't . . .

Past Conditional—Progressive Form
(If) I had been saying, . . . would have . . .
(+ past participle)

Neg. (If) hadn't been saying, . . . would
have . . . (+ past participle)
(If) had been saying, . . . wouldn't
have . . . (+ past participle)

Unreal Conditional
(If) I said, . . . would . . .

Neg. (If) didn't say, . . . would . . .
(If) said, . . . wouldn't . . .

Past Conditional
(If) I had said, . . . would have . . .
(+ past participle)

Neg. (If) hadn't said, . . . would have . . .
(+ past participle)
(If) had said, . . . wouldn't have . . .
(+ past participle)

These Verbs Follow the Same Pattern
lay
pay

These Verbs Follow a Different Pattern
betray (= act disloyally)
play
pray

Say your name and address at the tone. (automated phone message)

You don't say! (exclamation of surprise = Really_!)

Daddy says I mustn't say that word.

As the boss was saying the other day, Mitch deserves a promotion.

I don't know what the sign says—it's in Chinese.

Maria has been saying for years that Tom should stop smoking.

It's all been said before, but people never learn.

Irregular verb, active form: *see*

INFINITIVE/IMPERATIVE	**NEGATIVE**
(to) see/See . . . !	(to) not see/Don't see . . . !
Present Participle	**Past Participle**
seeing	seen
Neg. not seeing	**Neg.** not seen

PRESENT TENSES

Simple Present Tense
I see
you see
he/she/it sees
we see
you see
they see

Neg. don't/doesn't see

Present Progressive
I am seeing

Neg. (am) not/aren't/isn't seeing

Present Perfect
I have seen

Neg. haven't/hasn't seen

PAST TENSES

Simple Past Tense
I saw

Neg. didn't see

Past Perfect
I had seen

Neg. hadn't seen

Past Progressive
I was seeing

Neg. wasn't/weren't seeing

Past Perfect Progressive
I had been seeing

Neg. hadn't been seeing

FUTURE TENSES

Simple Future Tense
I will see

Neg. won't see

Future Progressive
I will be seeing

Neg. won't be seeing

Future Perfect
I will have seen

Neg. won't have seen

Immediate Future Tense
I am going to see

Neg. (am) not/aren't/isn't going to see

Immediate Future Progressive
I am going to be seeing

Neg. (am) not/aren't/isn't going to be seeing

CONDITIONALS

Future Conditional
(If) I see, . . . <u>will</u> . . .

Neg. (If) <u>don't</u>/<u>doesn't</u> see, . . . will . . .
(If) see, . . . <u>won't</u> . . .

Unreal Conditional—Progressive Form
(If) I <u>were</u> see<u>ing</u>, . . . <u>would</u> . . .

Neg. (If) <u>weren't</u> see<u>ing</u>, . . . <u>would</u> . . .
(If) <u>were</u> see<u>ing</u>, . . . <u>wouldn't</u> . . .

Past Conditional—Progressive Form
(If) I <u>had been</u> see<u>ing</u>, . . . <u>would have</u> . . .
(+ past participle)

Neg. (If) <u>hadn't been</u> see<u>ing</u>, . . . <u>would</u>
<u>have</u> . . . (+ past participle)
(If) <u>had been</u> see<u>ing</u>, . . . <u>wouldn't</u>
<u>have</u> . . . (+ past participle)

Unreal Conditional
(If) I s<u>aw</u>, . . . <u>would</u> . . .

Neg. (If) <u>didn't</u> see, . . . <u>would</u> . . .
(If) s<u>aw</u>, . . . <u>wouldn't</u> . . .

Past Conditional
(If) I <u>had</u> seen, . . . <u>would have</u> . . .
(+ past participle)

Neg. (If) <u>hadn't</u> see<u>n</u>, . . . <u>would have</u> . . .
(+ past participle)
(If) <u>had</u> seen, . . . <u>wouldn't</u> have . . .
(+ past participle)

These Verbs Follow the Same Pattern
foresee
oversee

These Verbs Follow a Different Pattern
agree
flee
free

See here, I don't like being spoken to that way!

(*see here* = exclamation of annoyance at listener—*somewhat* more popular in Britain than U.S.)

Would you **see** if you can reach Bob Carlson in Advertising?

(*see if . . . can . . .* = please try to . . .)

I **don't see** what Mary's age has to do with her work.

(= understand; agree with)

Don **is going to see** a doctor about his headaches.

(= meet/consult)

The marketing department will have to **see** about which market to target.

(*will have to see about* = make the decision about . . .)

Chris **was seeing** Barbara last week, but this week he**'s seeing** someone else.

(= dating)

We **haven't seen** Vince for ages.

(*for ages* = emphatic for *very long time*)

Those complaints **are being seen** to.

(*be seen to*/*see to* something = take care of a situation/problem)

Today's legal ruling **was seen** as a victory for consumers.

(*. . . is seen as* = . . . gives the impression of)

Irregular verb, active form: *send*

INFINITIVE/IMPERATIVE	NEGATIVE
(to) send/Send . . . !	(to) not send/Don't send . . . !
Present Participle	*Past Participle*
send<u>ing</u>	sen<u>t</u>
Neg. <u>not</u> send<u>ing</u>	*Neg.* <u>not</u> sen<u>t</u>

PRESENT TENSES

Simple Present Tense
I send
you send
he/she/it send<u>s</u>
we send
you send
they send

Neg. <u>don't</u>/<u>doesn't</u> send

Present Perfect
I <u>have</u> sen<u>t</u>

Neg. <u>haven't</u>/<u>hasn't</u> sent

Present Progressive
I <u>am</u> send<u>ing</u>

Neg. <u>(am)</u> no<u>t</u>/<u>aren't</u>/<u>isn't</u> send<u>ing</u>

PAST TENSES

Simple Past Tense
I sen<u>t</u>

Neg. <u>didn't</u> send

Past Perfect
I <u>had</u> sent

Neg. <u>hadn't</u> sent

Past Progressive
I <u>was</u> send<u>ing</u>

Neg. <u>wasn't</u>/<u>weren't</u> send<u>ing</u>

Past Perfect Progressive
I <u>had</u> <u>been</u> send<u>ing</u>

Neg. <u>hadn't</u> <u>been</u> sending

FUTURE TENSES

Simple Future Tense
I <u>will</u> send

Neg. <u>won't</u> send

Future Progressive
I <u>will</u> <u>be</u> send<u>ing</u>

Neg. <u>won't</u> <u>be</u> sending

Future Perfect
I <u>will</u> <u>have</u> sen<u>t</u>

Neg. <u>won't</u> <u>have</u> sent

Immediate Future Tense
I <u>am</u> <u>going</u> <u>to</u> send

Neg. <u>(am)</u> no<u>t</u>/<u>aren't</u>/<u>isn't</u> <u>going</u> <u>to</u> send

Immediate Future Progressive
I <u>am</u> <u>going</u> <u>to</u> <u>be</u> send<u>ing</u>

Neg. <u>(am)</u> no<u>t</u>/<u>aren't</u>/<u>isn't</u> <u>going</u> <u>to</u> <u>be</u>
send<u>ing</u>

CONDITIONALS

Future Conditional
(If) I send, . . . will . . .

Neg. (If) don't/doesn't send, . . . will . . .
(If) send, . . . won't . . .

Unreal Conditional—Progressive Form
(If) I were sending, . . . would . . .

Neg. (If) weren't sending, . . . would . . .
(If) were sending, . . . wouldn't . . .

Past Conditional—Progressive Form
(If) I had been sending, . . . would have . . . (+ past participle)

Neg. (If) hadn't been sending, . . . would have . . . (+ past participle)
(If) had been sending, . . . wouldn't have . . . (+ past participle)

Unreal Conditional
(If) I sent, . . . would . . .

Neg. (If) didn't send, . . . would . . .
(If) sent, . . . wouldn't . . .

Past Conditional
(If) I had sent, . . . would have . . . (+ past participle)

Neg. (If) hadn't sent, . . . would have . . . (+ past participle)
(If) had sent, . . . wouldn't have . . . (+ past participle)

These Verbs Follow a Different Pattern
apprehend (= catch criminal)
attend
blend (= mix)
defend

These Verbs Follow the Same Pattern
bend   lend
build   spend

Send In the next job applicant, please.

Don't send cash through the mail.

The boss *is sending* mixed messages about quality control.
(*send [out] mixed messages* = express conflicting opinions or decisions)

My assistant *was sending* you a fax when the lines went down.
(*went down* = electric lines damaged by storm, etc.)

Who *sent* you here?
(= told you to come)

How *will* you *be sending* the documents—by air?

We've already *sent* you the check.

Mom *has sent* me to the market three times today!
(= ask/tell someone to go on an errand)

Michael *is being sent* to head the firm's Singapore office.
(*is sent* = transferred; *head* = be in charge of)

Irregular verb, active form: *set*

INFINITIVE/IMPERATIVE	NEGATIVE
(to) set/Set . . . !	(to) not set/Don't set . . . !
Present Participle*	**Past Participle**
setting	set
Neg. not setting	**Neg.** not set

PRESENT TENSES

Simple Present Tense
I set
you set
he/she/it sets
we set
you set
they set

Neg. don't/doesn't set

Present Perfect
I have set

Neg. haven't/hasn't set

Present Progressive
I am setting

Neg. (am) not/aren't/isn't setting

PAST TENSES

Simple Past Tense
I set

Neg. didn't set

Past Perfect
I had set

Neg. hadn't set

Past Progressive
I was setting

Neg. wasn't/weren't setting

Past Perfect Progressive
I had been setting

Neg. hadn't been setting

FUTURE TENSES

Simple Future Tense
I will set

Neg. won't set

Future Progressive
I will be setting

Neg. won't be setting

Immediate Future Tense
I am going to set

Neg. (am) not/aren't/isn't going to set

Immediate Future Progressive
I am going to be setting

Neg. (am) not/aren't/isn't going to be setting

Note: *Spelling change: Irregular verbs ending in a single consonant following a single vowel double the last consonant before -*ing*.

Future Perfect
I will have set

Neg. won't have set

CONDITIONALS

Future Conditional
(If) I set, . . . will . . .

Neg. (If) don't/doesn't set, . . . will . . .
(If) set, . . . won't . . .

Unreal Conditional—Progressive Form
(If) I were setting, . . . would . . .

Neg. (If) weren't setting, . . . would . . .
(If) were setting, . . . wouldn't . . .

Unreal Conditional
(If) I set, . . . would . . .

Neg. (If) didn't set, . . . would . . .
(If) set, . . . wouldn't . . .

Past Conditional
(If) I had set, . . . would have . . .
(+ past participle)

Neg. (If) hadn't set, . . . would have . . .
(+ past participle)
(If) had set, . . . wouldn't have . . .
(+ past participle)

Past Conditional—Progressive Form
(If) I had been setting, . . . would have . . . (+ past participle)

Neg. (If) hadn't been setting, . . . would have . . . (+ past participle)
(If) had been setting, . . . wouldn't have . . . (+ past participle)

These Verbs Follow the Same Pattern

bet	hit	put
cost	hurt	quit
cut	let	shut

These Verbs Follow a Different Pattern
forget
last (= duration)
regret

In addition to many phrasal verbs and idiomatic uses, *set* has three
main meanings: (1) to place something on a horizontal surface, (2) to fix
a plan or procedure, or to establish a standard for achievement or quality; (3) to adjust a mechanical device such as an alarm or timer.

Our department *is setting* a high standard for the rest of the company.

Let's *set* a time for lunch—otherwise we'll never do it.

The hospital bills *have set* Monica
back quite a bit.

(*set . . . back* = reduce available money)

How much time *is* Bob *setting* aside
for basketball practice?

(*set aside* = reserve)

Have you *set* your alarm clock?

Irregular verb, active form: *show*

INFINITIVE/IMPERATIVE	*NEGATIVE*
(to) show/Show . . . !	(to) not show/Don't show . . . !
Present Participle	*Past Participle*
show<u>ing</u>	show<u>n</u>
Neg. <u>not</u> showing	*Neg.* <u>not</u> shown

PRESENT TENSES

Simple Present Tense
I show
you show
he/she/it show<u>s</u>
we show
you show
they show

Neg. <u>don't/doesn't</u> show

Present Progressive
I <u>am</u> showing

Neg. (<u>am</u>) <u>not/aren't/isn't</u> showing

Present Perfect
I <u>have</u> show<u>n</u>

Neg. <u>haven't/hasn't</u> shown

PAST TENSES

Simple Past Tense
I show<u>ed</u>

Neg. <u>didn't</u> show

Past Perfect
I <u>had</u> show<u>n</u>

Neg. <u>hadn't</u> show<u>n</u>

Past Progressive
I <u>was</u> showing

Neg. <u>wasn't/weren't</u> showing

Past Perfect Progressive
I <u>had</u> <u>been</u> showing

Neg. <u>hadn't</u> <u>been</u> showing

FUTURE TENSES

Simple Future Tense
I <u>will</u> show

Neg. <u>won't</u> show

Future Progressive
I <u>will</u> <u>be</u> showing

Neg. <u>won't</u> <u>be</u> showing

Immediate Future Tense
I <u>am</u> <u>going to</u> show

Neg. (<u>am</u>) <u>not/aren't/isn't</u> <u>going to</u> show

Immediate Future Progressive
I <u>am</u> <u>going to</u> <u>be</u> showing

Neg. (<u>am</u>) <u>not/aren't/isn't</u> <u>going to</u> <u>be</u> showing

Future Perfect
I will have shown

Neg. won't have shown

CONDITIONALS

Future Conditional
(If) I show, . . . will . . .

Neg. (If) don't/doesn't show, . . . will . . .
(If) show, . . . won't . . .

Unreal Conditional—Progressive Form
(If) I were showing, . . . would . . .

Neg. (If) weren't showing, . . . would . . .
(If) were showing, . . . wouldn't . . .

Past Conditional—Progressive Form
(If) I had been showing, . . . would
have . . . (+ past participle)

Neg. (If) hadn't been showing, . . . would
have . . . (+ past participle)
(If) had been showing, . . . wouldn't
have . . . (+ past participle)

Unreal Conditional
(If) I showed, . . . would . . .

Neg. (If) didn't show, . . . would . . .
(If) showed, . . . wouldn't . . .

Past Conditional
(If) I had shown, . . . would have . . .
(+ past participle)

Neg. (If) hadn't shown, . . . would
have . . . (+ past participle)
(If) had shown, . . . wouldn't have . . .
(+ past participle)

These Verbs Follow the Same Pattern
mow (= cut grass)
prove
sow

These Verbs Follow a Different Pattern
blow
know
throw
tow

Show me your proposal.
Show some respect for your teachers!
They'*re showing* the British version of *Gaslight* at the local theater.
Will you *show* me where the exit is, please?
Terry *is going to show* me how to play backgammon.
Has Brenda ever *shown* any interest in cooking?

Irregular verb, active form: *sit*

INFINITIVE/IMPERATIVE	*NEGATIVE*
(to) sit/Sit . . . !	(to) not sit/Don't sit . . . !
Present Participle*	*Past Participle*
sitting	sat
Neg. not sitting	*Neg.* not sat

PRESENT TENSES

Simple Present Tense
I sit
you sit
he/she/it sits
we sit
you sit
they sit

Neg. don't/doesn't sit

Present Progressive
I am sitting

Neg. (am) not/aren't/isn't sitting

Present Perfect
I have sat

Neg. haven't/hasn't sat

PAST TENSES

Simple Past Tense
I sat

Neg. didn't sit

Past Perfect
I had sat

Neg. hadn't sat

Past Progressive
I was sitting

Neg. wasn't/weren't sitting

Past Perfect Progressive
I had been sitting

Neg. hadn't been sitting

FUTURE TENSES

Simple Future Tense
I will sit

Neg. won't sit

Future Progressive
I will be sitting

Neg. won't be sitting

Immediate Future Tense
I am going to sit

Neg. (am) not/aren't/isn't going to sit

Immediate Future Progressive
I am going to be sitting

Neg. (am) not/aren't/isn't going to be sitting

Note: *Spelling change: Irregular verbs ending in a single consonant following a single vowel double the last consonant before -ing.

Future Perfect
I will have sat

Neg. won't have sat

CONDITIONALS

Future Conditional
(If) I sit, . . . will . . .

Neg. (If) don't/doesn't sit, . . . will . . .
(If) sit, . . . won't . . .

Unreal Conditional—Progressive Form
(If) I were sitting, . . . would . . .

Neg. (If) weren't sitting, . . . would . . .
(If) were sitting, . . . wouldn't . . .

Past Conditional—Progressive Form
(If) I had been sitting, would have . . .
(+ past participle)

Neg. (If) hadn't been sitting, . . . would
have . . . (+ past participle)
(If) had been sitting, . . . wouldn't have . . .
(+ past participle)

Unreal Conditional
(If) I sat, . . . would . . .

Neg. (If) didn't sit, . . . would . . .
(If) sat, . . . wouldn't . . .

Past Conditional
(If) I had sat, . . . would have . . .
(+ past participle)

Neg. (If) hadn't sat, . . . would have . . .
(+ past participle)
(If) had sat, . . . wouldn't have . . .
(+ past participle)

This Verb Follows the Same Pattern
spit

These Verbs Follow a Different Pattern
fit
knit
quit

Sit over here by me, Ellen.
Don't sit on that bench, it's broken.
Sit down, everyone, and let's eat.
Edward *sits* on the Board of three   (*sit on* = be a member of an official
corporations.   body)
Which of them *was sitting* in the driver's seat?
Have you ever *sat* in this chair?
If I *sit* on the aisle, I can stretch my legs out.

Irregular verb, active form: *sleep*

INFINITIVE/IMPERATIVE	*NEGATIVE*
(to) sleep/Sleep . . . !	(to) not sleep/Don't sleep . . . !
Present Participle	*Past Participle*
sleeping	slept
Neg. not sleeping	*Neg.* not slept

PRESENT TENSES

Simple Present Tense
I sleep
you sleep
he/she/it sleeps
we sleep
you sleep
they sleep

Neg. don't/doesn't sleep

Present Perfect
I have slept

Neg. haven't/hasn't slept

Present Progressive
I am sleeping

Neg. (am) not/aren't/isn't sleeping

PAST TENSES

Simple Past Tense
I slept

Neg. didn't sleep

Past Perfect
I had slept

Neg. hadn't slept

Past Progressive
I was sleeping

Neg. wasn't/weren't sleeping

Past Perfect Progressive
I had been sleeping

Neg. hadn't been sleeping

FUTURE TENSES

Simple Future Tense
I will sleep

Neg. won't sleep

Future Progressive
I will be sleeping

Neg. won't be sleeping

Immediate Future Tense
I am going to sleep

Neg. (am) not/aren't/isn't going to sleep

Immediate Future Progressive
I am going to be sleeping

Neg. (am) not/aren't/isn't going to be sleeping

Future Perfect
I will have slept

Neg. won't have slept

CONDITIONALS

Future Conditional
(If) I sleep, . . . will . . .

Neg. (If) don't/doesn't sleep, . . . will . . .
(If) sleep, . . . won't . . .

Unreal Conditional—Progressive Form
(If) I were sleeping, . . . would . . .

Neg. (If) weren't sleeping, . . . would . . .
(If) were sleeping, . . . wouldn't . . .

Past Conditional—Progressive Form
(If) I had been sleeping, . . . would have . . . (+ past participle)

Neg. (If) hadn't been sleeping, . . . would have . . . (+ past participle)
(If) had been sleeping, . . . wouldn't have . . . (+ past participle)

Unreal Conditional
(If) I slept, . . . would . . .

Neg. (If) didn't sleep, . . . would . . .
(If) slept, . . . wouldn't . . .

Past Conditional
(If) I had slept, . . . would have . . . (+ past participle)

Neg. (If) hadn't slept, . . . would have . . . (+ past participle)
(If) had slept, . . . wouldn't have . . . (+ past participle)

These Verbs Follow the Same Pattern
creep
keep
leap
sweep

This Verbs Follows a Different Pattern
seek

Sleep well.
Does Tony *sleep* late on Saturday?
Don't disturb the cat when it'*s sleeping*!
I hope you *slept* well.
Who'*s been sleeping* In my bed?   (*who's* = who has)
Andy *has been sleeping* badly for weeks.

Irregular verb, active form: *speak*

INFINITIVE/IMPERATIVE	*NEGATIVE*
(to) speak/Speak . . . !	(to) not speak/Don't speak . . . !
Present Participle	*Past Participle*
speaking	spoken
Neg. not speaking	*Neg.* not spoken

PRESENT TENSES

Simple Present Tense
I speak
you speak
he/she/it speaks
we speak
you speak
they speak

Neg. don't/doesn't speak

Present Perfect
I have spoken

Neg. haven't/hasn't spoken

Present Progressive
I am speaking

Neg. (am) not/aren't/isn't speaking

PAST TENSES

Simple Past Tense
I spoke

Neg. didn't speak

Past Perfect
I had spoken

Neg. hadn't spoken

Past Progressive
I was speaking

Neg. wasn't/weren't speaking

Past Perfect Progressive
I had been speaking

Neg. hadn't been speaking

FUTURE TENSES

Simple Future Tense
I will speak

Neg. won't speak

Future Progressive
I will be speaking

Neg. won't be speaking

Immediate Future Tense
I am going to speak

Neg. (am) not/aren't/isn't going to speak

Immediate Future Progressive
I am going to be speaking

Neg. (am) not/aren't/isn't going to be speaking

Future Perfect
I will have spoken

Neg. won't have spoken

CONDITIONALS

Future Conditional
(If) I speak, . . . will . . .

Neg. (If) don't/doesn't speak, . . . will . . .
(If) speak, . . . won't . . .

Unreal Conditional—Progressive Form
(If) I were speaking, . . . would . . .

Neg. (If) weren't speaking, . . . would . . .
(If) were speaking, . . . wouldn't . . .

Past Conditional—Progressive Form
(If) I had been speaking, . . . would
have . . . (+ past participle)

Neg. (If) hadn't been speaking, . . . would
have . . . (+ past participle)
(If) had been speaking, . . . wouldn't
have . . . (+ past participle)

Unreal Conditional
(If) I spoke, . . . would . . .

Neg. (If) didn't speak, . . . would . . .
(If) spoke, . . . wouldn't . . .

Past Conditional
(If) I had spoken, . . . would have . . .
(+ past participle)

Neg. (If) hadn't spoken, . . . would
have . . . (+ past participle)
(If) had spoken, . . . wouldn't have . . .
(+ past participle)

This Verb Follows the Same Pattern
break

These Verbs Follow a Different Pattern
creak
leak

Speak and *talk* are used fairly interchangeably except for foreign languages;
in that context, always use *speak.*

Don't speak to me during the show.

Speak to me, Dan! Are you all right?

Paula *speaks* five languages.

Am I *speaking* with the manager?

We didn't know you *spoke* Italian.

Louise *wasn't speaking* of anyone in particular.

Betty *hasn't spoken* to her father in years.

If my child *spoke* to me in that tone, I'*d* send him to his room.

Irregular verb, active form: *stand*

INFINITIVE/IMPERATIVE	NEGATIVE
(to) stand/Stand . . . !	(to) not stand/Don't stand . . . !
Present Participle	**Past Participle**
standing	stood
Neg. not standing	**Neg.** not stood

PRESENT TENSES

Simple Present Tense
I stand
you stand
he/she/it stands
we stand
you stand
they stand

Neg. don't/doesn't stand

Present Progressive
I am standing

Neg. (am) not/aren't/isn't standing

Present Perfect
I have stood

Neg. haven't/hasn't stood

PAST TENSES

Simple Past Tense
I stood

Neg. didn't stand

Past Progressive
I was standing

Neg. wasn't/weren't standing

Past Perfect
I had stood

Neg. hadn't stood

Past Perfect Progressive
I had been standing

Neg. hadn't been standing

FUTURE TENSES

Simple Future Tense
I will stand

Neg. won't stand

Immediate Future Tense
I am going to stand

Neg. (am) not/aren't/isn't going to stand

Future Progressive
I will be standing

Neg. won't be standing

Immediate Future Progressive
I am going to be standing

Neg. (am) not/aren't/isn't going to be standing

Future Perfect
I will have stood

Neg. won't have stood

CONDITIONALS

Future Conditional
(If) I stand, . . . will . . .

Neg. (If) don't/doesn't stand, . . . will . . .
(If) stand, . . . won't . . .

Unreal Conditional—Progressive Form
(If) I were standing, . . . would . . .

Neg. (If) weren't standing, . . . would . . .
(If) were standing, . . . wouldn't . . .

Past Conditional—Progressive Form
(If) I had been standing, . . . would have . .
. (+ past participle)

Neg. (If) hadn't been standing, . . . would
have . . . (+ past participle)
(If) had been standing, . . . wouldn't
have . . . (+ past participle)

Unreal Conditional
(If) I stood, . . . would . . .

Neg. (If) didn't stand, . . . would . . .
(If) stood, . . . wouldn't . . .

Past Conditional
(If) I had stood, . . . would have . . .
(+ past participle)

Neg. (If) hadn't stood, . . . would have . . .
(+ past participle)
(If) had stood, . . . wouldn't have . . .
(+ past participle)

These Verbs Follow the Same Pattern
misunderstand
understand
withstand

These Verbs Follow a Different Pattern
hand
land

Stand up straight, John.
Don't just **stand** there—help me!
Mary's friends can't **stand** her new
boyfriend.   (can't stand = dislike strongly.)
Each star in the American flag **stands**   (stand for = represent; symbolize)
for a state.
The house my grandfather was born in **is** still **standing**.
Dozens of people **were standing** at the entrance to the courthouse.
We**'ve been standing** in line for tickets since 6:00 A.M.!

Irregular verb, active form: *take*

INFINITIVE/IMPERATIVE	***NEGATIVE***
(to) take/Take . . . !	(to) not take/Don't take . . . !
Present Participle*	***Past Participle***
tak<u>ing</u>	take<u>n</u>
Neg. <u>not</u> tak<u>ing</u>	***Neg.*** <u>not</u> take<u>n</u>

PRESENT TENSES

Simple Present Tense
I take
you take
he/she/it take<u>s</u>
we take
you take
they take

Neg. <u>don't/doesn't</u> take

Present Progressive
I <u>am</u> tak<u>ing</u>

Neg. <u>(am) not/aren't/isn't</u> tak<u>ing</u>

Present Perfect
I <u>have</u> take<u>n</u>

Neg. <u>haven't/hasn't</u> take<u>n</u>

PAST TENSES

Simple Past Tense
I t<u>ook</u>

Neg. <u>didn't</u> take

Past Perfect
I <u>had</u> take<u>n</u>

Neg. <u>hadn't</u> take<u>n</u>

Past Progressive
I <u>was</u> tak<u>ing</u>

Neg. <u>wasn't/weren't</u> tak<u>ing</u>

Past Perfect Progressive
I <u>had</u> <u>been</u> tak<u>ing</u>

Neg. <u>hadn't</u> <u>been</u> tak<u>ing</u>

FUTURE TENSES

Simple Future Tense
I <u>will</u> take

Neg. <u>won't</u> take

Future Progressive
I <u>will</u> <u>be</u> tak<u>ing</u>

Neg. <u>won't</u> <u>be</u> tak<u>ing</u>

Immediate Future Tense
I <u>am</u> <u>going</u> <u>to</u> take

Neg. <u>(am) not/aren't/isn't</u> <u>going</u> <u>to</u> take

Immediate Future Progressive
I <u>am</u> <u>going</u> <u>to</u> <u>be</u> tak<u>ing</u>

Neg. <u>(am) not/aren't/isn't</u> <u>going</u> <u>to</u> <u>be</u>
tak<u>ing</u>

Note: *Spelling change: Verbs ending in -*e* following a consonant drop the -*e* before -*ing* endings.

Future Perfect
I will have taken

Neg. won't have taken

CONDITIONALS

Future Conditional
(If) I take, . . . will . . .

Neg. (If) don't/doesn't take, . . . will . . .
(If) take, . . . won't . . .

Unreal Conditional—Progressive Form
(If) I were taking, . . . would . . .

Neg. (If) weren't taking, . . . would . . .
(If) were taking, . . . wouldn't . . .

Past Conditional—Progressive Form
(If) I had been taking, . . . would have . . .
(+ past participle)

Neg. (If) hadn't been taking, . . . would
have . . . (+ past participle)
(If) had been taking, . . . wouldn't have . . .
(+ past participle)

Unreal Conditional
(If) I took, . . . would . . .

Neg. (If) didn't take, . . . would . . .
(If) took, . . . wouldn't . . .

Past Conditional
(If) I had taken, . . . would have . . .
(+ past participle)

Neg. (If) hadn't taken, . . . would have . . .
(+ past participle)
(If) had taken, . . . wouldn't have . . .
(+ past participle)

These Verbs Follow the Same Pattern
mistake
overtake (= reach and surpass level of
speed, skill, success, etc.)
shake
undertake (= assume responsibility for
future task)

These Verbs Follow a Different Pattern
break   fake   make

Please *take* me to the airport, driver.
It's easier *to take* the train.
How long *does* it *take* you to get ready for bed?
Vic *is taking* a new medicine for his allergies.
Sally *was taking* her cat to the vet when it ran away.
Who *took* the last cookie?
Terry and Mike *are going to take* Mike's mother with them to Aruba.
Mr. Williams *has taken* the 3:00 shuttle and *will take* a taxi to the hotel.
Take more mashed potatoes if you like them so much.

Irregular verb, active form: *teach*

INFINITIVE/IMPERATIVE	NEGATIVE
(to) teach/Teach . . . !	(to) not teach/Don't teach . . . !
Present Participle	**Past Participle**
teaching	taught
Neg. not teaching	**Neg.** not taught

PRESENT TENSES

Simple Present Tense*
I teach
you teach
he/she/it teaches
we teach
you teach
they teach

Neg. don't/doesn't teach

Present Perfect
I have taught

Neg. haven't/hasn't taught

Present Progressive
I am teaching

Neg. (am) not/aren't/isn't teaching

PAST TENSES

Simple Past Tense
I taught

Neg. didn't teach

Past Perfect
I had taught

Neg. hadn't taught

Past Progressive
I was teaching

Neg. wasn't/weren't teaching

Past Perfect Progressive
I had been teaching

Neg. hadn't been teaching

FUTURE TENSES

Simple Future Tense
I will teach

Neg. won't teach

Future Progressive
I will be teaching

Neg. won't be teaching

Immediate Future Tense
I am going to teach

Neg. (am) not/aren't/isn't going to teach

Immediate Future Progressive
I am going to be teaching

Neg. (am) not/aren't/isn't going to be teaching

Note: *Spelling change: Verbs ending in -*sh*, -*ch*, -*ss*, -*x*, and -*o* form the 3rd person singular with -*es* instead of -*s*.

210

Future Perfect
I will have taught

Neg. won't have taught

CONDITIONALS

Future Conditional
(If) I teach, . . . will . . .

Neg. (If) don't/doesn't teach, . . . will . . .
(If) teach, . . . won't . . .

Unreal Conditional—Progressive Form
(If) I were teaching, . . . would . . .

Neg. (If) weren't teaching, . . . would . . .
(If) were teaching, . . . wouldn't . . .

Past Conditional—Progressive Form
(If) I had been teaching, . . . would
have . . (+ past participle)

Neg. (If) hadn't been teaching, . . . would
have . . . (+ past participle)
(If) had been teaching, . . . wouldn't
have . . . (+ past participle)

Unreal Conditional
(If) I taught, . . . would . . .

Neg. (If) didn't teach, . . . would . . .
(If) taught, . . . wouldn't . . .

Past Conditional
(If) I had taught, . . . would have . . .
(+ past participle)

Neg. (If) hadn't taught, . . . would have . . .
(+ past participle)
(If) had taught, . . . wouldn't have . . .
(+ past participle)

This Verb Follows the Same Pattern
catch

These Verbs Follow a Different Pattern
preach (= give religious sermon, moralize,
    caution/warn)
reach

Would you *teach* me how to say that in French?
Anna *teaches* Italian at the local college.
I'm *teaching* my two-year-old (child) how to swim.
My parents *taught* me right from wrong.
This experience *has taught* me a lot.
If you *teach* me how to make bread, I'*ll teach* you how to make sushi.

Irregular verb, active form: *tell*

INFINITIVE/IMPERATIVE	NEGATIVE
(to) tell/Tell . . . !	(to) not tell/Don't tell . . . !
Present Participle	**Past Participle**
telling	told
Neg. not telling	**Neg.** not told

PRESENT TENSES

Simple Present Tense
I tell
you tell
he/she/it tells
we tell
you tell
they tell

Neg. don't/doesn't tell

Present Progressive
I am telling

Neg. (am) not/aren't/isn't telling

Present Perfect
I have told

Neg. haven't/hasn't told

PAST TENSES

Simple Past Tense
I told

Neg. didn't tell

Past Perfect
I had told

Neg. hadn't told

Past Progressive
I was telling

Neg. wasn't/weren't telling

Past Perfect Progressive
I had been telling

Neg. hadn't been telling

FUTURE TENSES

Simple Future Tense
I will tell

Neg. won't tell

Future Progressive
I will be telling

Neg. won't be telling

Immediate Future Tense
I am going to tell

Neg. (am) not/aren't/isn't going to tell

Immediate Future Progressive
I am going to be telling

Neg. (am) not/aren't/isn't going to be telling

Future Perfect
I will have told

Neg. won't have told

CONDITIONALS

Future Conditional
(If) I tell, . . . will . . .

Neg. (If) don't/doesn't tell, . . . will . . .
(If) tell, won't

Unreal Conditional—Progressive Form
(If) I were telling, . . . would . . .

Neg. (If) weren't telling, . . . would . . .
(If) were telling, . . . wouldn't . . .

Unreal Conditional
(If) I told, . . . would . . .

Neg. (If) didn't tell, . . . would . . .
(If) told, . . . wouldn't . . .

Past Conditional
(If) I had told, . . . would have . . .
(+ past participle)

Neg. (If) hadn't told, . . . would have . . .
(+ past participle)
(If) had told, . . . wouldn't have . . .
(+ past participle)

Past Conditional—Progressive Form
(If) I had been telling, . . . would have . . .
(+ past participle)

Neg. (If) hadn't been telling, . . . would have . . . (+ past participle)
(If) had been telling, . . . wouldn't have . . .
(+ past participle)

These Verbs Follow the Same Pattern
foretell (= predict future)
sell

These Verbs Follow a Different Pattern
call
fall
smell

Please *tell* Dr. Johnson that I'm here for my 3:00 appointment.

Tell me why you're upset.

Who can *tell* what may happen in the future?   (*can* + *tell* = estimate, predict, guess, know)

Peter *was telling* me the other day that he's very worried.

Sandra *tells* her mother everything.

Dolly *told* you that, didn't she?

Will you *tell* your husband about the accident?

If you *tell* me what time your flight comes in, I'*ll* meet you (at the airport).

Irregular verb, active form: *think*

INFINITIVE/IMPERATIVE	***NEGATIVE***
(to) think/Think . . . !	(to) not think/Don't think . . . !
Present Participle	***Past Participle***
thinking	thought
Neg. not thinking	***Neg.*** not thought

PRESENT TENSES

Simple Present Tense
I think
you think
he/she/it thinks
we think
you think
they think

Neg. don't/doesn't think

Present Progressive
I am thinking

Neg. (am) not/aren't/isn't thinking

Present Perfect
I have thought

Neg. haven't/hasn't thought

PAST TENSES

Simple Past Tense
I thought

Neg. didn't think

Past Perfect
I had thought

Neg. hadn't thought

Past Progressive
I was thinking

Neg. wasn't/weren't thinking

Past Perfect Progressive
I had been thinking

Neg. hadn't been thinking

FUTURE TENSES

Simple Future Tense
I will think

Neg. won't think

Future Progressive
I will be thinking

Neg. won't be thinking

Future Perfect
I will have thought

Neg. won't have thought

Immediate Future Tense
I am going to think

Neg. (am) not/aren't/isn't going to think

Immediate Future Progressive
I am going to be thinking

Neg. (am) not/aren't/isn't going to be thinking

CONDITIONALS

Future Conditional
(If) I think, . . . will . . .

Neg. (If) don't/doesn't think, . . . will . . .
(If) think, . . . won't . . .

Unreal Conditional—Progressive Form
(If) I were thinking, . . . would . . .

Neg. (If) weren't thinking, . . . would . . .
(If) were thinking, . . . wouldn't . . .

Past Conditional—Progressive Form
(If) I had been thinking, . . . would
have . . . (+ past participle)

Neg. (If) hadn't been thinking, . . . would
have . . . (+ past participle)
(If) had been thinking, . . . wouldn't
have . . . (+ past participle)

Unreal Conditional
(If) I thought, . . . would . . .

Neg. (If) didn't think, . . . would . . .
(If) thought, . . . wouldn't . . .

Past Conditional
(If) I had thought, . . . would have . . .
(+ past participle)

Neg. (If) hadn't thought, . . . would
have . . . (+ past participle)
(If) had thought, . . . wouldn't have . . .
(+ past participle)

These Verbs Follow the Same Pattern
bring   fight   seek
buy   rethink   teach

These Verbs Follow a Different Pattern
blink (= rapidly—usually involuntarily—
open and close eyes)
drink
shrink
wink (= deliberately close one eye as a
gesture)

Think about my suggestions.

Tom *thinks* (that) the company is
heading for trouble.

My wife *thinks* so, but I don't
(*think* so).

What *are* you *thinking* about?

(*be heading for* = going in the direction
of—used both literally and figuratively)

(expresses the speaker's or third
party's opinion—only used in response
to a preceding comment)

Linda and I *were thinking* (that) this house is too small for us.

Margaret *will* only *think* about leaving her job if she gets transferred.

I'm glad I *thought* of this . . . !

Have you *thought* about the future?

Frank *had thought* he would go into advertising, but later changed his mind.

Irregular verb, active form: *write*

INFINITIVE/IMPERATIVE	**NEGATIVE**
(to) write/Write . . . !	(to) not write/Don't write . . . !
Present Participle*	**Past Participle**
writing	written
Neg. not writing	**Neg.** not written

PRESENT TENSES

Simple Present Tense	**Present Progressive**
I write	I am writing
you write	
he/she/it writes	
we write	
you write	
they write	
Neg. don't/doesn't write	**Neg.** (am) not/aren't/isn't writing

Present Perfect
I have written

Neg. haven't/hasn't written

PAST TENSES

Simple Past Tense	**Past Progressive**
I wrote	I was writing
Neg. didn't write	**Neg.** wasn't/weren't writing
Past Perfect	**Past Perfect Progressive**
I had written	I had been writing
Neg. hadn't written	**Neg.** hadn't been writing

FUTURE TENSES

Simple Future Tense	**Immediate Future Tense**
I will write	I am going to write
Neg. won't write	**Neg.** (am) not/aren't/isn't going to write
Future Progressive	**Immediate Future Progressive**
I will be writing	I am going to be writing
Neg. won't be writing	**Neg.** (am) not/aren't/isn't going to be writing

Note: *Spelling change: Verbs ending in *-e* following a consonant drop the *-e* before *-ing* endings.

Future Perfect
I will have written

Neg. won't have written

CONDITIONALS

Future Conditional
(If) I write, . . . will . . .

Neg. (If) don't/doesn't write, . . . will . . .
(If) write, . . . won't . . .

Unreal Conditional—Progressive Form
(If) I were writing, . . . would . . .

Neg. (If) weren't writing, . . . would . . .
(If) were writing, . . . wouldn't . . .

Past Conditional—Progressive Form
(If) I had been writing, . . . would have . . .
(+ past participle)

Neg. (If) hadn't been writing, . . . would
have . . . (+ past participle)
(If) had been writing, . . . wouldn't
have . . . (+ past participle)

Unreal Conditional
(If) I wrote, . . . would . . .

Neg. (If) didn't write, . . . would . . .
(If) wrote, . . . wouldn't . . .

Past Conditional
(If) I had written, . . . would have . . .
(+ past participle)

Neg. (If) hadn't written, . . . would
have . . . (+ past participle)
(If) had written, . . . wouldn't have . . .
(+ past participle)

These Verbs Follow the Same Pattern
drive
ride
rise

These Verbs Follow a Different Pattern
excite
ignite (= light explosive; something
catches fire)
invite

Write to me while you're away.
Nora *is writing* her memoirs.
I *was writing* checks until 1:00 A.M.
Are you *going to write* those reports this week?
Have you *written* to Mother and Dad this month?
If Don *writes* to me, *will* you forward the letter?
This letter *is written* in Swedish.

Modals and "Semi-Modals"

In the following section, you will find complete conjugations for a number of modals and other verbs that are often used as if they were modals because they need another verb to complete their overall meaning in the sentence. A verb like *write* clearly states its meaning. A "semi-modal" like *want to* or *be able to* invariably makes us ask "want to do what," "be able to do what?" For that reason, all true modals, as well as "semi-modals" must be followed by a full verb. In actual conversations, when the full verb is understood, it is sometimes not repeated or explicitly stated (Yes, you *ought to;* I simply *must; Shouldn't* I; He *mustn't,* etc.), but there is no doubt about what the full verb is.

True modals seldom have a full array of tenses, and most "semi-modals" lack some or all of the progressive forms. It is important to keep in mind that while modals may have forms that we traditionally use to show past or future situations, they have no real tenses the way full verbs do. As a result, the various tense labels used in the individual conjugations that follow (such as "simple past" or present perfect") are only general indicators, not strict categories conforming to the rules of tense usage. For more about modals, see Part A, Section 6, *More Help—Modals*, page 20)

Another verb that often functions as a modal is the auxiliary *do*, followed by the sentence's main verb. In this sense, *do* is used for emphasis, like a verbal version of an underlined word in the written language (although this construction is perfectly proper in non-business written English as well). Here are some examples.

Do be quiet, children!
Do tell me all about your trip!
Do give me all the facts, Doctor.
Do visit us again in the spring.
The next time you're in our part of the world, do give us a call.
Even after that terrible meal, the restaurant owner said 'Do come back soon'!
Do promise me you'll be careful!
Do go and see Mother—she misses you.

This use of *do* is confined to immediate and distant future situations, and is always directed at the listener(s), never a third person. Although this construction is used in all English-speaking countries, it is especially (but not at all exclusively) popular in Britain.

Modal/semi-modal: *be able to*

INFINITIVE	*NEGATIVE*
(to) be able to (+ simple form)	(to) not be able to (+ simple form)
	(to) be unable to (+ simple form)
Present Participle	*Past Participle*
being able to (+ simple form)	having been able to (+ simple form)
Neg. not being able to (+ simple form)	*Neg.* not having been able to
being unable to (+ simple form)	(+ simple form)
	having been unable to (+ simple form)

PRESENT TENSES

Simple Present Tense
all persons: + simple form
I am able to
you are able to
he/she/it is able to
we are able to
you are able to
they are able to

Neg. (am) not/isn't/aren't able to
(+ simple form)
am/is/are unable to (+ simple form)

Present Progressive*

Present Perfect
I have been able to (+ simple form)

Neg. haven't/hasn't been able to
(+ simple form)
have/has been unable to (+ simple form)

PAST TENSES

Simple Past Tense
I was able to (+ simple form)/could
(+ simple form)

Neg. wasn't able to (+ simple form)
was unable to (+ simple form)

Past Perfect
I had been able to (+ simple form)

Neg. hadn't been able to (+ simple form)
had been unable to (+ simple form)

FUTURE TENSES

Simple Future Tense
I will be able to (+ simple form)
I am going to be able to (+ simple form)

Neg. won't be able to (+ simple form)
will be unable to (+ simple form)
(am) not/aren't/isn't going to be able to
(+ simple form)
am/is/are going to be unable to
(+ simple form)

Future Perfect
I will have been able to (+ simple form)
I am going to have been able to
(+ simple form)

Neg. won't have been able to
(+ simple form)
will have been unable to (+ simple form)
(am) not/aren't/isn't going to have been
able to (+ simple form)
am/is/are going to have been unable to
(+ simple form)

Note: ** Be able to* has no progressive forms, although it does have a present participle.

OTHER FORMS

Future Conditional
(If) I <u>am</u> able to (+ simple form), . . . <u>will</u> . . .

Neg. (If) <u>not</u> able to (+ simple form), . . . <u>will</u> . . .
(If) <u>un</u>able to (+ simple form), . . . <u>will</u> . . .
(If) able to (+ simple form), . . . <u>won't</u> . . .

Unreal Conditional
(If) I <u>were</u> able to (+ simple form), . . . <u>would</u> . . .

Neg. (If) <u>weren't</u> able to (+ simple form), . . . <u>would</u> . . .
(If) <u>were un</u>able to (+ simple form), . . . <u>would</u> . . .
(If) <u>were</u> able to (+ simple form), . . . <u>wouldn't</u> . . .

Past Conditional
(If) I <u>had been</u> able to (+ simple form), . . . <u>would have</u> . . . (+ past participle)

Neg. (If) <u>hadn't been</u> able to (+ simple form), . . . <u>would have</u> . . . (+ past participle)
(If) <u>had been un</u>able to (+ simple form), . . . <u>would have</u> . . . (+ past participle)
(If) had been able to (+ simple form), . . . <u>wouldn't have</u> . . . (+ past participle)

I'd like to *be able to* play the piano.

Who'*s able to* open this jar for me?

At your age, I *was able to* dance until dawn without feeling tired.

Tom *was unable to* join us last night because of work.

Lillian *has been able to* drive a car since she was in high school.

Bob *had been able to* get away with his wild spending until he lost his job.　　　(*get away with* = avoid punishment/consequences)

If I *were able to* live anywhere, I'*d* move to Tahiti.

Having been able to speak German was a big help to John.

Sue *was able to* get through last week without breaking her diet.

Modal/semi-modal: *can*

PRESENT TENSES

Simple Present Tense
all persons: + simple form
I can
you can
he/she/it can
we can
you can
they can

Neg. can't

Present Perfect*
can <u>have</u> (+ past participle)

Neg. can't <u>have</u> (+ past participle)

PAST TENSES

Simple Past Tense
I c<u>ould</u> (+ simple form)

Neg. c<u>ouldn't</u> (+ simple form)

Past Perfect
I c<u>ould have</u> (+ past participle)

Neg. c<u>ouldn't have</u> (+ past participle)

FUTURE TENSES

Simple Future Tense
I can (+ simple form + future time expression—*tomorrow, next week*, etc.)

Neg. can'<u>t</u> (+ simple form + future time expression—*tomorrow, next week*, etc.)

OTHER FORMS

Future Conditional
(I<u>f</u>) I can (+ simple form), . . . <u>will</u> . . .

Neg. (I<u>f</u>) can'<u>t</u> (+ simple form), . . . <u>will</u> . . .
(I<u>f</u>) can (+ simple form), . . . <u>won't</u> . . .

Unreal Conditional
(I<u>f</u>) I c<u>ould</u> (+ simple form), . . . <u>would</u> . . .

Neg. (I<u>f</u>) c<u>ouldn't</u> (+ simple form), . . . <u>would</u> . . .
(I<u>f</u>) c<u>ould</u> (+ simple form), . . . <u>wouldn't</u> . . .

Note: *Usually not used in the first person.

Past Conditional
(If) I could have (+ past participle), . . .
would have . . . (+ past participle)

Neg. (If) couldn't have (+ past participle), . . .
would have . . . (+ past participle)
(If) could have (+ past participle), . . .
wouldn't have . . . (+ past participle)

Can has three meanings: (1) to express ability; (2) to express actual or theoretical possibility, or impossibility/disbelief (usually in the negative); (3) to ask or grant permission.

Can Bobby come over to play?	(meaning 3)
This *can't* be happening!	(meaning 2)
Can you tell me where the bank is?	(meaning 1)
Maria *can* speak five languages	(meaning 1)
Anyone *can* join the club.	(meaning 2)
Can Granddad still read without glasses?	(meaning 1)
Bonnie *can* go to the movies if she's home before 10:00.	(meaning 3)
Fluffy *can't have been* run over!	(meaning 2)
If you *can* make the dinner, I *can* wash the dishes.	(meaning 2)

Modal/semi-modal: *could*

PRESENT TENSES

Simple Present Tense
all persons: + simple form
I could
you could
he/she/it could
we could
you could
they could

Present Perfect
I could <u>have</u> (+ past participle)

Neg. could<u>n't</u>

Neg. could<u>n't have</u> (+ past participle)

PAST TENSES

Simple Past Tense
I could (+ simple form)

Neg. could<u>n't</u> (+ simple form)

OTHER FORMS

Future Conditional
No separate form; use *can* if some
possibility exists.

Unreal Conditional
(<u>If</u>) I could (+ simple form), . . . <u>would</u> . . .

Neg. (<u>If</u>) could<u>n't</u> (+ simple form), . . .
<u>would</u> . . .
(<u>If</u>) could (+ simple form), . . . <u>wouldn't</u> . . .

Past Conditional
(<u>If</u>) I could <u>have</u> (+ past participle), . . . <u>would have</u> . . . (+ past participle)

Neg. (<u>If</u>) could<u>n't have</u> (+ past participle), . . . <u>would have</u> . . . (+ past participle)
(<u>If</u>) could <u>have</u> (+ past participle), . . . <u>wouldn't have</u> . . . (+ past participle)

Could has a number of different meanings: (1) to form the past tense of the modal *can*; (2) to ask permission or make very polite requests; (3) to make an imperative request gentler; (4) to express extreme disbelief/skepticism, unlikelihood, or impossibility (this meaning is almost always expressed in the negative, *couldn't*); (5) to express possibility—much like *can*—but only if a given set of circumstances exist; sentences with this meaning of *could* usually also contain words like *if* or *unless*. (for more details, see Part A, Section 6, *More Help-Modals*, page 20).

My son *could* already walk when he was eight months old.	(meaning 1)
Could you lend me $100 until my next paycheck?	(meaning 2)
How *could* Paul do such a terrible thing?	(meaning 4)
Do you think you *could* put that cigar out?	(meaning 3)
I *could* lend you some money if you pay me back by the 20th.	(meaning 5)
Boys, *couldn't* you please watch TV in your room?	(meaning 3)
You *couldn't* possibly be serious about this!	(meaning 4)
I *could have* gone with you *if* you *had* asked me earlier.	(meaning 5)
Ted *could* read Arabic while he was living in Saudi Arabia, but he can't read it any more.	(meaning 1)
Lois said she *couldn't* marry Dave unless he stopped smoking.	(meaning 5)
Could I have my salad dressing on the side, please?	(meaning 3)

Modal/semi-modal: *have got to*

INFINITIVE	**NEGATIVE**
(to) have got to (+ simple form)	Same as *have to*.

PRESENT TENSES

Simple Present Tense
all persons: + simple form
I have got to
you have got to
he/she/it has got to
we have got to
you have got to
they have got to

Present Progressive
Same as *have to*.

Neg. don't/doesn't have to (+ simple form)
*haven't/hasn't got to (+ simple form)

Neg. Same as *have to*.

Present Perfect
I have got to (+ simple form)

Present Perfect Progressive
Same as *have to*.

Neg.* haven't/hasn't got to (+ simple form)

Neg. Same as *have to*.

PAST TENSES

Simple Past Tense
I had got to (+ simple form)

Past Progressive
Same as *have to*.

Neg. hadn't got to (+ simple form)

Neg. Same as *have to*.

Past Perfect*
I had got to (+ simple form)

Past Perfect Progressive
Same as *have to*.

Neg.* hadn't got to (+ simple form)

Neg. Same as *have to*.

FUTURE TENSES

Simple Future Tense
Same as *have to*.

Future Progressive
Same as *have to*.

Neg. Same as *have to*.

Neg. Same as *have to*.

Note: *Grammar forms marked with an asterisk are exclusively British. Those that have the entry "Same as *have to*." are not used in American English except for *have to*. Other entries are used in both countries.

Future Perfect
Same as *have to.*

Neg. Same as *have to.*

Future Perfect Progressive
Same as *have to.*

Neg. Same as *have to.*

OTHER FORMS

Present Participle
Same as *have to.*

Neg. Same as *have to.*

Past Participle
Same as *have to.*

Neg. Same as *have to.*

Future Conditional
(If) I have got to (+ simple form), . . .
will . . .

Neg.* (If) haven't/hasn't got to (+ simple
form), . . . will . . .
(If) have/has got to (+ simple form), . . .
won't . . .

Unreal Conditional*
(If) I had got to (+ simple form), . . .
would . . .

Neg.* (If) hadn't got to (+ simple form), . . .
would . . .
(If) had got to (+ simple form), . . .
wouldn't . . .

Past Conditional
Same as *have to.*

Neg. Same as *have to.*

The only way *have got to* differs from *have to* in American English, is that it sounds more emphatic, urgent, or imperative than *have to.* On the other hand, *have got to* is far more common as an all-purpose modal of obligation in British English than in the United States. All sample sentences are American English.

I**'ve got to** stop smoking!

Charlie **has got to** study harder. (*or else* = if not, there will be negative consequences)

We**'ve got to** get to the bottom of this mystery.

I**'ve got to** find my plane ticket before the taxi arrives.

You**'ve got to** keep taking your medicine. (*keep* + present participle = continue doing/carry on doing)

We**'ve got to** end this bickering! (*bickering* = small arguments)

Modal/semi-modal: *have to*

INFINITIVE	**NEGATIVE**
(to) have to (+ simple form)	(to) not have to (+ simple form)
Present Participle	**Past Participle**
hav<u>ing</u> to (+ simple form)	hav<u>ing</u> <u>had</u> to (+ simple form)
Neg. <u>not</u> hav<u>ing</u> to (+ simple form)	**Neg.** <u>not</u> hav<u>ing</u> <u>had</u> to (+ simple form)

PRESENT TENSES

Simple Present Tense
all persons: + simple form
I have to
you have to
he/she/it ha<u>s</u> to
we have to
you have to
they have to

Neg. <u>don't</u>/<u>doesn't</u> have to (+ simple form)

Present Progressive
I <u>am</u> hav<u>ing</u> to (+ simple form)

Neg. (<u>am</u>) <u>not</u>/<u>aren't</u>/<u>isn't</u> hav<u>ing</u> to
(+ simple form)

Present Perfect
I <u>have</u> had to (+ simple form)

Neg. <u>haven't</u>/<u>hasn't</u> ha<u>d</u> to (+ simple form)

Present Perfect Progressive
I <u>have been</u> hav<u>ing</u> to (+ simple form)

Neg. <u>haven't</u>/<u>hasn't</u> <u>been</u> hav<u>ing</u> to
(+ simple form)

PAST TENSES

Simple Past Tense
I ha<u>d</u> to (+ simple form)

Neg. <u>didn't</u> have to (+ simple form)

Past Progressive
I <u>was</u> hav<u>ing</u> to (+ simple form)

Neg. <u>wasn't</u>/<u>weren't</u> hav<u>ing</u> to
(+ simple form)

Past Perfect
I <u>had</u> ha<u>d</u> to (+ simple form)

Neg. <u>hadn't</u> ha<u>d</u> to (+ simple form)

Past Perfect Progressive
I <u>had been</u> hav<u>ing</u> to (+ simple form)

Neg. <u>hadn't been</u> hav<u>ing</u> to
(+ simple form)

FUTURE TENSES

Simple Future Tense
I <u>will</u> have to (+ simple form)
I <u>am going to</u> have to (+ simple form)

Neg. <u>won't</u> have to (+ simple form)
(<u>am</u>) <u>not</u>/<u>aren't</u>/<u>isn't</u> <u>going to</u> have to
(+ simple form)

Future Progressive
I <u>will be</u> hav<u>ing</u> to (+ simple form)
I <u>am going to be</u> hav<u>ing</u> to (+ simple form)

Neg. <u>won't be</u> hav<u>ing</u> to (+ simple form)
(<u>am</u>) <u>not</u>/<u>aren't</u>/<u>isn't</u> <u>going to be</u> hav<u>ing</u> to
(+ simple form)

Note: Spelling change: Verbs ending in *-e* following a consonant drop the *-e* before *-ing* endings.
Although most modals have few or no progressive forms, *have to* has all the simple and perfect progressive tenses.

Future Perfect

I will have had to (+ simple form)
I am going to have had to
(+ simple form)*

Neg. won't have had to (+ simple form)
(am) not/aren't/isn't going to have had to
(+ simple form)

OTHER FORMS

Future Conditional

(If) I have to (+ simple form), . . . will . . .

Neg. (If) don't/doesn't have to
(+ simple form), . . . will . . .
(If) have to (+ simple form), . . . won't . . .

Unreal Conditional—Progressive Form

(If) I were having to (+ simple form), . . .
would . . .

Neg. (If) weren't having to
(+ simple form), . . . would . . .
(If) were having to (+ simple form), . . .
wouldn't . . .

Past Conditional—Progressive Form

(If) I had been having to (+ simple form), . . .
would have . . . (+ past participle)

Neg. (If) hadn't been having to
(+ simple form), . . . would have . . .
(+ past participle)
(If) had been having to (+ simple form), . . .
wouldn't have . . . (+ past participle)

Note: *Seldom used.

Unreal Conditional

(If) I had to (+ simple form), . . . would . . .

Neg. (If) didn't have to (+ simple form), . . .
would . . .
(If) had to (+ simple form), . . . wouldn't . . .

Past Conditional

(If) I had had to (+ simple form), . . .
would have . . . (+ past participle)

Neg. (If) hadn't had to (+ simple form), . . .
would have . . . (+ past participle)
(If) had had to (+ simple form), . . .
wouldn't have . . . (+ past participle)

Every morning, I *have to* get the newspaper from between the rose bushes.
Harry *has to* be at the bus stop by 7:00.
We *have to* stay at a hotel while the heating is being fixed.
Martha *had to* diet for weeks to fit into her wedding gown.
Jill said she *had to* bring her boss coffee six times a day, so she quit.
How often *have* you *had to* work late this month?
Bernie *has had to* wear sneakers for two months because of his broken foot.
Having to walk my dogs several times a day keeps me fit.
If Steve *had to* do the laundry, he'*d be* careful of his clothes.

Modal/semi-modal: *had better**

PRESENT TENSES

Simple Present Tense
all persons: + simple form
I had better
you had better
he/she/it had better
we had better
you had better
they had better

Simple Past Tense
I had better (+ simple form)

Neg. had better <u>not</u> (+ simple form)

NEGATIVE
had better <u>not</u> (+ simple form)
had<u>n't</u> better (+ simple form)

Note: *Only the above forms exist.

Similar in meaning to *should, had better* is one of several ways of giving advice in English. Some others are phrases such as *How about . . . ? How would it be if . . . ? What about . . . ? It might be better if . . .* , etc. *Had better* is the most emphatic of all, so it can sound very interfering if used too frequently.

I think you *had better* rest for a day or so.

The boss told Marvin that he'*d better* start looking for a new job.

Hadn't Sally *better* watch her weight?   (*watch . . . 's weight* = restrain eating; diet)

I *had better* get dinner started or Bill will be upset.

You'*d better* do something more than just read comic books if you want to graduate.

Our neighbors *had better* stop making noise at 3:00 A.M. or I'll call the police!

Tommy, you'*d better* eat all your spinach.

Modal/semi-modal: *like to*

INFINITIVE/IMPERATIVE	*NEGATIVE*
(to) like to (+ simple form)	(to) not like to (+ simple form)
Present Participle*	*Past Participle**
liking to (+ simple form)	having liked to (+ simple form)
Neg. not liking to (+ simple form)	*Neg.* not having liked to (+ simple form)

PRESENT TENSES

Simple Present Tense
all persons: + simple form
I like to
you like to
he/she/it likes to
we like to
you like to
they like to

Neg. don't/doesn't like to (+ simple form)

Present Perfect
I have liked to (+ simple form)

Neg. haven't/hasn't liked to
(+ simple form)

PAST TENSES

Simple Past Tense
I liked to (+ simple form)

Neg. didn't like to (+ simple form)

Past Perfect
I had liked to (+ simple form)

Neg. hadn't liked to (+ simple form)

Note: In addition to their use as semi-modals (always followed by *to* + the simple form), the verbs *like*, *need*, and *want* can also be followed by a noun or gerund (I *like* ice cream/*liking* sports . . . , he *needs* water/*needing* a drink, we *want* money/*wanting* affection, etc.)—in which case the *to* is dropped. When used before a verb, the imperative form is rare, but theoretically possible with *need* and *want*, but not with *like* (*Want* to succeed! *Need* to win!). There is no imperative form for any of these verbs when used before a noun.

*Spelling change: Regular verbs ending in -*e* following a consonant drop the -*e* before -*ing* endings and add -*d* for -*ed* endings.

FUTURE TENSES

Simple Future Tense*

Neg. won't like to (+ simple form)
(am) not/aren't/isn't going to like to
(+ simple form)

OTHER FORMS

Future Conditional
(If) I like to (+ simple form), . . . will . . .

Neg. (If) don't/doesn't like to (+ simple form), . . . will . . .
(If) like to (+ simple form), . . . won't . . .

Unreal Conditional
(If) I liked to (+ simple form), . . . would . . .

Neg. (If) didn't like to (+ simple form), . . . would . . .
(If) liked to (+ simple form), . . . wouldn't . . .

Past Conditional
(If) I had liked to (+ simple form), . . . would have . . . (+ past participle)

Neg. (If) hadn't liked to (+ simple form), . . . would have . . . (+ past participle)
(If) had liked to (+ simple form), . . . wouldn't have . . . (+ past participle)

Note: *There is no affirmative simple future tense for *like to* + verb, but the future is frequently expressed by the use of a gerund after *like* (I'll like living in London; He's going to like working In Marketing, etc.). The negative form, though infrequent, is sometimes used.

As with most modals, *like to* has no progressive forms. Also, the phrase *would like to* is not a tense form of *like to*, but a separate form with a substantially different usage: *like to* indicates general liking, but *would like to* indicates a specific situation.

Tony *likes to* play basketball.

We *used to like to* go to Manero's for dinner on Fridays.

Dad *liked to* tell silly stories.

If I *had liked to* come to these types of parties, I *would have* attended more of them.

Modal/semi-modal: *may*

PRESENT TENSES

Simple Present Tense
all persons: + simple form
I may
you may
he/she/it may
we may
you may
they may

Neg. may <u>not</u>*

Present Perfect
I may <u>have</u> (+ past participle)

Neg. may <u>not have</u> (+ past participle)

Present Perfect Progressive
I may <u>have been</u> (+ present participle)

Neg. may <u>not have been</u>
(+ present participle)

PAST TENSES

Simple Past Tense
I may <u>have</u> (+ past participle)

Neg. may <u>not have</u> (+ past participle)

Past Progressive
I may <u>have been</u> (+ present participle)

Neg. may <u>not have been</u>
(+ present participle)

FUTURE TENSES

Simple Future Tense
Same as simple present.

Neg. Same as simple present.

Note: *The contraction *mayn't* is never used in American English.

OTHER FORMS

Future Conditional

(If) I (+ simple form), . . . may . . .
(If) I may, . . . <u>will</u> . . . (+ simple form)

Neg. (If) <u>don't/doesn't</u> (+ simple form), . . . may <u>not</u> . . .
(If) may, . . . <u>won't</u> . . .

May has several meanings: (1) to express possibility; (2) to ask or grant permission (for granting permission *may* is more formal, *can* is often substituted informally); (3) to speculate about a situation. *May* and *might* are largely interchangeable when speculating on a possibility out of the speaker's control, but when the speaker is indicating his or her own possible future intentions/actions, the use of *might* shows less likelihood than *may*.

It *may* get cold later—take your jacket.	(meaning 3)
Nancy thinks she *may* break up with Tommy.	(meaning 1)
May I take another piece of cake?	(meaning 2)
I *may* leave before you're awake tomorrow.	(meaning 1)
Stock prices *may* start to decline.	(= go down) (meaning 3)
Students *may* take one hour to complete the test.	(meaning 2)
The floor is wet—a pipe *may have* burst.	(meaning 1)
Sam *may have* taken the wrong road coming here.	(meaning 3)
I *may not have been* thinking clearly when I agreed to this.	(meaning 3)

Modal/semi-modal: *might*

PRESENT TENSES

Simple Present Tense
all persons: + simple form
I might
you might
he/she/it might
we might
you might
they might

NEGATIVE
might not (+ simple form)

Present Progressive
might <u>be</u> (+ present participle)

Neg. might <u>not be</u> (+ present participle)

Present Perfect
I might <u>have</u> (+ past participle)

Neg. might <u>not have</u> (+ past participle)

Present Perfect Progressive
might <u>have been</u> (+ present participle)

Neg. might <u>not have been</u> (+ present participle)

PAST TENSES

Simple Past Tense
I might <u>have</u> (+ past participle)

Neg. might <u>not have</u> (+ past participle)

Past Progressive
might <u>have been</u> (+ present participle)

Neg. might <u>not have been</u> (+ present participle)

Past Perfect
Use present perfect form.

Neg. Use present perfect form.

Past Perfect Progressive
Use present perfect progressive form.

Neg. Use present perfect progressive form.

FUTURE TENSES

Simple Future Tense
Use simple present form.

Neg. Use simple present form.

Future Progressive
Use present progressive form.

Neg. Use present progressive form.

OTHER FORMS

Future Conditional
(<u>If</u>) I (+ simple form), . . . might . . .

Neg. (<u>If</u>) <u>don't</u>/<u>doesn't</u> (+ simple form), . . .
might . . .
(<u>If</u>) (+ simple form), . . . might <u>not</u> . . .

Unreal Conditional
(<u>If</u>) I (+ simple past form), . . . might . . .

Neg. (<u>If</u>) <u>didn't</u> (+ simple form), . . .
might . . .
(<u>If</u>) (+ simple past form), . . . might <u>not</u> . . .

Unreal Conditional—Progressive Form
(If) I <u>were</u> (+ present participle), . . . might . . .

Neg. (If) <u>weren't</u> (+ present participle), . . . might . . .
(If) <u>were</u> (+ present participle), . . . might <u>not</u> . . .

Past Conditional—Progressive Form
(If) I <u>had been</u> (+ present participle), . . . might <u>have</u> . . . (+ past participle)

Neg. (If) <u>hadn't been</u> (+ present participle), . . . might <u>have</u> . . . (+ past participle)
(If) <u>had been</u> (+ present participle), . . . might <u>not have</u> . . . (+ past participle)

Past Conditional
(If) I <u>had</u> (+ past participle), . . . might <u>have</u> . . . (+ past participle)

Neg. (If) <u>hadn't</u> (+ past participle), . . . might <u>have</u> . . . (+ past participle)
(If) <u>had</u> (+ past participle), . . . might <u>not have</u> . . . (+ past participle)

Might has several meanings: (1) to express possibility (in some cases, *might* and *may* are interchangeable—see usage note under entry for *may*); (2) to very politely ask a favor of someone, or for permission to do something—*not* for granting favors or permission; (3) to replace *may* when quoting someone's words to a third party.

Bill *might* want me to help him, but he'd be wrong.	(*he'd* = he would) (meaning 1)
When *might* we expect to hear from you?	(written or business style)(meaning 2)
Larry asked if he *might* bring a friend to our party.	(meaning 3)
Jane *might* have to work this Saturday.	(meaning 1)
Philip phoned to say he *might* be a little late.	(meaning 3)
If they apologized, we *might* speak to them again.	(meaning 1)

Modal/semi-modal: *must**

PRESENT TENSES

Simple Present Tense
all persons: + simple form
I must
you must
he/she/it must
we must
you must
they must

NEGATIVE
must <u>not</u> (+ simple form)
(= forbidden/prohibited)

Future Conditional
(<u>If</u>) I must, . . . <u>will</u> . . .

Neg. (<u>If</u>) <u>don't</u>/<u>doesn't</u> have to, . . . <u>will</u> . . .
(<u>If</u>) have to, . . . <u>won't</u> . . .

Note: *For all forms not given for *must*, see the entry for *have to*.

You *must* eat or you'll get sick.

Must we leave already?

The doctor told Fred he *mustn't* eat steak any more.

Passengers *must* have exact change.   (*exact change* = correct amount of coins)

Tell Frank he *must* confirm his plane reservation before Thursday.

The accounting department *must* get those forms to the tax people by Friday.

You *mustn't* think that.

Modal/semi-modal: *need to*

INFINITIVE/IMPERATIVE*	**NEGATIVE**
(to) need to (+ simple form)	(to) not need to (+ simple form)
Present Participle	**Past Participle**
need<u>ing</u> to (+ simple form)	hav<u>ing</u> need<u>ed</u> to (+ simple form)
Neg. <u>not</u> need<u>ing</u> to (+ simple form)	**Neg.** <u>not having</u> need<u>ed</u> to (+ simple form)

PRESENT TENSES

Simple Present Tense
all persons: + simple form
I need to
you need to
he/she/it need<u>s</u> to
we need to
you need to
they need to

Neg. <u>don't</u>/<u>doesn't</u> need to (+ simple form)

Present Perfect
I <u>have</u> need<u>ed</u> to (+ simple form)

Neg. <u>haven't</u>/<u>hasn't</u> need<u>ed</u> to
(+ simple form)

Present Perfect Progressive[†]
I <u>have been</u> need<u>ing</u> to (+ simple form)

Neg. <u>haven't</u>/<u>hasn't been</u> need<u>ing</u> to
(+ simple form)

PAST TENSES

Simple Past Tense
I need<u>ed</u> to (+ simple form)

Neg. <u>didn't</u> need to (+ simple form)

Past Perfect
I <u>had</u> need<u>ed</u> to (+ simple form)

Neg. <u>hadn't</u> need<u>ed</u> to (+ simple form)

Past Perfect Progressive[†]
I <u>had been</u> need<u>ing</u> to (+ simple form)

Neg. <u>hadn't been</u> need<u>ing</u> to
(+ simple form)

FUTURE TENSES

Simple Future Tense
I <u>will</u> need to (+ simple form)
I <u>am going to</u> need to (+ simple form)

Future Progressive[†]
I <u>will be</u> need<u>ing</u> to (+ simple form)
I <u>am going to be</u> need<u>ing</u> to
(+ simple form)

Note: *In addition to their use as semi-modals (always followed by *to* + the simple form), the verbs *like*, *need*, and *want* can also be followed by a noun or gerund (I *like* ice cream/*liking* sports . . . , he *needs* water/*needing* a drink, we *want* money/*wanting* affection, etc.)—in which case the *to* is dropped. When used before a verb, the imperative form is rare, but theoretically possible with *need* and *want*, but not with *like* (*Want* to succeed! *Need* to win!). There is no imperative form for any of these verbs when used before a noun.

Neg. <u>won't</u> need to (+ simple form)
(<u>am</u>) <u>not</u>/<u>aren't</u>/<u>isn't going to</u> need to
(+ simple form)

Neg. <u>won't be</u> needing to (+ simple form)
(<u>am</u>) <u>not</u>/<u>aren't</u>/<u>isn't going to be</u> needing
to (+ simple form)

Future Perfect
I <u>will have</u> need<u>ed</u> to (+ simple form)
I <u>am going to have</u> need<u>ed</u> to
(+ simple form)

Neg. <u>won't have</u> need<u>ed</u> to (+ simple form)
(<u>am</u>) <u>not</u>/<u>aren't</u>/<u>isn't going to have</u> need<u>ed</u>
to (+ simple form)

OTHER FORMS

Future Conditional
(<u>If</u>) I need to (+ simple form), . . . <u>will</u> . . .

Neg. (<u>If</u>) <u>don't</u>/<u>doesn't</u> need to
(+ simple form), . . . <u>will</u> . . .
(<u>If</u>) need to (+ simple form), . . . <u>won't</u> . . .

Unreal Conditional
(<u>If</u>) I need<u>ed</u> to (+ simple form), . . .
<u>would</u> . . .

Neg. (<u>If</u>) <u>didn't</u> need to (+ simple form),
. . . <u>would</u> . . .
(<u>If</u>) need<u>ed</u> to (+ simple form), . . .
<u>wouldn't</u> . . .

Past Conditional
(<u>If</u>) I <u>had</u> need<u>ed</u> to (+ simple form), . . . <u>would have</u> . . . (+ past participle)

Neg. (<u>If</u>) <u>hadn't</u> need<u>ed</u> to (+ simple form), . . . <u>would have</u> . . . (+ past participle)
(<u>If</u>) <u>had</u> need<u>ed</u> to (+ simple form), . . . <u>wouldn't have</u> . . . (+ past participle)

Note: ¹Although most modals have few or no progressive forms, *need to* has a future progressive as well as present perfect and past perfect progressive forms. The perfect forms especially are idiomatic, really meaning "I've noticed the necessity to . . . ," or "I've been intending to . . . ."

Mac understands what it's like *to need to* get away from the city.

Do you *need to* stop for gas before
we head north?

(*head north* = go in the northerly
direction)

Who *needs to* have this kind of pressure! I quit!

I *was needing to* hear some kind words when my favorite professor called.

This car *will be needing* some new tires soon.

If Don *had needed to* borrow money, he *would have* asked me first.

Modal/semi-modal: *want to*

INFINITIVE/IMPERATIVE*
(to) want to (+ simple form)

NEGATIVE
(to) not want to (+ simple form)

Present Participle
want<u>ing</u> to (+ simple form)

Past Participle
hav<u>ing</u> want<u>ed</u> to (+ simple form)

Neg. <u>not</u> want<u>ing</u> to (+ simple form)

Neg. <u>not having</u> want<u>ed</u> to (+ simple form)

PRESENT TENSES

Simple Present Tense
all persons: + simple form
I want to
you want to
he/she/it want<u>s</u> to
we want to
you want to
they want to

Neg. <u>don't</u>/<u>doesn't</u> want to (+ simple form)

Present Perfect
I <u>have</u> want<u>ed</u> to (+ simple form)

Present Perfect Progressive†
I <u>have been</u> want<u>ing</u> to (+ simple form)

Neg. <u>haven't</u>/<u>hasn't</u> want<u>ed</u> to
(+ simple form)

Neg. <u>haven't</u>/<u>hasn't been</u> want<u>ing</u> to
(+ simple form)

PAST TENSES

Simple Past Tense
I want<u>ed</u> to (+ simple form)

Past Perfect Progressive†
I <u>had been</u> want<u>ing</u> to (+ simple form)

Neg. <u>didn't</u> want to (+ simple form)

Neg. <u>hadn't been</u> want<u>ing</u> to (+ simple form)

Past Perfect
I <u>had</u> want<u>ed</u> to (+ simple form)

Neg. <u>hadn't</u> want<u>ed</u> to (+ simple form)

FUTURE TENSES

Simple Future Tense
I <u>will</u> want to (+ simple form)
I <u>am going to</u> want to (+ simple form)

Future Progressive
I <u>will be</u> want<u>ing</u> to (+ simple form)
I <u>am going to be</u> want<u>ing</u> to (+ simple form)

Note: *In addition to their use as semi-modals (always followed by *to* + the simple form), the verbs *like*, *need*, and *want* can also be followed by a noun or gerund (I *like* ice cream/*liking* sports . . . , he *needs* water/*needing* a drink, we *want* money/*wanting* affection, etc.)—in which case the *to* is dropped. When used before a verb, the imperative form is rare, but theoretically possible with *need* and *want*, but not with *like* (*Want* to succeed! *Need* to win!). There is no imperative form for any of these verbs when used before a noun.
†As with most modals, *want to* has no present or past progressive forms, but unlike the majority of modals, it does have a future progressive and both present and past perfect progressive forms.

Neg. <u>won't</u> want to (+ simple form)
(<u>am</u>) <u>not/aren't/isn't</u> <u>going to</u> want to
(+ simple form)

Future Perfect
I <u>will have</u> wan<u>ted</u> to (+ simple form)
I <u>am going to have</u> wan<u>ted</u> to (+ simple form)

Neg. <u>won't have</u> wan<u>ted</u> to (+ simple form)
(<u>am</u>) <u>not/aren't/isn't</u> <u>going to have</u> wan<u>ted</u> to (+ simple form)

Neg. <u>won't be</u> want<u>ing</u> to (+ simple form)
(<u>am</u>) <u>not/aren't/isn't</u> <u>going to be</u> want<u>ing</u> to (+ simple form)

OTHER FORMS

Future Conditional
(<u>If</u>) I want to (+ simple form), . . . <u>will</u> . . .

Neg. (<u>If</u>) <u>don't/doesn't</u> want to (+ simple form), . . . <u>will</u> . . .
(<u>If</u>) want to (+ simple form), . . . <u>won't</u> . . .

Past Conditional
(If) I <u>had</u> wan<u>ted</u> to (+ simple form), . . . <u>would have</u> . . . (+ past participle)

Neg. (<u>If</u>) <u>hadn't</u> wan<u>ted</u> to (+ simple form), . . . <u>would have</u> . . . (+ past participle)
(<u>If</u>) <u>had</u> wan<u>ted</u> to (+ simple form), . . . <u>wouldn't have</u> . . . (+ past participle)

Unreal Conditional
(<u>If</u>) I wan<u>ted</u> to (+ simple form), . . . <u>would</u> . . .

Neg. (<u>If</u>) <u>didn't</u> want to (+ simple form), . . . <u>would</u> . . .
(<u>If</u>) wan<u>ted</u> to (+ simple form), . . . <u>wouldn't</u> . . .

Past Conditional—Progressive Form
(<u>If</u>) I had <u>been</u> want<u>ing</u> to (+ simple form), . . . <u>would have</u> . . . (+ past participle)

Neg. (<u>If</u>) <u>hadn't been</u> want<u>ing</u> to (+ simple form), . . . <u>would have</u> . . . (+ past participle)
(<u>If</u>) <u>had been</u> want<u>ing</u> to (+ simple form), . . . <u>wouldn't have</u> . . . (+ past participle)

It's natural *to want to* be young again.

Who *wants to* join me for a swim?

Dad *wanted to* come with me, but his arthritis is worse.

We're *going to want to* find a house with a basement.

Mark *has wanted to* get this promotion very badly.

I've *been wanting to* come to this restaurant for years.

In high school, Helen *had wanted to* become a veterinarian, but then she began *to want to* study human medicine.

Having wanted to buy a new computer, Marilyn was sorry to have missed the sale.

Modal/semi-modal: *ought to*

PRESENT TENSES

Simple Present Tense
all persons: + simple form
I ought to
you ought to
he/she/it ought to
we ought to
you ought to
they ought to

NEGATIVE
ought not to (+ simple form)*

Present Progressive
I ought to <u>be</u> (+ present participle)

Neg. ought <u>not</u> to <u>be</u> (+ present participle)

Present Perfect
I ought to <u>have</u> (+ past participle)

Neg. ought <u>not</u> to <u>have</u> (+ past participle)

Present Perfect Progressive
I ought to <u>have been</u> (+ present participle)

Neg. ought <u>not</u> to <u>have been</u> (+ present participle)

PAST TENSES

Simple Past Tense
I ought to <u>have</u> (+ past participle)

Neg. ought <u>not</u> to <u>have</u> (+ past participle)*

Past Progressive
I ought to <u>have been</u> (+ past participle)

Neg. ought <u>not</u> to <u>have been</u> (+ past participle)

Past Perfect
Same as present perfect.

Neg. Same as present perfect.

Past Perfect Progressive
Same as present perfect progressive.

Neg. Same as present perfect progressive.

FUTURE TENSES

Simple Future Tense
Same as simple present.

Neg. Same as simple present.

Future Progressive
Same as present progressive.

Neg. Same as present progressive.

OTHER FORMS

Future Conditional
(<u>If</u>) I (+ simple form), . . . ought to . . .

Past Conditional
(<u>If</u>) I <u>had</u> (+ past participle), . . . ought to <u>have</u> . . . (+ past participle)

Note: *The contraction, *oughtn't*, is predominantly British. The form "didn't ought to have" is considered substandard.

Neg. (If) <u>don't</u>/<u>doesn't</u> (+ simple form), . . .
ought to . . .
(<u>If</u>) (+ simple form), . . . ought <u>not</u> to . . .

Neg. (<u>If</u>) <u>hadn't</u> (+ past participle), . . .
ought to <u>have</u> . . . (+ past participle)
(<u>If</u>) <u>had</u> (+ past participle), . . . ought <u>not</u>
to <u>have</u> . . . (+ past participle)

Ought to has three usages: (1) to express objective obligation (i.e., society's expectation); (2) to express the speaker's concept of what is the right, wise, sensible (or wrong, unwise, impractical) thing to do (usually for the listener, but often for the speaker or a third party as well); (3) to express logical expectation. In the second meaning, *ought to* is similar to *had better*, but the third meaning is identical to *should*.

In the sense of obligation, *should* and *ought to* are used fairly interchangeably. Unlike *should*, however, *ought to* carries a feeling that society at large obliges the action, whereas *should* is slightly more subjective.

I suppose I *ought to* do the laundry now.	(meaning 2)
Henry really *ought to* send his tax return in on time.	(meaning 1)
You really *ought not to* wear your hair so long around machinery.	(meaning 2)
People *ought not to* waste water by washing their cars at home.	(meaning 1)
Do you really think you *ought to* be smoking at your age, Tim?	(meaning 1)
I *ought not to have been* dancing with this bad back.	(meaning 2)
The floor *ought to have* gotten thoroughly dry by now.	(meaning 3)
Kate *ought to have* heard from her doctor by this time about her test results.	(meaning 3)

Modal/semi-modal: *should*

PRESENT TENSES

Simple Present Tense
all persons: + simple form
I should
you should
he/she/it should
we should
you should
they should

NEGATIVE
shouldn't (+ simple form)

Present Progressive
I should <u>be</u> (+ present participle)

Neg. shouldn't <u>be</u> (+ present participle)

Present Perfect
I should <u>have</u> (+ past participle)

Neg. shouldn't have (+ past participle)

Present Perfect Progressive
I should <u>have been</u> (+ present participle)

Neg. shouldn't have been
(+ present participle)

PAST TENSES

Simple Past Tense
I should <u>have</u> (+ past participle)

Neg. shouldn't have (+ past participle)

Past Progressive
I should <u>have been</u> (+ present participle)

Neg. shouldn't have been
(+ present participle)

Past Perfect
Same as present perfect.

Neg. Same as present perfect.

Past Perfect Progressive
Same as present perfect progressive.

Neg. Same as present perfect progressive.

FUTURE TENSES

Simple Future Tense
Same as simple present.

Neg. Same as simple present.

Future Progressive
Same as present progressive.

Neg. Same as present progressive.

OTHER FORMS

Future Conditional
(<u>If</u>) I (+ simple form), . . . should . . .

Neg. (<u>If</u>) <u>don't</u>/<u>doesn't</u> (+ simple form), . . . should . . .
(<u>If</u>) (+ simple form), . . . should<u>n't</u> . . .

Should has three usages: (1) to express objective obligation or customary behavior; (2) to express the speaker's judgement; (3) to express the speaker's expectation—often, but not always based on likelihood. In the sense of obligation, *should* and *ought to* are used fairly interchangeably. See usage note under entry for *ought to*.

Someone *should* tell Marjorie not to wear that color.	(meaning 2)
The instructions *should* be on the box.	(meaning 3)
Should you really have that rich dessert, Robin?	(meaning 2)
All of you *should* double-space your reports.	(meaning 1)
The firm's profits *should* rise dramatically over the next two quarters.	(meaning 3)
Ted *should* have reported the accident immediately.	(meaning 1)
It's after 11:00—Andy *should have* gotten home long before now.	(meaning 3)
I suppose I *shouldn't have been* arguing with George over politics.	(meaning 1)

Modal/semi-modal: *will*

PRESENT TENSES

Simple Present Tense
all persons: + simple form
I will
you will
he/she/it will
we will
you will
they will

Past Participle
having been willing (+ infinitive)

Neg. not having been willing (+ infinitive)

NEGATIVE
won't (+ simple form)

Present Participle
being willing (+ infinitive)

Neg. not being willing (+ infinitive)

Present Progressive
I am willing (+ infinitive)

Neg. (am) not/aren't/isn't willing
(+ infinitive)

PAST TENSES

Simple Past Tense
I would (+ simple form)

Neg. wouldn't (+ simple form)

Past Progressive
I was willing (+ infinitive)

Neg. wasn't/weren't willing (+ infinitive)

Past Perfect Progressive
I had been willing (+ infinitive)

Neg. hadn't been willing (+ infinitive)

FUTURE TENSES

Simple Future Tense
I will (+ simple form)
I would (+ simple form) (= implies some
conditions must first be met)

Neg. won't (+ simple form)
wouldn't (+ simple form) (= implies some
conditions must first be met)

Future Perfect
I will have (+ past participle)

Neg. won't have (+ infinitive)

Future Progressive
I'll be willing (+ infinitive)

Neg. won't be willing (+ infinitive)

OTHER FORMS

Future Conditional
(If) I (+ simple form), . . . will (+ simple form)

Neg. (If) don't/doesn't (+ simple form), . . . will . . .
(If) (+ simple form), . . . won't . . .

Unreal Conditional—Progressive Form
(If) I were willing (+ infinitive), . . . would . . .

Neg. (If) weren't willing (+ infinitive), . . . would . . .
(If) were willing (+ infinitive), . . . wouldn't . . .

Unreal Conditional
(If) I were willing (+ simple form), . . . would . . .

Neg. (If) weren't willing (+ infinitive), . . . would . . .
(If) were willing (+ infinitive), . . . wouldn't . . .

Past Conditional—Progressive Form
(If) I had been willing (+ infinitive), . . . would have . . . (+ past participle)

Neg. (If) hadn't been willing (+ infinitive), . . . would have . . . (+ past participle)
(If) had been willing (+ infinitive), . . . wouldn't have . . . (+ past participle)

Although it has very broad use as an auxiliary, implying future actions, *will*'s meaning as a modal is limited to (1) willingness—i.e., a mild form of wanting to do (or not minding doing) the action described by the full verb—or determination (the *will*) to do something; and (2) predicting probable situations or advisable results. In meaning 2, *would* is used for past situations, but *would* also has several other meanings of its own.

I'*ll* go to the store if you don't want to.	(meaning 1)
Terry *will* drive you if you need a driver.	(meaning 1)
Will we get back by 6:00?	(get back = return) (meaning 2)
All of us *were willing* to defer our bonuses to help the company.	(defer = postpone) (meaning 1)
It *will* start snowing by afternoon.	(meaning 2)
I *wouldn't* advise you to invest in that company.	(meaning 2)
Prices *would* have to fall before I'*d* be willing to buy a house.	(meaning 2)
The trip *will* only take you an hour— you'*ll* be home by 9:00.	(meaning 2)

Modal/semi-modal: *would*

PRESENT TENSES

Simple Present Tense
all persons: + simple form
I would
you would
he/she/it would
we would
you would
they would

Present Perfect
I would <u>have</u> (+ past participle)

Neg. would<u>n't have</u> (+ past participle)

NEGATIVE
wouldn't (+ simple form)

Present Perfect Progressive
I would <u>have been</u> (+ infinitive)

Neg. would<u>n't have been</u> (+ infinitive)

PAST TENSES

Simple Past Tense
I would <u>have</u> (+ past participle)

Neg. would<u>n't have</u> (+ past participle)

Past Progressive
I would <u>have been</u> (+ present participle)

Neg. would<u>n't have been</u>
(+ present participle)

FUTURE TENSES

Simple Future Tense
Same as simple present.

Neg. Same as simple present.

Future Perfect
Same as present perfect.

Neg. Same as present perfect.

Future Progressive
Same as present progressive.

Neg. Same as present progressive.

OTHER FORMS

Unreal Conditional
(<u>If</u>) I (+ simple past tense), . . . would . . .

Neg. (<u>If</u>) <u>don't/didn't</u>
(+ simple form), . . . would . . .
(<u>If</u>) (+ simple past tense), . . . would<u>n't</u> . . .

Unreal Conditional—Progressive Form
(<u>If</u>) I <u>were</u> (+ present participle), . . .
would . . .

Neg. (<u>If</u>) <u>weren't</u> (+ present participle), . . .
would . . .
(<u>If</u>) <u>were</u> (+ present participle), . . .
would<u>n't</u> . . .

Past Conditional

(If) I had (+ past participle), . . . would have . . . (+ past participle)

Neg. (If) hadn't (+ past participle), . . . would have . . . (+ past participle)
(If) had (+ past participle), . . . wouldn't have . . . (+ past participle)

Past Conditional—Progressive Form

(If) I had been (+ present participle), . . . would have . . . (+ past participle)

Neg. (If) hadn't been (+ present participle), . . . would have . . . (+ past participle)
(If) had been (+ present participle), . . . wouldn't have . . . (+ past participle)

Would has several meanings: (1) to replace *will* in past situations or in telling someone what a third person said; (2) to make a polite request; (3) to wish for something that is unlikely at the moment; (4) to theorize about another person's behavior or situation—particularly if negative; (5) to express future intentions that depend on other conditions.

Would you hold the ladder for me?	(meaning 2)
Florence was sure the painting *would* fall down.	(meaning 1)
We hoped you *wouldn't* mind if we brought our houseguest along.	(meaning 2)
If only those people next door *would* stop fighting!	(meaning 4)
I *would* move *if* houses in this town *weren't* so expensive.	(meaning 5)
Wouldn't it be nice to go skiing over Christmas?	(meaning 4)
Would everyone please start singing "Happy Birthday" when Ann comes in?	(meaning 2)
Mom wishes Dad *would* retire soon.	(meaning 3)

Causative Verbs

English has a group of verbs that are used, much like modals, to show situations in which one person wants something done, but "asks" a second person, sometimes nonverbally, to perform the action—usually a task, obligation, or service. These verbs are called causatives because in the relationship one person "causes"—i.e., creates a situation—in which another person or animal does something.

Causatives are often put in the same general category as another group of verbs known as permissives. These verbs show that the subject gives the human or animal object permission to do something. With causatives, the subject wants something, but only activates another to actually do it; with permissives, the subject "permits" someone or something to perform an action that he, she, or even it already wants to do.

Causatives have two forms, with a very rigid word order that must be strictly observed. In Form 1, the focus is strongly on the task or service, less on the "doer"; in Form 2, the focus shifts to the "doer," and the task or service becomes slightly less important than who actually does it. Some causatives—especially *have*, the most widely used of all—can be used with either Form 1 or Form 2 constructions. Most causatives, however, and all permissives, can only be used in Form 2 constructions. Remember that *only* the causative or permissive verb is conjugated.

- Form 1 uses the causative verb + the phrase describing the task + the past participle of the second verb + (optional) *by* + the *agent* (the "doer")

I *had* <u>my teeth</u> *cleaned* by the dentist.
We *are having* <u>the carpet</u> *taken up.*
Then we *are going to have* <u>tile</u> *laid* in the kitchen (by workmen).*
Up to now, the firm *has had* <u>the annual report</u> *written* by in-house staff.

- Form 2 uses the causative verb + the person or animal doing the action + the infinitive or simple form of the second verb[†] + the phrase describing the task

We usually *have* <u>Billy</u> *take out* the trash each morning.
My husband *has been having* <u>us</u> *help* him paint the living room.
I *have* <u>the dentist</u> *make* two sets of x-rays.

Note: *In a case like this, naming the agent is unnecessary unless the specific tile company were mentioned.

†Whether to use the infinitive or simple form varies with each causative or permissive verb. It isn't based on the second verb (see the individual conjugations and the list that follows). The infinitive/simple form distinction does not apply when any of these verbs are used in non-causative constructions.

CAUSATIVE VERBS

The following are the causative and permissive verbs you may encounter.

Causatives:

ask	Form 2; infinitive
cause	Form 2; infinitive
force	Form 2; infinitive
get	Form 1 & Form 2; infinitive
have*	Form 1 & Form 2; simple form
hire	Form 2; infinitive
make	Form 2; simple form
order	Form 2; infinitive
persuade	Form 2; infinitive
require	Form 2; infinitive
tell	Form 2; infinitive
want[†]	Form 2; infinitive
would like	Form 2; infinitive

Permissives:

allow	Form 2; infinitive
encourage	Form 2; infinitive
help	Form 2; infinitive
let	Form 2; simple form
permit	Form 2; infinitive

Note: *The use of *have*, which is neutral in tone, indicates that the task is either something the "doer" would ordinarily do, or could reasonably be expected of him/her. *Get*, however, indicates reluctance on the part of the "doer" (Form 2), or that the task was something of an effort (Form 1).

[†]Widely used in other, non-causative constructions. *Want to* + verb means the speaker intends to do the task; *Want* someone *to do* . . . means that the speaker wants another person to act on his/her wishes.

Causative verb forms 1 & 2: *get*

INFINITIVE/IMPERATIVE
(to) get (something) done/(someone) to
do (something)
Get (something) done!/Get (someone) to
do (something)!

NEGATIVE
(to) not get (something) done/(someone)
to do (something)
Don't get (something) done/(someone) to
do (something)!

Present Participle*
getting (something) done/(someone) to do
(something)

Neg. not getting (something) done/
(someone) to do (something)

Past Participle
gotten (something) done/(someone) to do
(something)

Neg. not gotten (something) done/(someone) to do (something)

PRESENT TENSES

Simple Present Tense
I get (something) done/(someone) to do
(something)
you get (something) done/(someone) to do (something)
he/she/it gets (something) done/(somone) to do (something)
we get (something) done/(someone) to do (something)
you get (something) done/(someone) to do (something)
they get (something) done/(someone) to do (something)

Neg. don't/doesn't get (something)
done/(someone) to do (something)

Present Progressive
I am getting (something) done/(someone)
to do (something)

Neg. (am) not/aren't/isn't getting (something) done/(someone) to do (something)

Present Perfect
I have gotten (something) done/(someone)
to do (something)

Neg. haven't/hasn't gotten (something)
done/(someone) to do (something)

Present Perfect Progressive
I have been getting (something)
done/(someone) do (something)

Neg. haven't been getting (something)
done/(someone) do (something)

PAST TENSES

Simple Past Tense
I got (something) done/(someone) to do
(something)

Neg. didn't get (something) done/(someone) to do (something)

Past Progressive
I was getting (something) done/(someone)
to do (something)

Neg. wasn't/weren't getting (something)
done/(someone) to do (something)

Past Perfect
I had gotten (something) done/(someone)
to do (something)

Neg. hadn't gotten (something)
done/(someone) to do (something)

Past Perfect Progressive
I had been getting (something)
done/(someone) to do (something)

Neg. hadn't been getting (something)
done/(someone) to do (something)

Note: *Spelling change: Irregular verbs ending in a single consonant following a single vowel double
the last consonant before -*ing*.

FUTURE TENSES

Simple Future Tense
I will get (something) done/(someone) to
do (something)

Neg. won't get (something) done/
(someone) to do (something)

Future Perfect
I will have gotten (something)
done/(someone) to do (something)

Neg. won't have gotten (something)
done/(someone) to do (something)

Future Progressive
I will be getting (something) done/
(someone) to do (something)

Neg. won't be getting (something)
done/(someone) to do (something)

OTHER FORMS

Future Conditional
(If) I get (something) done/(someone) to
do (something), . . . will . . .

Neg. (If) don't/doesn't get (something)
done/(someone) to do (something), . . .
will . . .

Unreal Conditional—Progressive Form
(If) I were getting (something)
done/(someone) to do (something), . . .
would . . .

Neg. (If) weren't getting (something)
done/(someone) to do (something), . . .
would . . .

Unreal Conditional
(If) I got (something) done/(someone) to
do (something), . . . would . . .

Neg. (If) didn't get (something)
done/(someone) to do (something), . . .
would . . .

Past Conditional
(If) I had gotten (something) done/
(someone) to do (something), . . .
would have . . . (+ past participle)

Neg. (If) hadn't gotten (something)
done/(someone) to do (something), . . .
would have . . . (+ past participle)

Past Conditional—Progressive Form
(If) I had been getting (something) done/(someone) to do (something), . . . would
have . . . (+ past participle)

Neg. (If) hadn't been getting (something) done/(someone) to do (something), . . . would
have . . . (+ past participle)

I *can't get* the new executive assistant to understand our filing system.
Why *don't* you *get* your hair cut tomorrow?
I'*m getting* the carpet cleaned right now.
Alan *will get* our tires changed this weekend.
At last I'*ve gotten* the company to give me a new printer!
We *will have gotten* the mattress replaced by your next visit.
If Hannah *doesn't get* Dr. Syms to give her stronger glasses, she'*ll* have a car accident.

Causative verb forms 1 & 2: *have*

INFINITIVE/IMPERATIVE
(to) have (something) done/(someone) do (something)
Have (something) done!/(someone) do (something)!

NEGATIVE
(to) not have (something) done/(someone) do (something)
Don't have (something) done/(someone) do (something)!

Present Participle*
hav*ing* (something) done/(someone) do (something)

Neg. not hav*ing* (something) done/(someone) do (something)

Past Participle
ha*d* (something) done/(someone) do (something)

Neg. not had (something) done/(someone) do (something)

PRESENT TENSES

Simple Present Tense
I have (something) done/(someone) do (something)
you have (something) done/(someone) do (something)
he/she/it ha*s* (something) done/(someone) do (something)
we have (something) done/(someone) do (something)
you have (something) done/(someone) do (something)
they have (something) done/(someone) do (something)

Neg. don't/doesn't have (something) done/(someone) do (something)

Present Progressive
I am hav*ing* (something) done/(someone) do (something)

Neg. (am) not/aren't/isn't hav*ing* (something) done/(someone) do (something)

Present Perfect
I have ha*d* (something) done/(someone) do (something)

Neg. haven't/hasn't had (something) done/(someone) do (something)

Present Perfect Progressive
I have been hav*ing* (something) done/(someone) do (something)

Neg. haven't been hav*ing* (something) done/(someone) do (something)

PAST TENSES

Simple Past Tense
I ha*d* (something) done/(someone) do (something)

Neg. didn't have (something) done/(someone) do (something)

Past Progressive
I wa*s* hav*ing* (something) done/(someone) do (something)

Neg. wasn't/weren't hav*ing* (something) done/(someone) do (something)

Past Perfect
I had had (something) done/(someone) do (something)

Neg. hadn't had (something) done/(someone) do (something)

Past Perfect Progressive
I had been hav*ing* (something) done/(someone) do (something)

Neg. hadn't been hav*ing* (something) done/(someone) do (something)

Note: *Spelling change: Verbs ending in *-e* following a consonant drop the *-e* before *-ing* endings.

FUTURE TENSES

Simple Future Tense
I <u>will</u> have (something) done/(someone) do (something)

Neg. <u>won't</u> have (something) done/(someone) do (something)

Future Progressive
I <u>will be</u> ha<u>ving</u> (something) done/(someone) do (something)

Neg. <u>won't be</u> ha<u>ving</u> (something) done/(someone) do (something)

Future Perfect
I <u>will have</u> ha<u>d</u> (something) done/(someone) do (something)

Neg. <u>won't have</u> had (something) done/(someone) do (something)

OTHER FORMS

Future Conditional
(<u>If</u>) I have (something) done/(someone) do (something), . . . <u>will</u> . . .

Neg. (<u>If</u>) <u>don't</u>/<u>doesn't</u> have (something) done/(someone) do (something), . . . <u>will</u> . . .

Unreal Conditional
(<u>If</u>) I ha<u>d</u> (something) done/(someone) do (something), . . . <u>would</u> . . .

Neg. (<u>If</u>) <u>didn't</u> have (something) done/(someone) do (something), . . . <u>would</u> . . .

Unreal Conditional—Progressive Form
(<u>If</u>) I <u>were</u> ha<u>ving</u> (something) done/(someone) do (something), . . . <u>would</u> . . .

Neg. (<u>If</u>) <u>weren't</u> ha<u>ving</u> (something) done/(someone) do (something), . . . <u>would</u> . . .

Past Conditional
(<u>If</u>) I <u>had</u> had (something) done/(someone) do (something), . . . <u>would have</u> . . . (+ past participle)

Neg. (<u>If</u>) <u>hadn't</u> had (something) done/(someone) do (something), . . . <u>would have</u> . . . (+ past participle)

Past Conditional—Progressive Form
(<u>If</u>) I <u>had been</u> ha<u>ving</u> (something) done/(someone) do (something), . . . <u>would have</u> . . . (+ past participle)

Neg. (<u>If</u>) <u>hadn't been</u> ha<u>ving</u> (something) done/(someone) do (something), . . . <u>would have</u> . . . (+ past participle)

This is the most universal of all the causative forms, except for its idiomatic equivalent, *get*.

I'd like to *have* you examine my right shoulder, Doctor.

Have this broken step fixed!

We'*re having* the students each bring a dish from their native countries.

The Sandersons finally *had* that old fence replaced last week.

Mike *will have* his whole office redecorated at company expense.

If only Mark *had had* Human Resources give the presentation, it *would have been* much more effective.

Causative verb form 2 only: *let*

INFINITIVE/IMPERATIVE
(to) let (someone) do (something)/Let (someone) do (something)!

NEGATIVE
(to) not let (someone) do (something)/Don't let (someone) do (something)!

Present Participle*
letting (someone) do (something)

Past Participle
let (someone) do (something)

Neg. not letting (someone) do (something)

Neg. not let (someone) do (something)

PRESENT TENSES

Simple Present Tense
I let (someone) do (something)
you let (someone) do (something)
he/she/it lets (someone) do (something)
we let (someone) do (something)
you let (someone) do (something)
they let (someone) do (something)

Present Progressive
I am letting (someone) do (something)

Neg. don't/doesn't let (someone) do (something)

Neg. (am) not/aren't/isn't letting (someone) do (something)

Present Perfect
I have let (someone) do (something)

Present Perfect Progressive
I have been letting (someone) do (something)

Neg. haven't/hasn't let (someone) do (something)

Neg. haven't been letting (someone) do (something)

PAST TENSES

Simple Past Tense
I let (someone) do (something)

Past Progressive
I was letting (someone) do (something)

Neg. didn't let (someone) do (something)

Neg. wasn't/weren't letting (someone) do (something)

Past Perfect
I had let (someone) do (something)

Past Perfect Progressive
I had been letting (someone) do (something)

Neg. hadn't let (someone) do (something)

Neg. hadn't been letting (someone) do (something)

Note: *Spelling change: Irregular verbs ending in a single consonant following a single vowel double the last consonant before -*ing*.

258

FUTURE TENSES

Simple Future Tense
I will let (someone) do (something)

Neg. won't let (someone) do (something)

Future Progressive
I will be letting (someone) do (something)

Neg. won't be letting (someone) do (something)

Future Perfect
I will have let (someone) do (something)

Neg. won't have let (someone) do (something)

OTHER FORMS

Future Conditional
(If) I let (someone) do (something), . . . will . . .

Neg. (If) don't/doesn't let (someone) do (something), . . . will . . .

Unreal Conditional—Progressive Form
(If) I were letting (someone) do (something), . . . would . . .

Neg. (If) weren't letting (someone) do (something), . . . would . . .

Unreal Conditional
(If) I let (someone) do (something), . . . would . . .

Neg. (If) didn't let (someone) do (something), . . . would . . .

Past Conditional
(If) I had let (someone) do (something), . . . would have . . . (+ past participle)

Neg. (If) hadn't let (someone) do (something), . . . would have . . . (+ past participle)

Past Conditional—Progressive Form
(If) I had been letting (someone) do (something), . . . would have . . . (+ past participle)

Neg. (If) hadn't been letting (someone) do (something), . . . would have . . . (+ past participle)

Let Charles slice the roast!
Don't let the cats jump up on the counters, Sarah!
It's about time Mom *let* us help her with the vacuuming.   (*about time* = should have happened before now)
I *let* the kids choose all their own clothes.
Mary's parents wisely *let* her make her own mistakes.
We*'ve* never *let* Billy stay out after 11:00.
If I *let* Harry choose the TV programs, we*'d* watch ten seconds of everything except football!

Causative verb form 2 only: *make*

INFINITIVE/IMPERATIVE	***NEGATIVE***
(to) make (someone) do (something)/Make (someone) do (something)!	(to) not make (someone) do (something)/Don't make (someone) do (something)!

Present Participle*
making (someone) do (something)

Past Participle
made (someone) do (something)

Neg. not making (someone) do (something)

Neg. not made (someone) do (something)

PRESENT TENSES

Simple Present Tense
I make (someone) do (something)
you make (someone) do (something)
he/she/it makes (someone) do (something)
we make (someone) do (something)
you make (someone) do (something)
they make (someone) do (something)

Present Progressive
I am making (someone) do (something)

Neg. don't/doesn't make (someone) do (something)

Neg. (am) not/aren't/isn't making (someone) do (something)

Present Perfect
I have made (someone) do (something)

Present Perfect Progressive
I have been making (someone) do (something)

Neg. haven't/hasn't made (someone) do (something)

Neg. haven't been making (someone) do (something)

PAST TENSES

Simple Past Tense
I made (someone) do (something)

Past Progressive
I was making (someone) do (something)

Neg. didn't make (someone) do (something)

Neg. wasn't/weren't making (someone) do (something)

Past Perfect
I had made (someone) do (something)

Past Perfect Progressive
I had been making (someone) do (something)

Neg. hadn't made (someone) do (something)

Neg. hadn't been making (someone) do (something)

FUTURE TENSES

Simple Future Tense
I will make (someone) do (something)

Future Progressive
I will be making (someone) do (something)

Neg. won't make (someone) do (something)

Neg. won't be making (someone) do (something)

Note: *Spelling change: Verbs ending in -*e* following a consonant drop the -*e* before -*ing* endings.

Future Perfect
I will have made (someone) do
(something)

Neg. won't have made (someone) do
(something)

OTHER FORMS

Future Conditional
(If) I make (someone) do (something), . . .
will . . .

Neg. (If) don't/doesn't make (someone) do
(something), . . . will . . .

Unreal Conditional—Progressive Form
(If) I were making (someone) do
(something), . . . would . . .

Neg. (If) weren't making (someone) do
(something), would

Unreal Conditional
(If) I made (someone) do (something), . . .
would . . .

Neg. (If) didn't make (someone) do
(something), . . . would . . .

Past Conditional
(If) I had made (someone) do
(something), . . . would have . . .
(+ past participle)

Neg. (If) hadn't made (someone) do
(something), . . . would have . . .
(+ past participle)

Past Conditional—Progressive Form
(If) I had been making (someone) do (something), . . . would have . . . (+ past participle)

Neg. (If) hadn't been making (someone) do (something), . . . would have . . . (+ past participle)

Make him stop teasing me, Mommy!
We want to *make* Eddy go to college, but he's decided to be a musician.
The professor *is making* me rewrite my entire thesis!
The coach *made* all the students run extra laps because the team lost.
Hurry up, Ted, or I'*ll make* you explain to my boss why I'm late for work.
Arthur says he *will make* the company pay for all the damage.
If I *had made* you eat everything on your plate, you'*d be* healthier today!

C
SUBJECT INDEX

SUBJECT INDEX

Note: Specific words are noted in *italics*.

A

Abstract subject (*it*), state-of-being verbs and, 14
Action verbs, 8–9, 11, 12
Actions
  completed, 31, 39–40
  continuing, 38–39
  duration of, 36
  future, 37
  habitual, 30, 31–32
  incomplete, 35
  intersecting, 35
  ongoing, 35
  parallel, 35
  recurring, 31–32
  relationships between, 39–40
  results of, 44–45
  subject's control of, 11–12
Adjectives
  modals used with adjective phrase, 23
  participles as, 7
  sense verbs and, 12
Adverbs of degree, 12
Affirmative form, 3
Agent, use of passive voice and, 44, 45, 46
Agreement, *will*-form and, 32
Already, use in present perfect tense, 39
Auxiliaries, 15–19
  in forming tenses, 62
  in passive voice, 43, 45
  in past conditional tense, 42
  in progressive tenses, 34, 35, 36, 38
  (*See also* Modals)

C

Change
  active verbs and, 8
  in conjugating irregular verbs, 116–117
  state-of-being verbs and, 10
Clarity, in using passive voice, 46
Cognitive verbs, 10–11
Commands, imperatives and, 5
Completed actions
  past perfect tense and, 39–40
  simple past tense and, 31

Complex sentences, 3, 50–51
Conditional tenses, 29, 41
  future conditional, 29, 40–41
  past conditional, 17, 29, 42
  unreal conditional tense, 29, 41
Conjugation, 62
  of auxiliaries, 15
  of passive voice, 43
  of phrasal verbs, 52
Conjugation patterns, 62, 116–117
Connections, present perfect tense and, 38
Context
  contractions and, 26
  of phrasal verbs, 57
  use of passive voice and, 45
Continuing actions
  future progressive tense and, 36
  present perfect progressive tense and, 38
  present perfect tense and, 38–39
Contractions, 25–27
Contrary-to-fact situations, 41
Could, contractions with, 26

D

Daily activities, action verbs and, 8
Determination, *will*-form and, 32
Direct objects, 47
Do, negative contractions with, 27
Duration of action, 36

E

Emotion verbs, 10–11

F

Factual information
  passive voice and, 44
  simple present tense and, 30
Finite verbs, modals and, 20, 22, 23
Fixed plans, *going-to* form and, 34
Frequent situations, present progressive tense and, 35
Full verbs, 15, 20, 22, 23
Future actions, 37
Future conditional tense, 29, 40–41
Future perfect tense, 16, 18–19, 29, 40
Future progressive tense, 15, 17–19, 29, 36–37